MAISIE CLIFTON

1919

PRELUDE

This story would never have been written if I hadn't become pregnant. Mind you, I had always planned to lose my virginity on the works outing to Weston-super-Mare, just not to that particular man.

Arthur Clifton was born in Still House Lane, just like me; even went to the same school, Merrywood Elementary, but as I was two years younger than him he didn't know I existed. All the girls in my class had a crush on him, and not just because he captained the school football team.

Although Arthur had never shown any interest in me while I was at school, that changed soon after he'd returned from the Western Front. I'm not even sure he realized who I was when he asked me for a dance that Saturday night at the Palais but, to be fair, I had to look twice before I recognized him because he'd grown a pencil mustache and had his hair slicked back like Ronald Colman. He didn't look at another girl that night, and after we'd danced the last waltz I knew it would only be a matter of time before he asked me to marry him.

Arthur held my hand as we walked back home, and when we reached my front door he tried to kiss me. I turned away. After all, the Reverend Watts had told me often enough that I had to stay pure until the day I was married, and Miss Monday, our choir mistress, warned me that men only wanted one thing, and once they'd got it, they quickly lost interest. I often wondered if Miss Monday spoke from experience.

The following Saturday, Arthur invited me to the flicks to see Lillian Gish in *Broken Blossoms,* and although I allowed him to put

3

an arm around my shoulder, I still didn't let him kiss me. He didn't make a fuss. Truth is, Arthur was rather shy.

The next Saturday I did allow him to kiss me, but when he tried to put a hand inside my blouse, I pushed him away. In fact I didn't let him do that until he'd proposed, bought a ring and the Reverend Watts had read the banns a second time.

My brother Stan told me that I was the last known virgin on our side of the River Avon, though I suspect most of his conquests were in his mind. Still, I decided the time had come, and when better than the works outing to Weston-super-Mare with the man I was going to marry in a few weeks' time?

However, as soon as Arthur and Stan got off the charabanc, they headed straight for the nearest pub. But I'd spent the past month planning for this moment, so when I got off the coach, like a good girl guide, I was prepared.

I was walking toward the pier feeling pretty fed up when I became aware someone was following me. I looked around and was surprised when I saw who it was. He caught up with me and asked if I was on my own.

"Yes," I said, aware that by now Arthur would be on his third pint.

When he put a hand on my bum, I should have slapped his face, but for several reasons I didn't. To start with, I thought about the advantages of having sex with someone I wasn't likely to come across again. And I have to admit I was flattered by his advances.

By the time Arthur and Stan would have been downing their eighth pints, he'd booked us into a guest house just off the seafront. They seemed to have a special rate for visitors who had no plans to spend the night. He started kissing me even before we'd reached the first landing, and once the bedroom door was closed he quickly undid the buttons of my blouse. It obviously wasn't his first time. In fact, I'm pretty sure I wasn't the first girl he'd had on a works outing. Otherwise, how did he know about the special rates?

I must confess I hadn't expected it to be all over quite so quickly. Once he'd climbed off me, I disappeared into the bathroom, while he sat on the end of the bed and lit up a fag. Perhaps it would be better the second time, I thought. But when I came back out, he was nowhere to be seen. I have to admit I was disappointed.

I might have felt more guilty about being unfaithful to Arthur if he hadn't been sick all over me on the journey back to Bristol.

The next day I told my mum what had happened, without letting on who the bloke was. After all, she hadn't met him, and was never likely to. Mum told me to keep my mouth shut as she didn't want to have to cancel the wedding, and even if I did turn out to be pregnant, no one would be any the wiser, as Arthur and I would be married by the time anyone noticed.

HARRY CLIFTON

1920–1933

1

I was told my father was killed in the war.

Whenever I questioned my mother about his death, she didn't say any more than that he'd served with the Royal Gloucestershire Regiment and had been killed fighting on the Western Front only days before the Armistice was signed. Grandma said my dad had been a brave man, and once when we were alone in the house she showed me his medals. My grandpa rarely offered an opinion on anything, but then he was deaf as a post so he might not have heard the question in the first place.

The only other man I can remember was my uncle Stan, who used to sit at the top of the table at breakfast time. When he left of a morning I would often follow him to the city docks, where he worked. Every day I spent at the dockyard was an adventure. Cargo ships coming from distant lands and unloading their wares: rice, sugar, bananas, jute and many other things I'd never heard of. Once the holds had been emptied, the dockers would load them with salt, apples, tin, even coal (my least favorite, because it was an obvious clue to what I'd been doing all day and annoyed my mother), before they set off again to I knew not where. I always wanted to help my uncle Stan unload whatever ship had docked that morning, but he just laughed, saying, "All in good time, my lad." It couldn't be soon enough for me, but, without any warning, school got in the way.

I was sent to Merrywood Elementary when I was six and I thought it was a complete waste of time. What was the point of school when I could learn all I needed to at the docks? I wouldn't have bothered to go back the following day if my mother hadn't dragged me to the front gates, deposited me and returned at four o'clock that afternoon to take me home.

I didn't realize Mum had other plans for my future, which didn't include joining Uncle Stan in the shipyard.

Once Mum had dropped me off each morning, I would hang around in the yard until she was out of sight, then slope off to the docks. I made sure I was always back at the school gates when she returned to pick me up in the afternoon. On the way home, I would tell her everything I'd done at school that day. I was good at making up stories, but it wasn't long before she discovered that was all they were: stories.

One or two other boys from my school also used to hang around the docks, but I kept my distance from them. They were older and bigger, and used to thump me if I got in their way. I also had to keep an eye out for Mr. Haskins, the chief ganger, because if he ever found me loitering, to use his favorite word, he would send me off with a kick up the backside and the threat: "If I see you loiterin' round here again, my lad, I'll report you to the headmaster."

Occasionally Haskins decided he'd seen me once too often and I'd be reported to the headmaster, who would leather me before sending me back to my classroom. My form master, Mr. Holcombe, never let on if I didn't show up for his class, but then he was a bit soft. Whenever my mum found out I'd been playing truant, she couldn't hide her anger and would stop my halfpenny-a-week pocket money. But despite the occasional punch from an older boy, regular leatherings from the headmaster and the loss of my pocket money, I still couldn't resist the draw of the docks.

I made only one real friend while I "loitered" around the dockyard. His name was Old Jack Tar. Mr. Tar lived in an abandoned railway carriage at the end of the sheds. Uncle Stan told me to keep away from Old Jack because he was a stupid, dirty old tramp. He didn't look that dirty to me, certainly not as dirty as Stan, and it wasn't long before I discovered he wasn't stupid either.

After lunch with my uncle Stan, one bite of his Marmite sandwich, his discarded apple core and a swig of beer, I would be back at school in time for a game of football; the only activity I considered it worth turning up for. After all, when I left school I was going to captain Bristol City, or build a ship that would sail around the world. If Mr. Holcombe kept his mouth shut and the ganger didn't report me to the headmaster, I could go for days without being found out, and as long as I avoided the coal barges and was standing by the school gate at four o'clock every afternoon, my mother would never be any the wiser.

◄◦►

Every other Saturday, Uncle Stan would take me to watch Bristol City at Ashton Gate. On Sunday mornings, Mum used to cart me off to Holy Nativity Church, something I couldn't find a way of getting out of. Once the Reverend Watts had given the final blessing, I would run all the way to the recreation ground and join my mates for a game of football before returning home in time for dinner.

By the time I was seven it was clear to anyone who knew anything about the game of football that I was never going to get into the school team, let alone captain Bristol City. But that was when I discovered that God had given me one small gift, and it wasn't in my feet.

To begin with, I didn't notice that anyone who sat near me in church on a Sunday morning stopped singing whenever I opened my mouth. I wouldn't have given it a second thought if Mum hadn't suggested I join the choir. I laughed scornfully; after all, everyone knew the choir was only for girls and sissies. I would have dismissed the idea out of hand if the Reverend Watts hadn't told me that choirboys were paid a penny for funerals and tuppence for weddings; my first experience of bribery. But even after I'd reluctantly agreed to take a vocal test, the devil decided to place an obstacle in my path, in the form of Miss Eleanor E. Monday.

I would never have come across Miss Monday if she hadn't been the choir mistress at Holy Nativity. Although she was only five feet three, and looked as though a gust of wind might blow her away, no one tried to take the mickey. I have a feeling that even the devil would have been frightened of Miss Monday, because the Reverend Watts certainly was.

I agreed to take a vocal test, but not before my mum had handed over a month's pocket money in advance. The following Sunday I stood in line with a group of other lads and waited to be called.

"You will always be on time for choir practice," Miss Monday announced, fixing a gimlet eye on me. I stared back defiantly. "You will never speak, unless spoken to." I somehow managed to remain silent. "And during the service, you will concentrate at all times." I reluctantly nodded. And then, God bless her, she gave me a way out. "But most importantly," she declared, placing her hands on her hips, "within twelve weeks, you will be expected to pass a reading and writing test, so that I can be sure you are able to tackle a new anthem or an unfamiliar psalm."

I was pleased to have fallen at the first hurdle. But as I was to discover, Miss Eleanor E. Monday didn't give up easily.

"What piece have you chosen to sing, child?" she asked me when I reached the front of the line.

"I haven't chosen anything," I told her.

She opened a hymn book, handed it to me and sat down at the piano. I smiled at the thought that I might still be able to make the second half of our Sunday morning football game. She began to play a familiar tune, and when I saw my mother glaring at me from the front row of pews, I decided I'd better go through with it, just to keep her happy.

"*All things bright and beautiful, all creatures great and small. All things wise and wonderful . . .*" A smile had appeared on Miss Monday's face long before I reached "*the Lord God made them all.*"

"What's your name, child?" she asked.

"Harry Clifton, miss."

"Harry Clifton, you will report for choir practice on Mondays, Wednesdays and Fridays at six o'clock sharp." Turning to the boy standing behind me, she said, "Next!"

I promised my mum I'd be on time for the first choir practice, even though I knew it would be my last, as Miss Monday would soon realize I couldn't read or write. And it would have been my last, if it hadn't been obvious to anyone listening that my singing voice was in a different class to that of any other boy in the choir.

In fact, the moment I opened my mouth, everyone fell silent, and the looks of admiration, even awe, that I had desperately sought on the football field, were happening in church. Miss Monday pretended not to notice.

After she dismissed us, I didn't go home, but ran all the way to the docks so I could ask Mr. Tar what I should do about the fact that I couldn't read or write. I listened carefully to the old man's advice, and the next day I went back to school and took my place in Mr. Holcombe's class. The schoolmaster couldn't hide his surprise when he saw me sitting in the front row, and was even more surprised when I paid close attention to the morning lesson for the first time.

Mr. Holcombe began by teaching me the alphabet, and within days I could write out all twenty-six letters, if not always in the correct order. My mum would have helped me when I got home in the afternoon but, like the rest of my family, she also couldn't read or write.

Uncle Stan could just about scrawl his signature, and although he could tell the difference between a packet of Wills's Star and Wild Woodbines, I was fairly sure he couldn't actually read the labels. Despite his unhelpful mutterings, I set about writing the alphabet on any piece of scrap paper I could find. Uncle Stan didn't seem to notice that the torn-up newspaper in the privy was always covered in letters.

Once I'd mastered the alphabet, Mr. Holcombe introduced me to a few simple words: "dog," "cat," "mum" and "dad." That was when I first asked him about my dad, hoping that he might be able to tell me something about him. After all, he seemed to know everything. But he seemed puzzled that I knew so little about my own dad. A week later he wrote my first four-letter word on the blackboard, "book," and then five, "house," and six, "school." By the end of the month, I could write my first sentence, "The quick brown fox jumps over the lazy dog," which, Mr. Holcombe pointed out, contained every letter in the alphabet. I checked, and he turned out to be right.

By the end of term I could spell "anthem," "psalm" and even "hymn," although Mr. Holcombe kept reminding me I still dropped my aitches whenever I spoke. But then we broke up for the holidays and I began to worry I would never pass Miss Monday's demanding test without Mr. Holcombe's help. And that might have been the case, if Old Jack hadn't taken his place.

─◦─

I was half an hour early for choir practice on the Friday evening when I knew I would have to pass my second test if I hoped to continue as a member of the choir. I sat silently in the stalls, hoping Miss Monday would pick on someone else before she called on me.

I had already passed the first test with what Miss Monday had described as flying colors. We had all been asked to recite *The Lord's Prayer*. This was not a problem for me, because for as long as I could remember my mum knelt by my bed each night and repeated the familiar words before tucking me up. However, Miss Monday's next test was to prove far more demanding.

By this time, the end of our second month, we were expected to read a psalm out loud, in front of the rest of the choir. I chose Psalm 121, which I also knew off by heart, having sung it so often in the past. *I will lift up mine eyes unto the hills, from whence cometh my help.* I could only hope that my help cometh from the Lord. Although I was able to turn to the correct page in the psalm book, as I could now count from one to a hundred, I feared Miss Monday would realize that I was unable to follow every verse line by line. If she did, she didn't let on, because I remained in the choir stalls for another month while two other miscreants—her word, not that I knew what it meant until I asked Mr. Holcombe the next day—were dispatched back to the congregation.

When the time came for me to take the third and final test, I was ready for it. Miss Monday asked those of us who remained to write out the Ten Commandments in the correct order without referring to the Book of Exodus.

The choir mistress turned a blind eye to the fact that I placed theft ahead of murder, couldn't spell "adultery," and certainly didn't know what it meant. Only after two other miscreants were summarily dismissed for lesser offenses did I realize just how exceptional my voice must be.

On the first Sunday of Advent, Miss Monday announced that she had selected three new trebles—or "little angels," as the Reverend Watts was wont to describe us—to join her choir, the remainder having been rejected for committing such unforgivable sins as chattering during the sermon, sucking a gobstopper and, in the case of two boys, being caught playing conkers during the "Nunc Dimittis."

The following Sunday, I dressed up in a long blue cassock with a ruffled white collar. I alone was allowed to wear a bronze medallion of the Virgin Mother around my neck, to show that I had been selected as the treble soloist. I would have proudly worn the medallion all the way back home, even to school the next morning, to show off to the rest of the lads, if only Miss Monday hadn't retrieved it at the end of each service.

On Sundays I was transported into another world, but I feared this state of delirium could not last forever.

2

WHEN UNCLE STAN rose in the morning, he somehow managed to wake the entire household. No one complained, as he was the breadwinner in the family, and in any case he was cheaper and more reliable than an alarm clock.

The first noise Harry would hear was the bedroom door slamming. This would be followed by his uncle tramping along the creaky wooden landing, down the stairs and out of the house. Then another door would slam as he disappeared into the privy. If anyone was still asleep, the rush of water as Uncle Stan pulled the chain, followed by two more slammed doors before he returned to the bedroom, served to remind them that Stan expected his breakfast to be on the table by the time he walked into the kitchen. He had a wash and a shave only on Saturday evenings before going off to the Palais or the Odeon. He took a bath four times a year on quarter-day. No one was going to accuse Stan of wasting his hard-earned cash on soap.

Maisie, Harry's mum, would be next up, leaping out of bed moments after the first slammed door. There would be a bowl of porridge on the stove by the time Stan came out of the privy. Grandma followed shortly afterward, and would join her daughter in the kitchen before Stan had taken his place at the head of the table. Harry had to be down within five minutes of the first slammed door if he hoped to get any breakfast. The last to arrive in the kitchen would be Grandpa, who was so deaf he often managed to sleep through Stan's early morning ritual. This daily routine in the Clifton household never varied. When you've only got one outside privy, one sink and one towel, order becomes a necessity.

By the time Harry was splashing his face with a trickle of cold water, his mother would be serving breakfast in the kitchen: two thickly sliced pieces of bread covered in lard for Stan, and four thin slices for the rest of the family, which she would toast if there was any coal left in the sack dumped outside the front door every Monday. Once Stan had finished his porridge, Harry would be allowed to lick the bowl.

A large brown pot of tea was always brewing on the hearth, which Grandma would pour into a variety of mugs through a silver-plated Victorian tea strainer she had inherited from her mother. While the other members of the family enjoyed a mug of unsweetened tea—sugar was only for high days and holidays— Stan would open his first bottle of beer, which he usually gulped down in one draft. He would then rise from the table and burp loudly before picking up his lunch box, which Grandma had prepared while he was having his breakfast: two Marmite sandwiches, a sausage, an apple, two more bottles of beer and a packet of five coffin nails. Once Stan had left for the docks, everyone began to talk at once.

Grandma always wanted to know who had visited the tea shop where her daughter worked as a waitress: what they ate, what they were wearing, where they sat; details of meals that were cooked on a stove in a room lit by electric light bulbs that didn't leave any candle wax, not to mention customers who sometimes left a thruppenny-bit tip, which Maisie had to split with the cook.

Maisie was more concerned to find out what Harry had done at school the previous day. She demanded a daily report, which didn't seem to interest Grandma, perhaps because she'd never been to school. Come to think of it, she'd never been to a tea shop either.

Grandpa rarely commented, because after four years of loading and unloading an artillery field gun, morning, noon and night, he was so deaf he had to satisfy himself with watching their lips move and nodding from time to time. This could give outsiders the impression he was stupid, which the rest of the family knew to their cost he wasn't.

The family's morning routine only varied at weekends. On Saturdays, Harry would follow his uncle out of the kitchen, always remaining a pace behind him as he walked to the docks. On Sunday, Harry's mum would accompany the boy to Holy Nativity Church, where, from the third row of the pews, she would bask in the glory of the choir's treble soloist.

But today was Saturday. During the twenty-minute walk to the docks, Harry never opened his mouth unless his uncle spoke. Whenever he did, it invariably turned out to be the same conversation they'd had the previous Saturday.

"When are you goin' to leave school and do a day's work, young'un?" was always Uncle Stan's opening salvo.

"Not allowed to leave until I'm fourteen," Harry reminded him. "It's the law."

"A bloody stupid law, if you ask me. I'd packed up school and was workin' on the docks by the time I were twelve," Stan would announce as if Harry had never heard this profound observation before. Harry didn't bother to respond, as he already knew what his uncle's next sentence would be. "And what's more I'd signed up to join Kitchener's army before my seventeenth birthday."

"Tell me about the war, Uncle Stan," said Harry, aware that this would keep him occupied for several hundred yards.

"Me and your dad joined the Royal Gloucestershire Regiment on the same day," Stan said, touching his cloth cap as if saluting a distant memory. "After twelve weeks' basic training at Taunton Barracks, we was shipped off to Wipers to fight the Boche. Once we got there, we spent most of our time cooped up in rat-infested trenches waiting to be told by some toffee-nosed officer that when the bugle sounded, we was going over the top, bayonets fixed, rifles firing as we advanced toward the enemy lines." This would be followed by a long pause, after which Stan would add, "I was one of the lucky ones. Got back to Blighty all ship-shape and Bristol fashion." Harry could have predicted his next sentence word for word, but remained silent. "You just don't know how lucky you are, my lad. I lost two brothers, your uncle Ray and your uncle Bert, and your father not only lost a brother, but his father, your other grandad, what you never met. A proper man, who could down a pint of beer faster than any docker I've ever come across."

If Stan had looked down, he would have seen the boy mouthing his words, but today, to Harry's surprise, Uncle Stan added a sentence he'd never uttered before. "And your dad would still be alive today, if only management had listened to me."

Harry was suddenly alert. His dad's death had always been the subject of whispered conversations and hushed tones. But Uncle Stan clammed up, as if he realized he'd gone too far. Maybe next week, thought Harry, catching his uncle up and keeping in step with him as if they were two soldiers on a parade ground.

"So who are City playin' this afternoon?" asked Stan, back on script.

"Charlton Athletic," Harry replied.

"They're a load of old cobblers."

"They trounced us last season," Harry reminded his uncle.

"Bloody lucky, if you ask me," said Stan, and didn't open his mouth again. When they reached the entrance to the dockyard, Stan clocked in before heading off to the pen where he was working with a gang of other dockers, none of whom could afford to be a minute late. Unemployment was at an all-time high and too many young men were standing outside the gates waiting to take their place.

Harry didn't follow his uncle, because he knew that if Mr. Haskins caught him hanging around the sheds he would get a clip round the ear, followed by a boot up the backside from his uncle for annoying the ganger. Instead, he set off in the opposite direction.

Harry's first port of call every Saturday morning was Old Jack Tar, who lived in the railway carriage at the other end of the dockyard. He had never told Stan about his regular visits because his uncle had warned him to avoid the old man at all costs.

"Probably hasn't had a bath in years," said a man who washed once a quarter, and then only after Harry's mother complained about the smell.

But curiosity had long ago got the better of Harry, and one morning he'd crept up to the railway carriage on his hands and knees, lifted himself up and peeped through a window. The old man was sitting in first class, reading a book.

Old Jack turned to face him and said, "Come on in, lad." Harry jumped down, and didn't stop running until he reached his front door.

The following Saturday, Harry once again crawled up to the carriage and peered inside. Old Jack seemed to be fast asleep, but then Harry heard him say, "Why don't you come in, my boy? I'm not going to bite you."

Harry turned the heavy brass handle and tentatively pulled open the carriage door, but he didn't step inside. He just stared at the man seated in the center of the carriage. It was hard to tell how old he was because his face was covered in a well-groomed salt-and-pepper beard, which made him look like the sailor on the Players Please packet. But he looked at Harry with a warmth in his eyes that Uncle Stan had never managed.

"Are you Old Jack Tar?" Harry ventured.

"That's what they call me," the old man replied.

"And is this where you live?" Harry asked, glancing around the carriage, his eyes settling on a stack of old newspapers piled high on the opposite seat.

"Yes," he replied. "It's been my home for these past twenty years. Why don't you close the door and take a seat, young man?"

Harry gave the offer some thought before he jumped back out of the carriage and once again ran away.

The following Saturday, Harry did close the door, but he kept hold of the handle, ready to bolt if the old man as much as twitched a muscle. They stared at each other for some time before Old Jack asked, "What's your name?"

"Harry."

"And where do you go to school?"

"I don't go to school."

"Then what are you hoping to do with your life, young man?"

"Join my uncle on the docks, of course," Harry replied.

"Why would you want to do that?" said the old man.

"Why not?" Harry bristled. "Don't you think I'm good enough?"

"You're far too good," replied Old Jack. "When I was your age," he continued, "I wanted to join the army, and nothing my old man could say or do would dissuade me." For the next hour Harry stood, mesmerized, while Old Jack Tar reminisced about the docks, the city of Bristol, and lands beyond the sea that he couldn't have been taught about in geography lessons.

The following Saturday, and for more Saturdays than he would remember, Harry continued to visit Old Jack Tar. But he never once told his uncle or his mother, for fear they would stop him going to see his first real friend.

—◇—

When Harry knocked on the door of the railway carriage that Saturday morning, Old Jack had clearly been waiting for him, because his usual Cox's Orange Pippin had been placed on the seat opposite. Harry picked it up, took a bite and sat down.

"Thank you, Mr. Tar," Harry said as he wiped some juice from his chin. He never asked where the apples came from; it just added to the mystery of the great man.

How different he was from Uncle Stan, who repeated the little he knew again and again, whereas Old Jack introduced Harry to new words, new experiences, even new worlds every week. He often wondered why Mr. Tar wasn't a schoolmaster—he seemed to know even more than Miss Monday, and almost as much as Mr. Holcombe. Harry was convinced that Mr. Holcombe knew everything, because he never failed to answer any question Harry put to him. Old Jack smiled across at him, but didn't speak until Harry had finished his apple and thrown the core out of the window.

"What have you learned at school this week," the old man asked, "that you didn't know a week ago?"

"Mr. Holcombe told me there are other countries beyond the sea that are part of the British Empire, and they are all reigned over by the King."

"He's quite right," said Old Jack. "Can you name any of those countries?"

"Australia. Canada. India." He hesitated. "And America."

"No, not America," said Old Jack. "That used to be the case, but it isn't any more, thanks to a weak Prime Minister and a sick King."

"Who was the King, and who was the Prime Minister?" demanded Harry angrily.

"King George III was on the throne in 1776," said Old Jack, "but to be fair, he was a sick man, while Lord North, his Prime Minister, simply ignored what was taking place in the colonies, and, sadly, in the end our own kith and kin took up arms against us."

"But we must have beaten them?" said Harry.

"No, we didn't," said Old Jack. "Not only did they have right on their side—not that that's a prerequisite for victory—"

"What does prerequisite mean?"

"Required as a pre-condition," said Old Jack, who then continued as if he hadn't been interrupted. "But they were also led by a brilliant general."

"What was his name?"

"George Washington."

"You told me last week that Washington was the capital of America. Was he named after the city?"

"No, the city was named after him. It was built on an area of marshland known as Columbia, through which the Potomac River flows."

"Is Bristol named after a man too?"

"No," chuckled Old Jack, amused by how quickly Harry's inquisitive mind could switch from subject to subject. "Bristol was originally called Brigstowe, which means the site of a bridge."

"So when did it become Bristol?"

"Historians differ in their opinions," said Old Jack, "although Bristol Castle was built by Robert of Gloucester in 1109, when he saw the opportunity to trade wool with the Irish. After that, the city developed into a trading port. Since then it's been a center of shipbuilding for hundreds of years, and grew even more quickly when the navy needed to expand in 1914."

"My dad fought in the Great War," said Harry with pride. "Did you?"

For the first time, Old Jack hesitated before answering one of Harry's questions. He just sat there, not saying a word. "I'm sorry, Mr. Tar," said Harry. "I didn't mean to pry."

"No, no," said Old Jack. "It's just that I haven't been asked that question for some years." Without another word, he opened his hand to reveal a sixpence.

Harry took the little silver coin and bit it, something he'd seen his uncle do. "Thank you," he said before pocketing it.

"Go and buy yourself some fish and chips from the dockside café, but don't tell your uncle, because he'll only ask where you got the money."

In truth, Harry had never told his uncle anything about Old Jack. He'd once heard Stan tell his mum, "The loony ought to be locked up." He'd asked Miss Monday what a loony was, because he couldn't find the word in the dictionary, and when she told him, he realized for the first time just how stupid his uncle Stan must be.

"Not necessarily stupid," Miss Monday counseled, "simply ill-informed and therefore prejudiced. I have no doubt, Harry," she added, "that you'll meet many more such men during your lifetime, some of them in far more exalted positions than your uncle."

3

MAISIE WAITED UNTIL she heard the front door slam and was confident that Stan was on his way to work before she announced, "I've been offered a job as a waitress at the Royal Hotel."

No one seated round the table responded, as conversations at breakfast were supposed to follow a regular pattern and not take anyone by surprise. Harry had a dozen questions he wanted to ask but waited for his grandma to speak first. She simply busied herself with pouring another cup of tea, as if she hadn't heard her daughter in the first place.

"Will someone please say something?" said Maisie.

"I didn't even realize you were looking for another job," ventured Harry.

"I wasn't," said Maisie. "But last week a Mr. Frampton, the manager of the Royal, dropped into Tilly's for coffee. He came back several times, and then he offered me a job!"

"I thought you were happy at the tea shop," said Grandma, finally joining in. "After all, Miss Tilly pays well, and the hours suit."

"I am happy," said Harry's mum, "but Mr. Frampton's offering me five pounds a week, and half of all the tips. I could be bringing home as much as six pounds on a Friday." Grandma sat there with her mouth wide open.

"Will you have to work nights?" asked Harry, once he'd finished licking Stan's porridge bowl.

"No, I won't," Maisie said, ruffling her son's hair, "and what's more I'll get one day off a fortnight."

"Are your clothes posh enough for a grand hotel like the Royal?" asked Grandma.

"I'll be supplied with a uniform, and a fresh white apron every morning. The hotel even has its own laundry."

"I don't doubt it," said Grandma, "but I can think of one problem we're all going to have to learn to live with."

"And what's that, Mum?" asked Maisie.

"You could end up earnin' more than Stan, and he's not going to like that, not one little bit."

"Then he'll just have to learn to live with it, won't he?" said Grandpa, offering an opinion for the first time in weeks.

—◇—

The extra money was going to come in useful, especially after what had happened at the Holy Nativity. Maisie had been about to leave the church after the service when Miss Monday walked purposefully down the aisle toward her.

"Can I have a private word with you, Mrs. Clifton?" she asked, before turning and walking back down the aisle toward the vestry. Maisie chased after her like a child in the Pied Piper's wake. She feared the worst. What had Harry been up to this time?

Maisie followed the choir mistress into the vestry and felt her legs give way when she saw the Reverend Watts, Mr. Holcombe and another gentleman standing there. As Miss Monday closed the door quietly behind her, Maisie began to shake uncontrollably.

The Reverend Watts placed an arm around her shoulder. "There's nothing for you to worry about, my dear," he assured her. "On the contrary, I hope you will feel we are the bearers of glad tidings," he added, offering her a seat. Maisie sat down, but still couldn't stop shaking.

Once everyone was seated, Miss Monday took over. "We wanted to talk to you about Harry, Mrs. Clifton," she began. Maisie pursed her lips; what could the boy possibly have done to bring three such important people together?

"I'll not beat about the bush," the choir mistress continued. "The music master at St. Bede's has approached me and asked if

Harry would consider entering his name for one of their choral scholarships."

"But he's very happy at Holy Nativity," said Maisie. "In any case, where is St. Bede's Church? I've never even heard of it."

"St. Bede's is not a church," said Miss Monday. "It's a choir school that supplies choristers for St. Mary Redcliffe, which was famously described by Queen Elizabeth as the fairest and godliest church in all the land."

"So would he have to leave his school, as well as the church?" asked Maisie in disbelief.

"Try to look upon it as an opportunity that might change his whole life, Mrs. Clifton," said Mr. Holcombe, speaking for the first time.

"But wouldn't he have to mix with posh, clever boys?"

"I doubt if there will be many children at St. Bede's cleverer than Harry," said Mr. Holcombe. "He's the brightest lad I've ever taught. Although we get the occasional boy into the grammar school, none of our pupils has ever been offered the chance of a place at St. Bede's before."

"There's something else you need to know before you make up your mind," said the Reverend Watts. Maisie looked even more anxious. "Harry would have to leave home during term time, because St. Bede's is a boarding school."

"Then it's out of the question," said Maisie. "I couldn't afford it."

"That shouldn't prove a problem," said Miss Monday. "If Harry is offered a scholarship, the school would not only waive any fees, but also award him a bursary of ten pounds a term."

"But is this one of those schools where the fathers wear suits and ties, and the mothers don't work?" asked Maisie.

"It's worse than that," said Miss Monday, trying to make light of it. "The masters wear long black gowns and mortarboards on their heads."

"Still," said the Reverend Watts joining in, "at least there would be no more leatherings for Harry. They're far more refined at St. Bede's. They just cane the boys."

Only Maisie didn't laugh. "But why would he want to leave

home?" she asked. "He's settled at Merrywood Elementary, and he won't want to give up being senior chorister at Holy Nativity."

"I must confess that my loss would be even greater than his," said Miss Monday. "But then, I'm sure our Lord would not want me to stand in the way of such a gifted child, simply because of my own selfish desires," she added quietly.

"Even if I agree," said Maisie, playing her last card, "that doesn't mean Harry will."

"I had a word with the boy last week," admitted Mr. Holcombe. "Of course he was apprehensive about such a challenge, but if I recall, his exact words were 'I'd like to have a go, sir, but only if you think I'm good enough.' But," he added before Maisie could respond, "he also made it clear that he wouldn't even consider the idea unless his mother agreed."

<o>

Harry was both terrified and excited by the thought of taking the entrance exam, but just as anxious about failing and letting so many people down as he was about succeeding and having to leave home.

During the following term, he never once missed a lesson at Merrywood, and when he returned home each evening, he went straight up to the bedroom he shared with Uncle Stan, where, with the aid of a candle, he studied for hours that until then he hadn't realized existed. There were even occasions when his mother found Harry sound asleep on the floor, open books scattered around him.

Every Saturday morning he continued to visit Old Jack, who seemed to know a great deal about St. Bede's, and continued to teach Harry about so many other things, almost as if he knew where Mr. Holcombe had left off.

On Saturday afternoons, much to the disgust of Uncle Stan, Harry no longer accompanied him to Ashton Gate to watch Bristol City, but returned to Merrywood, where Mr. Holcombe gave him extra lessons. It would be years before Harry worked out that Mr. Holcombe was also forgoing his regular visits to support the Robins, in order to teach him.

As the day of the examination drew nearer, Harry became even more frightened of failure than of the possibility of success.

On the appointed day, Mr. Holcombe accompanied his star pupil to the Colston Hall, where the two-hour examination would take place. He left Harry at the entrance to the building, with the words, "Don't forget to read each question twice before you even pick up your pen," a piece of advice he'd repeated several times during the past week. Harry smiled nervously, and shook hands with Mr. Holcombe as if they were old friends.

He entered the examination hall to find about sixty other boys standing around in small groups, chattering. It was clear to Harry that many of them already knew each other, while he didn't know anyone. Despite this, one or two of them stopped talking and glanced at him as he made his way to the front of the hall trying to look confident.

"Abbott, Barrington, Cabot, Clifton, Deakins, Fry . . ."

Harry took his place at a desk in the front row, and just moments before the clock struck ten, several masters in long black gowns and mortarboards swept in and placed examination papers on the desks in front of each candidate.

"Gentlemen," said a master standing at the front of the hall, who had not taken part in the distribution of the papers, "my name is Mr. Frobisher, and I am your invigilator. You have two hours in which to answer one hundred questions. Good luck."

A clock he couldn't see struck ten. All around him, pens dipped into inkwells and began to scratch furiously across paper, but Harry simply folded his arms, leaned on the desk and read each question slowly. He was among the last to pick up his pen.

Harry couldn't know that Mr. Holcombe was pacing up and down on the pavement outside, feeling far more nervous than his pupil. Or that his mother was glancing up at the clock in the foyer of the Royal Hotel every few minutes as she served morning coffee. Or that Miss Monday was kneeling in silent prayer before the altar at Holy Nativity.

Moments after the clock had struck twelve, the examination papers were gathered up and the boys were allowed to leave the hall, some laughing, some frowning, others thoughtful.

When Mr. Holcombe first saw Harry, his heart sank. "Was it that bad?" he asked.

Harry didn't reply until he was certain no other boy could overhear his words. "Not at all what I expected," he said.

"What do you mean?" asked Mr. Holcombe anxiously.

"The questions were far too easy," replied Harry.

Mr. Holcombe felt that he had never been paid a greater compliment in his life.

—◄○►—

"Two suits, madam, gray. One blazer, navy. Five shirts, white. Five stiff collars, white. Six pairs of calf-length socks, gray. Six sets of undergarments, white. And one St. Bede's tie." The shop assistant checked the list carefully. "I think that covers everything. Oh, no, the boy will also need a school cap." He reached under the counter, opened a drawer and removed a red and black cap which he placed on Harry's head. "A perfect fit," he pronounced. Maisie smiled at her son with considerable pride. Harry looked every inch a St. Bede's boy. "That will be three pounds, ten shillings and six pence, madam."

Maisie tried not to look too dismayed. "Is it possible to purchase any of these items secondhand?" she whispered.

"No, madam, this is not a secondhand shop," said the assistant, who had already decided that this customer would not be allowed to open an account.

Maisie opened her purse, handed over four pound notes and waited for the change. She was relieved that St. Bede's had paid the first term's bursary in advance, especially as she still needed to buy two pairs of leather shoes, black with laces, two pairs of gym shoes, white with laces, and one pair of slippers, bedroom.

The assistant coughed. "The boy will also need two pairs of pajamas and a dressing gown."

"Yes, of course," said Maisie, hoping she had enough money left in her purse to cover the cost.

"And am I to understand that the boy is a choral scholar?" asked the assistant, looking more closely at his list.

"Yes, he is," Maisie replied proudly.

"Then he'll also require one cassock, red, two surplices, white, and a St. Bede's medallion." Maisie wanted to run out of the shop. "Those items will be supplied by the school when he attends his first choir practice," the assistant added before handing over her change. "Will you be requiring anything else, madam?"

"No, thank you," said Harry, who picked up the two bags, grabbed his mother by the arm and led her quickly out of T. C. Marsh, Tailors of Distinction.

◄◦►

Harry spent the Saturday morning before he was due to report to St. Bede's with Old Jack.

"Are you nervous about going to a new school?" asked Old Jack.

"No, I'm not," said Harry defiantly. Old Jack smiled. "I'm terrified," he admitted.

"So is every new bug, as you'll be called. Try to treat the whole thing as if you're starting out on an adventure to a new world, where everyone begins as equals."

"But the moment they hear me speak, they'll realize I'm not their equal."

"Possibly, but the moment they hear you sing, they'll realize they're not *your* equal."

"Most of them will have come from rich families, with servants."

"That will only be a consolation for the more stupid ones," said Old Jack.

"And some of them will have brothers at the school, and even fathers and grandfathers who were there before them."

"Your father was a fine man," said Old Jack, "and none of them will have a better mother, of that I can assure you."

"You knew my father?" said Harry, unable to mask his surprise.

"Knew would be an exaggeration," said Old Jack, "but I observed him from afar, as I have many others who have worked at the docks. He was a decent, courageous, God-fearing man."

"But do you know how he died?" asked Harry, looking Old Jack in the eye, hoping he would at last get an honest reply to the question that had troubled him for so long.

"What have you been told?" asked Old Jack cautiously.

"That he was killed in the Great War. But as I was born in 1920, even I can work out that that can't be possible."

Old Jack didn't speak for some time. Harry remained on the edge of his seat.

"He was certainly badly wounded in the war, but you're right, that was not the cause of his death."

"Then how did he die?" asked Harry.

"If I knew, I'd tell you," replied Old Jack. "But there were so many rumors flying around at the time that I wasn't sure whom to believe. However, there are several men, and three in particular, who undoubtedly know the truth about what happened that night."

"My uncle Stan must be one of them," said Harry, "but who are the other two?"

Old Jack hesitated, before he replied, "Phil Haskins and Mr. Hugo."

"Mr. Haskins? The ganger?" said Harry. "He wouldn't give me the time of day. And who's Mr. Hugo?"

"Hugo Barrington, the son of Sir Walter Barrington."

"The family who own the shipping line?"

"The same," replied Old Jack, fearing he'd gone too far.

"And are they also decent, courageous, God-fearing men?"

"Sir Walter is among the finest men I've ever known."

"But what about his son, Mr. Hugo?"

"Not cut from the same cloth, I fear," said Old Jack, without further explanation.

4

THE SMARTLY DRESSED boy sat next to his mother on the back seat of the tram.

"This is our stop," she said when the tram came to a halt. They got off, and began to walk slowly up the hill toward the school, going a little slower with each step.

Harry held on to his mother with one hand, while he clutched a battered suitcase with the other. Neither of them spoke as they watched several hansom cabs, as well as the occasional chauffeur-driven car, pull up outside the front gates of the school.

Fathers were shaking hands with their sons, while fur-draped mothers embraced their offspring before giving them a peck on the cheek, like a bird finally having to acknowledge her fledglings were about to fly the nest.

Harry didn't want his mother to kiss him in front of the other boys, so he let go of her hand when they were still fifty yards from the gate. Maisie, sensing his discomfort, bent down and kissed him quickly on the forehead. "Good luck, Harry. Make us all proud of you."

"Good-bye, Mum," he said, fighting back the tears.

Maisie turned and began to walk back down the hill, tears flooding down her own cheeks.

Harry walked on, recalling his uncle's description of going over the top at Ypres before charging toward the enemy lines. *Never look back, or you're a dead man.* Harry wanted to look back, but he knew if he did, he would not stop running until he was safely on the tram. He gritted his teeth and kept on walking.

"Did you have a good hols, old chap?" one of the boys was asking a friend.

"Topping," the other replied. "The pater took me to Lord's for the Varsity match."

Was Lord's a church, Harry wondered, and if so, what sort of match could possibly take place in a church? He marched resolutely on through the school gates, coming to a halt when he recognized a man holding a clipboard standing by the front door of the school.

"And who are you, young man?" he asked, giving Harry a welcoming smile.

"Harry Clifton, sir," he replied, removing his cap just as Mr. Holcombe had instructed him to do whenever a master or a lady spoke to him.

"Clifton," he said, running a finger down a long list of names. "Ah, yes." He placed a tick by Harry's name. "First generation, choral scholar. Many congratulations, and welcome to St. Bede's. I'm Mr. Frobisher, your housemaster, and this is Frobisher House. If you leave your suitcase in the hall, a prefect will accompany you to the refectory where I'll be addressing all the new boys before supper."

Harry had never had supper before. "Tea" was always the last meal in the Clifton household, before being sent to bed the moment it was dark. Electricity hadn't yet reached Still House Lane, and there was rarely enough money left over to spend on candles.

"Thank you, sir," said Harry, before making his way through the front door and into a large, highly polished wood-paneled hall. He put his case down and stared up at a painting of an old man with gray hair and bushy white sideburns, dressed in a long black gown with a red hood draped around his shoulders.

"What's your name?" barked a voice from behind him.

"Clifton, sir," said Harry, turning to see a tall boy wearing long trousers.

"You don't call me sir, Clifton. You call me Fisher. I'm a prefect, not a master."

"Sorry, sir," said Harry.

"Leave your case over there and follow me."

Harry placed his secondhand, battered suitcase next to a row of leather trunks. His was the only one that didn't have a set of initials stamped on it. He followed the prefect down a long corridor that was lined with photographs of old school teams and display cabinets filled with silver cups, to remind the next generation of past glories. When they reached the refectory, Fisher said, "You can sit anywhere you like, Clifton. Just be sure to stop talking the moment Mr. Frobisher enters the refectory."

Harry hesitated for some time before deciding which of the four long tables he would sit at. A number of boys were already milling around in clusters, talking quietly. Harry walked slowly to the far corner of the room and took a place at the end of the table. He looked up to see several boys pouring into the hall, looking just as perplexed as he felt. One of them came and sat next to Harry, while another sat opposite him. They continued chatting to each other as if he wasn't there.

Without warning, a bell rang and everyone stopped talking as Mr. Frobisher entered the refectory. He took his place behind a lectern Harry hadn't noticed and tugged at the lapels of his gown.

"Welcome," he began, doffing his mortarboard to the assembled gathering, "on this, the first day of your first term at St. Bede's. In a few moments' time you will experience your first school meal, and I can promise you that it doesn't get any better." One or two of the boys laughed nervously. "Once you have finished supper, you will be taken up to your dormitories, where you will unpack. At eight o'clock, you will hear another bell. Actually it's the same bell, just being rung at a different time." Harry smiled, although most of the boys hadn't caught Mr. Frobisher's little joke.

"Thirty minutes later, the same bell will ring again, and you will then go to bed, but not before you've washed and brushed your teeth. You will then have thirty minutes to read before lights out, after which you will go to sleep. Any child caught talking after lights out will be punished by the duty prefect. You will not hear another bell," continued Mr. Frobisher, "until six thirty tomorrow morning, when you will rise, wash and dress in time to report back to the refectory before seven. Any child who is late will forgo his breakfast.

"Morning assembly will be held at eight o'clock in the great hall, where the headmaster will address us. This will be followed by your first lesson at eight thirty. There will be three sixty-minute lessons during the morning, with ten-minute breaks between them, giving you time to change classrooms. This will be followed by lunch at twelve.

"In the afternoon there will only be two more lessons before games, when you will play football." Harry smiled for a second time. "This is compulsory for everyone who is not a member of the choir." Harry frowned. No one had told him that choristers didn't get to play football. "After games or choir practice, you will return to Frobisher House for supper, which will be followed by an hour of prep before you retire to bed, when once again you can read until lights out—but only if the book has been approved by Matron," added Mr. Frobisher. "This must all sound very bemusing to you"—Harry made a mental note to look up the word in the dictionary Mr. Holcombe had presented him with. Mr. Frobisher once again tugged at the lapels of his gown before continuing. "But don't worry, you'll soon get used to our traditions at St. Bede's. That's all I'm going to say for the moment. I'll now leave you to enjoy your supper. Goodnight, boys."

"Goodnight, sir," some boys had the courage to reply as Mr. Frobisher left the room.

Harry didn't move a muscle as several women in pinafores marched up and down the tables placing bowls of soup in front of each boy. He watched attentively as the boy opposite him picked up a strangely shaped spoon, dipped it into his soup and pushed it away from him before putting it to his mouth. Harry attempted to imitate the motion, but only ended up spilling several drops of soup on the table, and when he did manage to transfer what was left into his mouth, most of it dribbled down his chin. He wiped his mouth with his sleeve. This didn't attract much attention, but when he slurped loudly with each mouthful, several of the boys stopped eating and stared at him. Embarrassed, Harry placed the spoon back on the table and left his soup to go cold.

The second course was a fishcake, and Harry didn't move until he'd seen which fork the boy opposite him picked up. He was surprised to notice that the boy placed his knife and fork on the plate between each mouthful, while Harry clung on to his as firmly as if they were pitchforks.

A conversation struck up between the boy opposite him and the boy next to him, on the subject of riding to hounds. Harry didn't join in, partly because the nearest he'd been to sitting on a horse was a halfpenny ride on a donkey one afternoon on an outing to Weston-super-Mare.

Once the plates had been whisked away, they were replaced with puddings, or what his mum called treats, because he didn't get them often. Yet another spoon, yet another taste, yet another mistake. Harry didn't realize that a banana wasn't like an apple, so to the astonishment of all those around him, he tried to eat the skin. For the rest of the boys, their first lesson might well be tomorrow at 8:30 a.m., but Harry's was already taking place.

After supper had been cleared away, Fisher returned and, as duty prefect, led his charges up a wide wooden staircase to the dormitories on the first floor. Harry entered a room with thirty beds neatly lined up in three rows of ten. Each had a pillow, two sheets and two blankets. Harry had never had two of anything.

"This is the new bugs' dorm," said Fisher with disdain. "It's where you'll remain until you're civilized. You'll find your names in alphabetical order, at the foot of each bed."

Harry was surprised to find his suitcase on the bed and wondered who'd put it there. The boy next to him was already unpacking.

"I'm Deakins," he said, pushing his spectacles further up his nose so he could take a closer look at Harry.

"I'm Harry. I sat next to you during exams last summer. I couldn't believe you answered all the questions in just over an hour."

Deakins blushed.

"That's why he's a scholar," said the boy on the other side of Harry.

Harry swung around. "Are you a scholar, too?" he asked.

"Good heavens, no," said the boy as he continued to unpack. "The only reason they let me into St. Bede's was because my father and grandfather were here before me. I'm the third generation to go to the school. Was your father here by any chance?"

"No," said Harry and Deakins in unison.

"Stop chattering!" shouted Fisher, "and get on with unpacking your cases."

Harry opened his suitcase and began taking his clothes out and placing them neatly in the two drawers next to his bed. His mother had put a bar of Fry's Five Boys chocolate in between his shirts. He hid it under the pillow.

A bell sounded. "Time to get undressed!" declared Fisher. Harry had never undressed in front of another boy, let alone a room full of them. He faced the wall, took off his clothes slowly and quickly pulled on his pajamas. Once he'd tied the cord of his dressing gown, he followed the other boys into the washroom. Once again, he watched carefully as they washed their faces with flannels before brushing their teeth. He didn't have a flannel or a toothbrush. The boy from the next bed rummaged around in his wash bag and handed him a brand-new toothbrush and a tube of toothpaste. Harry didn't want to take them until the boy said, "My mother always packs two of everything."

"Thank you," said Harry. Although he cleaned his teeth quickly, he was still among the last to return to the dormitory. He climbed into bed, two clean sheets, two blankets and a soft pillow. He had just looked across to see that Deakins was reading *Kennedy's Latin Primer* when the other boy said, "This pillow is brick hard."

"Would you like to swap with me?" Harry asked.

"I think you'll find they're all the same," the boy said with a grin, "but thanks."

Harry took his bar of chocolate from under the pillow and broke it into three pieces. He handed one piece to Deakins, and another to the boy who'd given him the toothbrush and toothpaste.

"I see your mater's far more sensible than mine," he said after taking a bite. Another bell. "By the way, my name's Giles Barrington. What's yours?"

"Clifton. Harry Clifton."

Harry didn't sleep for more than a few minutes at a time, and it wasn't just because his bed was so comfortable. Could it be possible that Giles was related to one of the three men who knew the truth about how his father had died? And if so, was he cut from the same cloth as his father, or his grandfather?

Suddenly Harry felt very lonely. He unscrewed the top of the toothpaste Barrington had given him and began to suck it until he fell asleep.

—◦—

When the now-familiar bell rang at 6:30 next morning, Harry climbed slowly out of bed, feeling sick. He followed Deakins into the washroom, to find Giles was testing the water. "Do you think this place has ever heard of hot water?" he asked.

Harry was just about to reply when the prefect hollered, "No talking in the washroom!"

"He's worse than a Prussian general," said Barrington, clicking his heels. Harry burst out laughing.

"Who was that?" asked Fisher, glaring at the two boys.

"Me," said Harry immediately.

"Name?"

"Clifton."

"Open your mouth again, Clifton, and I'll slipper you."

Harry had no idea what being slippered meant, but he had a feeling it wouldn't be pleasant. Once he'd brushed his teeth, he walked quickly back into the dorm and dressed without another word. After he'd done up his tie—something else he hadn't quite mastered—he caught up with Barrington and Deakins as they made their way down the stairs to the refectory.

Nobody said a word, as they weren't sure if they were allowed to talk while they were on the staircase. When they sat down for breakfast in the refectory, Harry slipped in between his two new friends, and watched as bowls of porridge were placed in front of each boy. He was relieved to find there was only one spoon in front of him, so he couldn't make a mistake this time.

Harry gulped down his porridge so quickly it was as if he was afraid Uncle Stan would appear and snatch it away from him. He was the first to finish, and without a moment's thought he put his spoon down on the table, picked up his bowl and began to lick it. Several other boys stared at him in disbelief, some pointed, while others sniggered. He turned a bright shade of crimson and put the bowl back down. He would have burst into tears, if Barrington hadn't picked up his own bowl and begun licking it.

5

THE REVEREND SAMUEL OAKSHOTT MA (Oxon) stood, feet apart, at the center of the stage. He peered benignly down on his flock, for that was certainly how the headmaster of St. Bede's viewed the pupils.

Harry, seated in the front row, stared up at the frightening figure who towered above him. Dr. Oakshott was well over six feet tall, and had a head of thick, graying hair and long bushy sideburns that made him look even more forbidding. His deep blue eyes pierced right through you and he never seemed to blink, while the criss-cross of lines on his forehead hinted at great wisdom. He cleared his throat before addressing the boys.

"Fellow Bedeans," he began. "We are once again gathered together at the beginning of a new school year, no doubt prepared to face whatever challenges should confront us. For the senior boys," he turned his attention to the back of the hall, "you don't have a moment to lose if you hope to be offered a place at the school of your first choice. Never settle for second best.

"For the middle school," his eyes moved to the center of the hall, "this will be a time when we discover which of you is destined for greater things. When you return next year, will you be a prefect, a monitor, a house captain or a captain of sport? Or will you simply be among the also-rans?" Several boys bowed their heads.

"Our next duty is to welcome the new boys, and do everything in our power to make them feel at home. They are being handed the baton for the first time as they begin life's long race. Should the pace prove to be too demanding, one or two of you may fall by the wayside," he warned, staring down at the front three rows. "St. Bede's is not a school for the faint-hearted. So be sure never to forget the words of the great Cecil Rhodes: *If you are lucky enough to have been born an Englishman, you have drawn first prize in the lottery of life.*"

The assembled gathering burst into spontaneous applause as the headmaster left the stage, followed by a crocodile of masters whom he led down the center aisle, out of the great hall and into the morning sunshine.

Harry, his spirits raised, was determined not to let the headmaster down. He followed the senior boys out of the hall, but the moment he stepped out into the quad, his exuberance was dampened. A posse of older boys were hanging around in one corner, hands in pockets to indicate they were prefects.

"There he is," said one of them, pointing at Harry.

"So that's what a street urchin looks like," said another.

A third, whom Harry recognized as Fisher, the prefect who had been on duty the previous night, added, "He's an animal, and it's nothing less than our duty to see that he's returned to his natural habitat as quickly as possible."

Giles Barrington ran after Harry. "If you ignore them," he said, "they'll soon get bored and start picking on someone else." Harry wasn't convinced, and ran ahead to the classroom where he waited for Barrington and Deakins to join him.

A moment later, Mr. Frobisher entered the room. Harry's first thought was, does he also think I'm a street urchin, unworthy of a place at St. Bede's?

"Good morning, boys," said Mr. Frobisher.

"Good morning, sir," replied the boys as their form master took his place in front of the blackboard. "Your first lesson this morning," he said, "will be history. As I am keen to get to know you, we will start with a simple test to discover how much you have already learned, or perhaps how little. How many wives did Henry the Eighth have?"

Several hands shot up. "Abbott," he said, looking at a chart on his desk and pointing to a boy in the front row.

"Six, sir," came back the immediate reply.

"Good, but can anyone name them?" Not quite as many hands were raised. "Clifton?"

"Catherine of Aragon, Anne Boleyn, Jane Seymour, then another Anne I think," he said before coming to a halt.

"Anne of Cleves. Can anyone name the missing two?" Only one hand remained in the air. "Deakins," said Frobisher after checking his chart.

"Catherine Howard and Catherine Parr. Anne of Cleves and Catherine Parr both outlived Henry."

"Very good, Deakins. Now, let's turn the clock forward a couple of centuries. Who commanded our fleet at the Battle of Trafalgar?" Every hand in the room shot up. "Matthews," he said, nodding at a particularly insistent hand.

"Nelson, sir."

"Correct. And who was Prime Minister at the time?"

"The Duke of Wellington, sir," said Matthews, not sounding quite as confident.

"No," said Mr. Frobisher, "it wasn't Wellington, although he was a contemporary of Nelson's." He looked around the class, but only Clifton's and Deakins's hands were still raised. "Deakins."

"Pitt the Younger, 1783 to 1801, and 1804 to 1806."

"Correct, Deakins. And when was the Iron Duke Prime Minister?"

"1828 to 1830, and again in 1834," said Deakins.

"And can anyone tell me what his most famous victory was?"

Barrington's hand shot up for the first time. "Waterloo, sir!" he shouted before Mr. Frobisher had time to select anyone else.

"Yes, Barrington. And whom did Wellington defeat at Waterloo?"

Barrington remained silent.

"Napoleon," whispered Harry.

"Napoleon, sir," said Barrington confidently.

"Correct, Clifton," said Frobisher, smiling. "And was Napoleon also a Duke?"

"No, sir," said Deakins, after no one else had attempted to

answer the question. "He founded the first French Empire, and appointed himself Emperor."

Mr. Frobisher was not surprised by Deakins's response, as he was an open scholar, but he was impressed by Clifton's knowledge. After all, he was a choral scholar, and over the years he had learned that gifted choristers, like talented sportsmen, rarely excel outside their own field. Clifton was already proving an exception to that rule. Mr. Frobisher would have liked to know who had taught the boy.

When the bell rang for the end of class, Mr. Frobisher announced, "Your next lesson will be geography with Mr. Henderson, and he is not a master who likes to be kept waiting. I recommend that during the break you find out where his classroom is, and are seated in your places long before he enters the room."

Harry stuck close to Giles, who seemed to know where everything was. As they strolled across the quad together, Harry became aware that some of the boys lowered their voices when they passed, and one or two even turned to stare at him.

Thanks to countless Saturday mornings spent with Old Jack, Harry held his own in the geography lesson, but in maths, the final class of the morning, no one came close to Deakins, and even the master had to keep his wits about him.

When the three of them sat down for lunch, Harry could feel a hundred eyes watching his every move. He pretended not to notice, and simply copied everything Giles did. "It's nice to know there's something I can teach you," Giles said as he peeled an apple with his knife.

Harry enjoyed his first chemistry lesson later that afternoon, especially when the master allowed him to light a Bunsen burner. But he didn't excel at nature studies, the final lesson of the day, because Harry was the only boy whose home didn't have a garden.

When the final bell sounded, the rest of the class went off for games, while Harry reported to the chapel for his first choir practice. Once again, he noticed everyone was staring at him, but this time it was for all the right reasons.

But no sooner had he walked out of the chapel than he was subjected to the same sotto voce jibes from boys who were making their way back from the playing fields.

"Isn't that our little street urchin?" said one.

"Pity he doesn't have a toothbrush," said another.

"Sleeps down at the docks at night, I'm told," said a third.

Deakins and Barrington were nowhere to be seen as Harry hurried back to his house, avoiding any gatherings of boys on the way.

During supper, the gawping eyes were less obvious, but only because Giles had made it clear to everyone within earshot that Harry was his friend. But Giles was unable to help when they all went up to the dormitory after prep and found Fisher standing by the door, clearly waiting for Harry.

As the boys began to undress, Fisher announced in a loud voice, "I'm sorry about the smell, gentlemen, but one of your form comes from a house without a bath." One or two of the boys sniggered, hoping to ingratiate themselves with Fisher. Harry ignored him. "Not only does this guttersnipe not have a bath, he doesn't even have a father."

"My father was a good man who fought for his country in the war," said Harry proudly.

"What makes you think I was talking about you, Clifton?" said Fisher. "Unless of course you're also the boy whose mother works —" he paused—"as a hotel waitress."

"An hotel," said Harry, correcting him.

Fisher grabbed a slipper. "Don't you ever answer me back, Clifton," he said angrily. "Bend down and touch the end of your bed." Harry obeyed, and Fisher administered six strokes with such ferocity that Giles had to turn away. Harry crept into bed, fighting to hold back the tears.

Before Fisher switched off the light, he added, "I'll look forward to seeing you all again tomorrow night, when I will continue with my bedtime tale of the Cliftons of Still House Lane. Wait until you hear about Uncle Stan."

The following night, Harry learned for the first time that his uncle had spent eighteen months in prison for burglary. This revelation was worse than being slippered. He crept into bed wondering if his father could still be alive but in jail, and that was the real reason no one at home ever talked about him.

Harry hardly slept for a third night running, and no amount of success in the classroom, or admiration in the chapel, could stop him continually thinking about the next inevitable encounter with Fisher. The slightest excuse, a drop of water spilled on the washroom floor, a pillow that wasn't straight, a sock that had fallen around his ankle, would ensure that Harry could expect six of the best from the duty prefect; a punishment that would be administered in front of the rest of the dorm, but not before Fisher had added another episode from the Clifton Chronicles. By the fifth night, Harry had had enough, and even Giles and Deakins could no longer console him.

During prep on Friday evening, while the other boys were turning the pages of their *Kennedy's Latin Primer,* Harry ignored Caesar and the Gauls and went over a plan that would ensure Fisher never bothered him again. By the time he climbed into bed that night, after Fisher had discovered a Fry's wrapper by his bed and slippered him once again, Harry's plan was in place. He lay awake long after lights out, and didn't stir until he was certain every boy was asleep.

Harry had no idea what time it was when he slipped out of bed. He dressed without making a sound, then crept between the beds until he reached the far side of the room. He pushed the window open, and the rush of cold air caused the boy in the nearest bed to turn over. Harry climbed out onto the fire escape and slowly closed the window before making his way down to the ground. He walked around the edge of the lawn, taking advantage of any shadows to avoid a full moon that seemed to beam down on him like a searchlight.

Harry was horrified to discover that the school gates were locked. He crept along the wall, searching for the slightest crack or indentation that would allow him to climb over the top and escape to freedom. At last he spotted a missing brick and was able to lever himself up until he was straddling the wall. He lowered himself down the other side, clinging on by the tips of his fingers, said a silent prayer, then let go. He landed on the ground in a heap, but didn't seem to have broken anything.

Once he'd recovered, he began to run down the road, slowly at first, but then he speeded up and didn't stop running until he reached the docks. The night shift was just coming off duty and Harry was relieved to find his uncle was not among them.

After the last docker had disappeared out of sight, he walked slowly along the quayside, past a line of moored ships that stretched as far as the eye could see. He noticed that one of the funnels proudly displayed the letter B, and thought about his friend who would be fast asleep. Would he ever . . . his thoughts were interrupted when he came to a halt outside Old Jack's railway carriage.

He wondered if the old man was also fast asleep. His question was answered when a voice said, "Don't just stand there, Harry, come inside before you freeze to death." Harry opened the carriage door to find Old Jack striking a match and trying to light a candle. Harry slumped into the seat opposite him. "Have you run away?" asked Old Jack.

Harry was so taken aback by his direct question that he didn't answer immediately. "Yes, I have," he finally spluttered.

"And no doubt you've come to tell me why you've made this momentous decision."

"I didn't make the decision," said Harry. "It was made for me."

"By whom?"

"His name is Fisher."

"A master or a boy?"

"My dormitory prefect," said Harry, wincing. He then told Old Jack everything that had happened during his first week at St. Bede's.

Once again, the old man took him by surprise. When Harry came to the end of his story, Jack said, "I blame myself."

"Why?" asked Harry. "You couldn't have done more to help me."

"Yes I could," said Old Jack. "I should have prepared you for a brand of snobbery that no other nation on earth can emulate. I should have spent more time on the significance of the old school tie, and less on geography and history. I had rather hoped things just might have changed after the war to end all wars, but they clearly haven't at St. Bede's." He fell into a thoughtful silence before finally asking, "So what are you going to do next, my boy?"

"Run away to sea. I'll take any boat that will have me," said Harry, trying to sound enthusiastic.

"What a good idea," said Old Jack. "Why not play straight into Fisher's hands?"

"What do you mean?"

"Just that nothing will please Fisher more than to be able to tell his friends that the street urchin had no guts, but then, what do you expect from the son of a docker whose mother is a waitress?"

"But Fisher's right. I'm not in his class."

"No, Harry, the problem is that Fisher already realizes he's not in your class, and never will be."

"Are you saying I should go back to that horrible place?" said Harry.

"In the end, only you can make that decision," said Old Jack, "but if you run away every time you come up against the Fishers of this world, you'll end up like me, one of life's also-rans, to quote the headmaster."

"But you're a great man," said Harry.

"I might have been," said Old Jack, "if I hadn't run away the moment I came across my Fisher. But I settled for the easy way out, and only thought about myself."

"But who else is there to think about?"

"Your mother for a start," said Old Jack. "Don't forget all the sacrifices she made to give you a better start in life than she ever dreamed was possible. And then there's Mr. Holcombe, who when he discovers you've run away will only blame himself. And don't forget Miss Monday, who called in favors, twisted arms and spent countless hours to make sure you were good enough to win that choral scholarship. And when you come to weigh up the pros and cons, Harry, I suggest you place Fisher on one side of the scales and Barrington and Deakins on the other, because I suspect that Fisher will quickly fade into insignificance, while

Barrington and Deakins will surely turn out to be close friends for the rest of your life. If you run away, they will be forced to listen to Fisher continually reminding them that you weren't the person they thought you were."

Harry remained silent for some time. Finally, he rose slowly to his feet. "Thank you, sir," he said. Without another word he opened the carriage door and let himself out.

He walked slowly down the quayside, once again staring up at the vast cargo ships, all of which would soon be departing for distant ports. He kept on walking until he reached the dockyard gates, where he broke into a run and headed back toward the city. By the time he reached the school gates they were already open, and the clock on the great hall was about to chime eight times.

Despite the telephone call, Mr. Frobisher would have to walk across to the headmaster's house and report that one of his boys was missing. As he looked out of his study window, he caught a glimpse of Harry nipping in and out between the trees as he made his way cautiously toward the house. Harry tentatively opened the front door as the final chime rang out, and came face to face with his housemaster.

"Better hurry, Clifton," Mr. Frobisher said, "or you'll miss breakfast."

"Yes, sir," said Harry, and ran down the corridor. He reached the dining room just before the doors were closed and slipped into place between Barrington and Deakins.

"For a moment I thought I'd be the only one licking my bowl this morning," said Barrington. Harry burst out laughing.

He didn't come across Fisher that day, and was surprised to find that another prefect had replaced him on dorm duty that night. Harry slept for the first time that week.

6

THE ROLLS-ROYCE DROVE through the gates of the Manor House and up a long driveway lined with tall oaks, standing like sentinels. Harry had counted six gardeners even before he set eyes on the house.

During their time at St. Bede's, Harry had picked up a little about how Giles lived when he returned home for the holidays, but nothing had prepared him for this. When he saw the house for the first time, his mouth opened, and stayed open.

"Early eighteenth century would be my guess," said Deakins.

"Not bad," said Giles, "1722, built by Vanbrugh. But I'll bet you can't tell me who designed the garden. I'll give you a clue: it's later than the house."

"I've only ever heard of one landscape gardener," said Harry, still staring at the house. "Capability Brown."

"That's exactly why we chose him," said Giles, "simply so that my friends would have heard of the fellow two hundred years later."

Harry and Deakins laughed as the car came to a halt in front of a three-story mansion built from golden Cotswold stone. Giles jumped out before the chauffeur had a chance to open the back door. He ran up the steps with his two friends following less certainly in his wake.

The front door was opened long before Giles reached the top step, and a tall man, elegantly dressed in a long black coat, pinstripe trousers and a black tie, gave a slight bow as the young master shot past him. "Happy birthday, Mr. Giles," he said.

"Thank you, Jenkins. Come on, chaps!" shouted Giles as he

disappeared into the house. The butler held open the door to allow Harry and Deakins to follow.

As soon as Harry stepped into the hall, he found himself transfixed by the portrait of an old man who appeared to be staring directly down at him. Giles had inherited the man's beak-like nose, fierce blue eyes and square jaw. Harry looked around at the other portraits that adorned the walls. The only oil paintings he'd seen before were in books: the *Mona Lisa,* the *Laughing Cavalier* and *Night Watch.* He was looking at a landscape by an artist called Constable when a woman swept into the hall wearing what Harry could only have described as a ball gown.

"Happy birthday, my darling," she said.

"Thank you, Mater," said Giles, as she bent down to kiss him. It was the first time Harry had ever seen his friend look embarrassed. "These are my two best friends, Harry and Deakins." As Harry shook hands with a woman who wasn't much taller than he was, she gave him such a warm smile that he immediately felt at ease.

"Why don't we all go through to the drawing room," she suggested, "and have some tea?" She led the boys across the hall and into a large room that overlooked the front lawn.

When Harry entered, he didn't want to sit down but to look at the paintings that hung on every wall. However, Mrs. Barrington was already ushering him toward the sofa. He sank down into the plush cushions and couldn't stop himself staring out of the bay window onto a finely cut lawn that was large enough to play a game of cricket on. Beyond the lawn, Harry could see a lake where contented mallards swam aimlessly around, clearly not worried about where their next meal would be coming from. Deakins sat himself down on the sofa next to Harry.

Neither of them spoke as another man, this one dressed in a short black jacket, entered the room, followed by a young woman in a smart blue uniform, not unlike the one his mother wore at the hotel. The maid carried a large silver tray which she placed on an oval table in front of Mrs. Barrington.

"Indian or China?" Mrs. Barrington asked, looking at Harry.

Harry wasn't sure what she meant.

"We'll all have Indian, thank you, Mother," said Giles.

Harry thought Giles must have taught him everything there was to know about etiquette as practiced in polite society, but Mrs. Barrington had suddenly raised the bar to a new level.

Once the under-butler had poured three cups of tea, the maid placed them in front of the boys, along with a side plate. Harry stared at a mountain of sandwiches, not daring to touch. Giles took one and put it on his plate. His mother frowned. "How many times have I told you, Giles, always to wait until your guests decide what they would like before you help yourself?"

Harry wanted to tell Mrs. Barrington that Giles always took the lead, just so that he would know what to do and, more important, what not to do. Deakins selected a sandwich and put it on his plate. Harry did the same. Giles waited patiently until Deakins had picked up his sandwich and taken a bite.

"I do hope you like smoked salmon," said Mrs. Barrington.

"Spiffing," said Giles, before his friends had a chance to admit that they had never tasted smoked salmon before. "We only get fish paste sandwiches at school," he added.

"So, tell me how you're all getting on at school," said Mrs. Barrington.

"Room for improvement, is how I think the Frob describes my efforts," said Giles, as he took another sandwich. "But Deakins is top of everything."

"Except for English," said Deakins, speaking for the first time, "Harry pipped me in that subject by a couple of percent."

"And did you pip anyone in anything, Giles?" asked his mother.

"He came second in maths, Mrs. Barrington," said Harry, coming to Giles's rescue. "He has a natural gift for figures."

"Just like his grandfather," said Mrs. Barrington.

"That's a nice picture of you above the fireplace, Mrs. Barrington," said Deakins.

She smiled. "It's not me, Deakins, it's my dear mother." Deakins bowed his head before Mrs. Barrington quickly added, "But what a charming compliment. She was considered a great beauty in her day."

"Who painted it?" asked Harry, coming to Deakins's rescue.

"László," replied Mrs. Barrington. "Why do you ask?"

"Because I was wondering if the portrait of the gentleman in the hall might be by the same artist."

"How very observant of you, Harry," said Mrs. Barrington. "The painting you saw in the hall is of my father, and was indeed also painted by László."

"What does your father do?" asked Harry.

"Harry never stops asking questions," said Giles. "One just has to get used to it."

Mrs. Barrington smiled. "He imports wines to this country, in particular, sherries from Spain."

"Just like Harvey's," said Deakins, his mouth full of cucumber sandwich.

"Just like Harvey's," repeated Mrs. Barrington. Giles grinned. "Do have another sandwich, Harry," said Mrs. Barrington, noticing that his eyes were fixed on the plate.

"Thank you," said Harry, unable to choose between smoked salmon, cucumber, or egg and tomato. He settled for salmon, wondering what it would taste like.

"And how about you, Deakins?"

"Thank you, Mrs. Barrington," he said, and took another cucumber sandwich.

"I can't go on calling you Deakins," said Giles's mother. "It makes you sound like one of the servants. Do tell me your Christian name."

Deakins bowed his head again. "I prefer to be called Deakins," he said.

"It's Al," said Giles.

"Such a nice name," said Mrs. Barrington, "although I expect your mother calls you Alan."

"No, she doesn't," said Deakins, his head still bowed. The other two boys looked surprised by this revelation, but said nothing. "My name's Algernon," he finally spluttered.

Giles burst out laughing.

Mrs. Barrington paid no attention to her son's outburst. "Your mother must be an admirer of Oscar Wilde," she said.

"Yes, she is," said Deakins. "But I wish she'd called me Jack, or even Ernest."

"I wouldn't let it worry you," said Mrs. Barrington. "After all, Giles suffers from a similar indignity."

"Mother, you promised you wouldn't—"

"You must get him to tell you his middle name," she said, ignoring the protest. When Giles didn't respond, Harry and Deakins looked at Mrs. Barrington hopefully. "Marmaduke," she declared with a sigh. "Like his father and grandfather before him."

"If either of you tell anyone about this when we get back to school," Giles said, looking at his two friends, "I swear I'll kill you, and I mean, kill you." Both boys laughed.

"Do you have a middle name, Harry?" asked Mrs. Barrington.

Harry was about to reply when the drawing-room door flew open and a man who couldn't have been mistaken for a servant strode into the room carrying a large parcel. Harry looked up at a man who could only have been Mr. Hugo. Giles leaped up and ran toward his father, who handed him the parcel and said, "Happy birthday, my boy."

"Thank you, Papa," said Giles, and immediately began to untie the ribbon.

"Before you open your present, Giles," said his mother, "perhaps you should first introduce your guests to Papa."

"Sorry, Papa. These are my two best friends, Deakins and Harry," said Giles, placing the gift on the table. Harry noticed that Giles's father had the same athletic build and restless energy he'd assumed was uniquely his son's.

"Pleased to meet you, Deakins," said Mr. Barrington, shaking him by the hand. He then turned to Harry. "Good afternoon, Clifton," he added, before sitting down in the empty chair next to his wife. Harry was puzzled that Mr. Barrington didn't shake hands with him. And how did he know his name was Clifton?

Once the under-butler had served Mr. Barrington with a cup of tea, Giles removed the wrapping from his present and let out a yelp of delight when he saw the Roberts radio. He pushed the plug into a wall socket and began to tune the radio to different stations. The boys applauded and laughed with each new sound that was emitted from the large wooden box.

"Giles tells me that he came second in mathematics this term," said Mrs. Barrington, turning to her husband.

"Which doesn't make up for him being bottom in almost every other subject," he retorted. Giles tried not to look embarrassed, as he continued to search for another station on his radio.

"But you should have seen the goal he scored against Avonhurst," said Harry. "We're all expecting him to captain the eleven next year."

"Goals aren't going to get him into Eton," said Mr. Barrington, not looking at Harry. "It's time the boy buckled down and worked harder."

No one spoke for some time, until Mrs. Barrington broke the silence. "Are you the Clifton who sings in the choir at St. Mary Redcliffe?" she asked.

"Harry's the treble soloist," said Giles. "In fact, he's a choral scholar."

Harry became aware that Giles's father was now staring at him.

"I thought I recognized you," said Mrs. Barrington. "Giles's grandfather and I attended a performance of the *Messiah* at St. Mary's, when the choir of St. Bede's joined forces with Bristol Grammar School. Your "I Know That My Redeemer Liveth" was quite magnificent, Harry."

"Thank you, Mrs. Barrington," said Harry, blushing.

"Are you hoping to go on to Bristol Grammar School after you leave St. Bede's, Clifton?" asked Mr. Barrington.

Clifton again, thought Harry. "Only if I win a scholarship, sir," he replied.

"But why is that important?" asked Mrs. Barrington. "Surely you will be offered a place, like any other boy?"

"Because my mother wouldn't be able to afford the fees, Mrs. Barrington. She's a waitress at the Royal Hotel."

"But wouldn't your father—"

"He's dead," said Harry. "He was killed in the war." He

watched carefully to see how Mr. Barrington would react, but like a good poker player he gave nothing away.

"I'm sorry," said Mrs. Barrington. "I didn't realize."

The door opened behind Harry and the under-butler entered, carrying a two-tier birthday cake on a silver tray which he placed on the center of the table. After Giles had succeeded in blowing out all twelve candles with one puff, everyone applauded.

"And when's your birthday, Clifton?" asked Mr. Barrington.

"It was last month, sir," Harry replied.

Mr. Barrington looked away.

The under-butler removed the candles before handing the young master a large cake knife. Giles cut deep into the cake and placed five uneven slices on the tea plates the maid had laid out on the table.

Deakins devoured the lumps of icing that had fallen onto his plate before taking a bite of the cake. Harry followed Mrs. Barrington's lead. He picked up the small silver fork by the side of his plate, using it to remove a tiny piece of his cake before placing it back on the plate.

Only Mr. Barrington didn't touch his cake. Suddenly, without warning, he rose from his place and left without another word.

Giles's mother made no attempt to conceal her surprise at her husband's behavior, but she said nothing. Harry never took his eyes off Mr. Hugo as he left the room, while Deakins, having finished his cake, turned his attention back to the smoked salmon sandwiches, clearly oblivious to what was going on around him.

Once the door was closed, Mrs. Barrington continued to chat as if nothing unusual had happened. "I'm sure you'll win a scholarship to Bristol Grammar, Harry, especially considering everything Giles has told me about you. You're obviously a very clever boy, as well as a gifted singer."

"Giles does have a tendency to exaggerate, Mrs. Barrington," said Harry. "I can assure you only Deakins is certain of winning a scholarship."

"But doesn't BGS offer grants for music scholars?" she asked.

"Not for trebles," said Harry. "They won't take the risk."

"I'm not sure I understand," said Mrs. Barrington. "Nothing can take away the years of choral training you've been put through."

"True, but sadly no one can predict what will happen when your voice breaks. Some trebles end up as basses or baritones, and the really lucky ones become tenors, but there's no way of telling in advance."

"Why not?" asked Deakins, taking an interest for the first time.

"There are plenty of treble soloists who can't even get a place in their local choir once their voice has broken. Ask Master Ernest Lough. Every household in England has heard him sing "Oh, for the wings of a dove," but after his voice broke no one ever heard from him again."

"You're just going to have to work harder," said Deakins between mouthfuls. "Don't forget the grammar school awards twelve scholarships every year, and I can only win one of them," he added matter-of-factly.

"But that's the problem," said Harry. "If I'm going to work any harder, I'll have to give up the choir, and without my bursary, I'd have to leave St. Bede's, so . . ."

"You're between a rock and a hard place," said Deakins.

Harry had never heard the expression before and decided to ask Deakins later what it meant.

"Well, one thing's for certain," said Mrs. Barrington, "Giles isn't likely to win a scholarship to any school."

"Maybe not," said Harry. "But Bristol Grammar isn't likely to turn down a left-handed batsman of his caliber."

"Then we'll have to hope that Eton feels the same way," said Mrs. Barrington, "because that's where his father wants him to go."

"I don't want to go to Eton," said Giles, putting down his fork. "I want to go to BGS and be with my friends."

"I'm sure you'll make a lot of new friends at Eton," said his mother. "And it would be a great disappointment to your father if you didn't follow in his footsteps."

The under-butler coughed. Mrs. Barrington looked out of the

window to see a car drawing up at the bottom of the steps. "I think the time has come for you all to return to school," she said. "I certainly don't want to be responsible for anyone being late for prep."

Harry looked longingly at the large plate of sandwiches and the half-finished birthday cake but reluctantly rose from his place and began to walk toward the door. He glanced back once and could have sworn he saw Deakins put a sandwich in his pocket. He took one last look out of the window and was surprised to notice, for the first time, a gangly young girl with long pigtails who was curled up in the corner reading a book.

"That's my frightful sister, Emma," said Giles. "She never stops reading. Just ignore her." Harry smiled at Emma, but she didn't look up. Deakins didn't give her a second look.

Mrs. Barrington accompanied the three boys to the front door, where she shook hands with Harry and Deakins. "I do hope you'll both come again soon," she said. "You're such a good influence on Giles."

"Thank you very much for having us to tea, Mrs. Barrington," Harry said. Deakins just nodded. Both boys looked away when she hugged her son and gave him a kiss.

As the chauffeur drove down the long driveway toward the gates, Harry looked out of the back window at the house. He didn't notice Emma staring out of the window at the disappearing car.

7

THE SCHOOL TUCK shop was open between four and six every Tuesday and Thursday afternoon.

Harry rarely visited the "Emporium," as it was known by the boys, since he only had two shillings' pocket money a term, and he knew his mother wouldn't appreciate any little extras appearing on his end-of-term account. However, on Deakins's birthday, Harry made an exception to this rule, as he intended to purchase a one-penny bar of fudge for his friend.

Despite Harry's rare visits to the tuck shop, a bar of Fry's Five Boys chocolate could be found on his desk every Tuesday and Thursday evening. Although there was a school rule that no boy could spend more than sixpence a week in the tuck shop, Giles would also leave a packet of Licorice Allsorts for Deakins, making it clear to his friends that he expected nothing in return.

When Harry arrived at the tuck shop that Tuesday, he joined a long queue of boys waiting to be served. His mouth watered as he stared at the neatly stacked rows of chocolate, fudge, jelly babies, licorice and, the latest craze, Smiths potato crisps. He'd considered buying a packet for himself, but after a recent introduction to Mr. Wilkins Micawber, he had been left in no doubt about the value of sixpence.

As Harry ogled the Emporium's treasures, he heard Giles's voice and noticed that he was a few places ahead of him in the queue. He was just about to hail his friend when he saw Giles remove a bar of chocolate from a shelf and slip it into his trouser pocket. A few moments later, a packet of chewing gum followed. When Giles reached the front of the queue, he placed on the counter a box of Licorice Allsorts, 2d, and a bag of crisps, 1d, which Mr. Swivals, the master in charge of the shop, entered neatly in his ledger against the name of Barrington. The two other items remained in Giles's pocket, unaccounted for.

Harry was horrified, and before Giles could turn round, he slipped out of the shop, not wanting his friend to spot him. Harry walked slowly around the school block, trying to work out why Giles would want to steal anything, when he could so obviously afford to pay. He assumed there had to be some simple explanation, although he couldn't imagine what it might be.

Harry went up to his study just before prep, to find the pilfered bar of chocolate on his desk, and Deakins tucking into a box of Licorice Allsorts. He found it difficult to concentrate on the causes of the Industrial Revolution while he tried to decide what, if anything, he should do about his discovery.

By the end of prep, he'd made his decision. He placed the unopened bar of chocolate in the top drawer of his desk, having decided he would return it to the tuck shop on Thursday, without telling Giles.

Harry didn't sleep that night, and after breakfast he took Deakins to one side and explained why he hadn't been able to give him a birthday present. Deakins couldn't hide his disbelief.

"My dad's been having the same problem in his shop," said Deakins. "It's called shoplifting. The *Daily Mail* is blaming it on the Depression."

"I don't think Giles's family will have been affected much by the Depression," said Harry with some feeling.

Deakins nodded thoughtfully. "Perhaps you should tell the Frob?"

"Sneak on my best friend?" said Harry. "Never."

"But if Giles is caught he could be expelled," said Deakins. "The least you can do is warn him you've found out what he's up to."

"I'll think about it," said Harry. "But in the meantime I'm

going to return anything Giles gives me to the tuck shop without letting him know."

Deakins leaned over. "Could you take my stuff back as well?" he whispered. "I never go to the tuck shop, so I wouldn't know what to do."

Harry agreed to take on the responsibility, and after that he went to the tuck shop twice a week and placed Giles's unwanted gifts back on the shelves. He had concluded that Deakins was right and that he would have to confront his friend before he was caught, but decided to put it off until the end of term.

—◇—

"Good shot, Barrington," said Mr. Frobisher as the ball crossed the boundary. A ripple of applause broke out around the ground. "Mark my words, headmaster, Barrington will play for Eton against Harrow at Lord's."

"Not if Giles has anything to do with it," Harry whispered to Deakins.

"What are you doing for the summer hols, Harry?" asked Deakins, seemingly oblivious to all that was going on around him.

"I don't have any plans to visit Tuscany this year, if that's what you're asking," Harry replied with a grin.

"I don't think Giles really wants to go either," said Deakins. "After all, the Italians have never understood cricket."

"Well, I'd be happy to change places with him," said Harry. "It doesn't bother me that Michelangelo, Da Vinci and Caravaggio were never introduced to the finer subtleties of leg break bowling, not to mention all that pasta he'll be expected to wade through."

"So where are you going?" asked Deakins.

"A week on the Riviera of the West," said Harry with bravado. "The grand pier at Weston-super-Mare is usually the high spot, followed by fish and chips at Coffins café. Care to join me?"

"Can't spare the time," said Deakins, who clearly thought Harry was being serious.

"And why's that?" asked Harry, playing along.

"Too much work to do."

"You intend to go on working during the holidays?" asked Harry in disbelief.

"Work *is* a holiday for me," said Deakins. "I enjoy it every bit as much as Giles does his cricket, and you do your singing."

"But where do you work?"

"In the municipal library, clot. They have everything I need."

"Can I join you?" asked Harry, sounding just as serious. "I need all the help I can get if I'm to have any chance of winning a scholarship to BGS."

"Only if you agree to remain silent at all times," said Deakins. Harry would have laughed, but he knew his friend didn't consider work a laughing matter.

"But I desperately need some help with my Latin grammar," said Harry. "I still don't understand the consecutive clause, let alone subjunctives, and if I don't manage a pass mark in the Latin paper, it's curtains, even if I do well in every other subject."

"I'd be willing to help you with your Latin," said Deakins, "if you do me a favor in return."

"Name it," said Harry, "though I can't believe you're hoping to perform a solo at this year's carol service."

"Good shot, Barrington," said Mr. Frobisher again. Harry joined in the applause. "That's his third half-century this season, headmaster," added Mr. Frobisher.

"Don't be frivolous, Harry," said Deakins. "The truth is, my dad needs someone to take over the morning paper round during the summer holidays, and I've suggested you. The pay is a shilling a week, and as long as you can report to the shop by six o'clock every morning, the position's yours."

"Six o'clock?" said Harry scornfully. "When you've got an uncle who wakes up the whole house at five, that's the least of your problems."

"Then you'd be willing to take on the job?"

"Yes, of course," said Harry. "But why don't you want it? A bob a week is not to be sniffed at."

"Don't remind me," said Deakins, "but I can't ride a bicycle."

"Oh hell," said Harry. "I don't even have a bicycle."

"I didn't say I didn't *have* a bicycle," sighed Deakins, "I said I couldn't ride one."

"Clifton," said Mr. Frobisher as the cricketers walked off the ground for tea, "I'd like to see you in my study after prep."

◄○►

Harry had always liked Mr. Frobisher, who was one of the few masters who treated him as an equal. He also didn't appear to have any favorites, while some of the other beaks left him in no doubt that a docker's son should never have been allowed to enter the hallowed portals of St. Bede's however good his voice was.

When the bell rang at the end of prep, Harry put down his pen and walked across the corridor to Mr. Frobisher's study. He had no idea why his housemaster wanted to see him, and hadn't given the matter a great deal of thought.

Harry knocked on the study door.

"Come," said the voice of a man who never wasted words. Harry opened the door and was surprised not to be greeted with the usual Frob smile.

Mr. Frobisher stared up at Harry as he came to a halt in front of his desk. "It has been brought to my attention, Clifton, that you have been stealing from the tuck shop." Harry's mind went blank as he tried to think of a response that wouldn't condemn Giles. "You were seen by a prefect, removing goods from the shelves," continued Frobisher in the same uncompromising tone, "and then slipping out of the shop before you reached the front of the queue."

Harry wanted to say, "Not removing, sir, returning," but all he managed was, "I have never taken anything from the tuck shop, sir." Despite the fact that he was telling the truth, he could still feel his cheeks reddening.

"Then how do you explain your twice weekly visits to the Emporium, when there isn't a single entry against your name in Mr. Swivals's ledger?"

Mr. Frobisher waited patiently, but Harry knew if he told the truth, Giles would surely be expelled.

"And this bar of chocolate and packet of Licorice Allsorts were found in the top drawer of your desk, not long after the tuck shop had closed."

Harry looked down at the sweets, but still said nothing.

"I'm waiting for an explanation, Clifton," said Mr. Frobisher. After another long pause, he added, "I am of course aware that you have far less pocket money than any other boy in your class, but that is no excuse for stealing."

"I have never stolen anything in my life," said Harry.

It was Mr. Frobisher's turn to look dismayed. He rose from behind his desk. "If that is the case, Clifton—and I want to believe you—you will report back to me after choir practice with a full explanation of how you came to be in possession of tuck you clearly didn't pay for. Should you fail to satisfy me, we will both be paying a visit to the headmaster, and I have no doubt what his recommendation will be."

Harry left the room. The moment he closed the door behind him, he felt sick. He made his way back to his study, hoping Giles wouldn't be there. When he opened the door, the first thing he saw was another bar of chocolate on his desk.

Giles looked up. "Are you feeling all right?" he asked when he saw Harry's flushed face. Harry didn't reply. He placed the bar of chocolate in a drawer and left for choir practice without saying a word to either of his friends. Giles's eyes never left him, and once the door was closed, he turned to Deakins and asked casually, "What's his problem?" Deakins went on writing as if he hadn't heard the question. "Didn't you hear me, cloth ears?" said Giles. "Why's Harry in a sulk?"

"All I know is that he had an appointment to see the Frob."

"Why?" asked Giles, sounding more interested.

"I've no idea," said Deakins, who didn't stop writing.

Giles stood up and strolled across the room to Deakins's side. "What aren't you telling me?" he demanded, grabbing him by the ear.

Deakins dropped his pen, nervously touched the bridge of his glasses and pushed them further up his nose, before he eventually squeaked, "He's in some sort of trouble."

"What sort of trouble?" asked Giles, twisting the ear.

"I think he might even be expelled," whimpered Deakins.

Giles let go of his ear and burst out laughing. "Harry, expelled?" he scoffed. "The Pope's more likely to be defrocked." He would have returned to his desk if he hadn't noticed beads of sweat appearing on Deakins's forehead. "What for?" he asked more quietly.

"The Frob thinks he's been stealing from the tuck shop," said Deakins.

If Deakins had looked up, he would have seen that Giles had turned ashen white. A moment later, he heard the door close. He picked up his pen and tried to concentrate, but for the first time in his life, he didn't finish his prep.

—◦—

When Harry came out of choir practice an hour later, he spotted Fisher leaning on the wall, unable to mask a smile. That was when he realized who must have reported him. He ignored Fisher and strolled back to his house as if he didn't have a care in the world, whereas in fact he felt like a man mounting the gallows, knowing that unless he ditched his closest friend, a stay of execution would not be possible. He hesitated before knocking on his housemaster's door.

The "Come" was far gentler than it had been earlier that afternoon, but when Harry entered the room he was greeted with the same uncompromising stare. He bowed his head.

"I owe you a sincere apology, Clifton," said Frobisher, rising from behind his desk. "I now realize that you were not the culprit."

Harry's heart was still beating fast, but his anxiety was now for Giles. "Thank you, sir," he said, his head still bowed. He had so many questions he would have liked to ask the Frob, but he knew none of them would be answered.

Mr. Frobisher stepped out from behind his desk and shook hands with Harry, something he'd never done before. "You'd better hurry, Clifton, if you hope to get any supper."

When Harry came out of the Frob's study, he walked slowly

toward the dining room. Fisher was standing by the door, a surprised look on his face. Harry walked straight past him and took his place on the end of the bench next to Deakins. The seat opposite him was empty.

8

GILES DIDN'T SHOW up for supper, and his bed wasn't slept in that night. If St. Bede's hadn't lost their annual fixture against Avonhurst by thirty-one runs, Harry suspected that not many boys or even masters would have noticed he was missing.

But, unfortunately for Giles, it was a home match, so everyone had an opinion on why the school's opening batsman had not taken his guard at the crease, not least Fisher, who was telling anyone who cared to listen that the wrong man had been rusticated.

<o>

Harry hadn't been looking forward to the holidays; not just because he wondered if he'd ever see Giles again, but also because it meant returning to No. 27 Still House Lane and once again having to share a room with his uncle Stan, who more often than not returned home drunk.

After spending the evening going over old exam papers, Harry would climb into bed around ten. He quickly fell asleep, only to be woken sometime after midnight by his uncle, who was often so drunk he couldn't find his own bed. The sound of Stan trying to pee into a chamberpot, and not always hitting the target, was something that would remain etched in Harry's mind for the rest of his life.

Once Stan had collapsed on to his bed—he rarely bothered to get undressed—Harry would try to fall asleep a second time, often to be woken a few minutes later by loud drunken snores.

He longed to be back at St. Bede's, sharing a dormitory with twenty-nine other boys.

Harry still hoped that in an unguarded moment Stan might let slip some more details about his father's death, but most of the time he was too incoherent to answer even the simplest question. On one of the rare occasions when he was sober enough to speak, he told Harry to bugger off and warned him that if he raised the subject again, he'd thrash him.

The only good thing about sharing a room with Stan was that there was never any chance of his being late for his paper round. Harry's days at Still House Lane fell into a well-ordered routine: up at five, one slice of toast for breakfast—he no longer licked his uncle's bowl—report to Mr. Deakins at the newsagent's by six, stack the papers in the correct order, then deliver them. The whole exercise took about two hours, allowing him to be back home in time for a cup of tea with Mum before she went off to work. At around eight thirty Harry would set off for the library, where he would meet up with Deakins, who was always sitting on the top step waiting for someone to open the doors.

In the afternoon, Harry would report for choir practice at St. Mary Redcliffe, as part of his obligation to St. Bede's. He never considered it an obligation because he enjoyed singing so much. In fact, he'd more than once whispered, "Please God, when my voice breaks, let me be a tenor, and I'll never ask for anything else."

After he returned home for tea in the evening, Harry would work at the kitchen table for a couple of hours before going to bed, dreading his uncle's return every bit as much as he had Fisher's in his first week at St. Bede's. At least Fisher had departed for Colston's Grammar School, so Harry assumed their paths would never cross again.

—◦—

Harry was looking forward to his final year at St. Bede's, although he wasn't in any doubt just how much his life would change if he and his two friends ended up going their separate ways: Giles to he knew not where, Deakins to Bristol Grammar, while if he failed to win a scholarship to BGS, he might well have to return to Merrywood Elementary, and then, at the age of fourteen, leave school and look for a job. He tried not to think about the consequences of failure, despite Stan never missing an opportunity to remind him he could always find work at the docks.

"The boy should never have been allowed to go to that stuck-up school in the first place," he regularly told Maisie once she'd placed his bowl of porridge in front of him. "It's given him ideas above his station," he added, as if Harry wasn't there. A view that Harry felt Fisher would have happily agreed with, but then he'd long ago come to the conclusion that Uncle Stan and Fisher had a lot in common.

"But surely Harry should be given the chance to better himself?" countered Maisie.

"Why?" said Stan. "If the docks was good enough for me and his old man, why aren't they good enough for him?" he demanded with a finality that brooked no argument.

"Perhaps the boy's cleverer than both of us," suggested Maisie. This silenced Stan for a moment, but after another spoonful of porridge, he declared, "Depends on what you mean by clever. After all, there's clever and then there's clever." He took another spoonful, but added nothing more to this profound observation.

Harry would cut his slice of toast into four pieces as he listened to his uncle play the same record again and again every morning. He never spoke up for himself, as clearly Stan had already made up his mind on the subject of Harry's future and nothing was going to budge him. What Stan didn't realize was that his constant jibes only inspired Harry to work even harder.

"Can't hang around here all day," would be Stan's final comment, especially if he felt he was losing the argument. "Some of us have a job to do," he added as he rose from the table. No one bothered to argue. "And another thing," he said as he opened the kitchen door. "None of you've noticed the boy's gone soft. He doesn't even lick my porridge bowl no longer. God knows what they've been teachin' him at that school." The door slammed behind him.

"Take no notice of your uncle," said Harry's mother. "He's just jealous. He doesn't like the fact that we're all so proud of you. And even he'll have to change his tune when you win that scholarship, just like your friend Deakins."

"But that's the problem, Mum," said Harry. "I'm not like Deakins, and I'm beginning to wonder if it's all worth it."

The rest of the family stared at Harry in silent disbelief, until Grandpa piped up for the first time in days. "I wish I'd been given the chance to go to Bristol Grammar School."

"Why's that, Grandpa?" shouted Harry.

"Because if I had, we wouldn't have had to live with your uncle Stan all these years."

—◇—

Harry enjoyed his morning paper round, and not just because it got him out of the house. As the weeks went by, he came to know several of Mr. Deakins's regulars, some of whom had heard him sing at St. Mary's and would wave when he delivered their paper, while others offered him a cup of tea, even an apple. Mr. Deakins had warned him that there were two dogs he should avoid on the round; within a fortnight, both of them were wagging their tails when he got off his bicycle.

Harry was delighted to discover that Mr. Holcombe was one of Mr. Deakins's regular customers, and they often had a word when he dropped off his copy of *The Times* each morning. His first teacher left Harry in no doubt that he didn't want to see him back at Merrywood, and added that if he needed any extra tuition, he was free most evenings.

When Harry returned to the newsagent's after his round, Mr. Deakins would always slip a penny bar of Fry's chocolate into his satchel before sending him on his way. It reminded him of Giles. He often wondered what had become of his friend. Neither he nor Deakins had heard from Giles since the day Mr. Frobisher had asked to see Harry after prep. Then, before he left the shop to go home, he always paused in front of the display cabinet to admire a watch he knew he'd never be able to afford. He didn't even bother to ask Mr. Deakins how much it cost.

There were only two regular breaks in Harry's weekly routine.

He would always try to spend Saturday morning with Old Jack, taking with him copies of all the previous week's *Times,* and on Sunday evenings, once he'd fulfilled his duties at St. Mary's, he would rush across the city so he could be at Holy Nativity in time for Evensong.

A frail Miss Monday would beam with pride during the treble solo. She only hoped she would live long enough to see Harry go up to Cambridge. She had plans to tell him about the choir at King's College, but not until he'd won a place at Bristol Grammar.

-◦-

"Is Mr. Frobisher going to make you a prefect?" asked Old Jack, even before Harry had sunk into his usual seat on the opposite side of the carriage.

"I've no idea," replied Harry. "Mind you, the Frob always says," he added, tugging his lapels, *"Clifton, in life you get what you deserve, no more and certainly no less."*

Old Jack chuckled, and just stopped himself saying, "Not a bad imitation of the Frob." He satisfied himself with, "Then my bet is you're about to become a prefect."

"I'd rather win a scholarship to BGS," said Harry, suddenly sounding older than his years.

"And what about your friends, Barrington and Deakins?" Old Jack asked, trying to lighten the mood. "Are they also destined for higher things?"

"They'll never make Deakins a prefect," said Harry. "He can't even take care of himself, let alone anyone else. In any case, he's hoping to be the library monitor, and as no one else wants the job, Mr. Frobisher shouldn't lose too much sleep over that appointment."

"And Barrington?"

"I'm not sure he'll be coming back next term," said Harry wistfully. "Even if he does, I'm fairly certain they won't make him a prefect."

"Don't underestimate his father," said Old Jack. "That man will undoubtedly have found a way to ensure that his son returns on the first day of term. And I wouldn't put money on his not being a prefect."

"Let's hope you're right," said Harry.

"And if I am, I presume he will then follow his father to Eton?"

"Not if he has any say in it. Giles would prefer to go to BGS with Deakins and me."

"If he doesn't get into Eton, they're unlikely to offer him a place at the grammar school. Their entrance exam is one of the hardest in the country."

"He told me he's got a plan."

"It had better be a good one, if he hopes to fool his father as well as the examiners."

Harry didn't comment.

"How's your mother?" asked Old Jack, changing the subject, as it was clear that the boy didn't want to go any further down that path.

"She's just been promoted. She's now in charge of all the waitresses in the Palm Court room, and reports directly to Mr. Frampton, the hotel manager."

"You must be very proud of her," said Old Jack.

"Yes, I am, sir, and what's more, I'm going to prove it."

"What do you have in mind?"

Harry let him in to his secret. The old man listened attentively, and nodded his approval from time to time. He could see one small problem, but it wasn't insurmountable.

—◁◦▷—

When Harry returned to the shop having completed his last paper round before going back to school, Mr. Deakins gave him a shilling bonus. "You're the best paper boy I've ever had," he said.

"Thank you, sir," said Harry, pocketing the money. "Mr. Deakins, can I ask you a question?"

"Yes, of course, Harry."

Harry walked over to the cabinet, where two watches were displayed side by side on the top shelf. "How much is that one?" he asked, pointing to the Ingersoll.

Mr. Deakins smiled. He'd been waiting for Harry to ask that question for some weeks, and had his answer well prepared. "Six shillings," he said.

Harry couldn't believe it. He'd been sure that such a magnificent object would cost more than double that. But despite his having put aside half his earnings each week, even with Mr. Deakins's bonus, he was still a shilling short.

"You do realize, Harry, that it's a lady's watch?" said Mr. Deakins.

"Yes, I do, sir," said Harry. "I was hoping to give it to my mother."

"Then you can have it for five shillings."

Harry couldn't believe his luck.

"Thank you, sir," he said as he handed over four shillings, one sixpence, one thruppence and three pennies, leaving him with empty pockets.

Mr. Deakins took the watch out of the display cabinet, discreetly removed the sixteen-shilling price tag and then placed it in a smart box.

Harry left the shop whistling. Mr. Deakins smiled and placed the ten-shilling note in the till, delighted that he'd fulfilled his part of the bargain.

9

THE BELL WENT.

"Time to get undressed," said the duty prefect in the new boys' dorm on the first evening of term. They all looked so small and helpless, Harry thought. One or two of them were clearly fighting back tears, while others were looking around, uncertain what they should do next. One boy was facing the wall, shaking. Harry walked quickly across to him.

"What's your name?" Harry asked gently.

"Stevenson."

"Well, I'm Clifton. Welcome to St. Bede's."

"And I'm Tewkesbury," said a boy standing on the other side of Stevenson's bed.

"Welcome to St. Bede's, Tewkesbury."

"Thank you, Clifton. Actually, my father and grandfather were here, before they went on to Eton."

"I don't doubt it," said Harry. "And I'll bet they captained Eton against Harrow at Lord's," he added, immediately regretting his words.

"No, my father was a wet bob," said Tewkesbury unperturbed, "not a dry bob."

"A wet bob?" said Harry.

"He captained Oxford against Cambridge in the boat race."

Stevenson burst into tears.

"What's the matter?" asked Harry, sitting down on the bed beside him.

"My dad's a tram driver."

Everyone else stopped unpacking and stared at Stevenson.

"Is that right?" said Harry. "Then I'd better let you into a secret," he added, loud enough to be sure that every boy in the dormitory could hear his words. "I'm the son of a dock worker. I wouldn't be surprised to discover that you're the new choral scholar."

"No," said Stevenson, "I'm an open scholar."

"Many congratulations," said Harry, shaking him by the hand. "You follow in a long and noble tradition."

"Thank you. But I have a problem," the boy whispered.

"And what's that, Stevenson?"

"I don't have any toothpaste."

"Don't worry about that, old chap," said Tewkesbury, "my mother always packs a spare one."

Harry smiled as the bell rang again. "Everyone into bed," he said firmly as he walked across the dormitory toward the door.

He heard a voice whisper, "Thank you for the toothpaste."

"Think nothing of it, old chap."

"Now," said Harry as he flicked off the light, "I don't want to hear another word from any of you until the bell goes at six thirty tomorrow morning." He waited for a few moments before he heard someone whispering. "I meant it—not another word." He smiled as he walked down the staircase to join Deakins and Barrington in the senior prefects' study.

Harry had been surprised by two things when he arrived back at St. Bede's on the first day of term. No sooner had he walked through the front door than Mr. Frobisher took him to one side.

"Congratulations, Clifton," he said softly. "It won't be announced until assembly tomorrow morning, but you're to be the new school captain."

"It should have been Giles," said Harry without thinking.

"Barrington will be captain of games, and—"

Harry had leaped in the air the moment he heard the news that his friend would be returning to St. Bede's. Old Jack had been right when he said Mr. Hugo would find a way to make sure his son was back for the first day of term.

When Giles walked into the front hall a few moments later, the two boys shook hands, and Harry never once referred to the subject that must have been on both their minds.

"What are the new bugs like?" Giles asked as Harry entered the study.

"One of them reminds me of you," said Harry.

"Tewkesbury, no doubt."

"You know him?"

"No, but Papa was at Eton at the same time as his father."

"I told him I was the son of a docker," said Harry as he slumped into the only comfortable chair in the room.

"Did you now?" said Giles. "And did he tell you he's the son of a cabinet minister?"

Harry said nothing.

"Are there any others I should keep an eye out for?" asked Giles.

"Stevenson," said Harry. "He's a cross between Deakins and me."

"Then we'd better lock the fire-escape door before he makes a dash for it."

Harry often thought about where he might be now if Old Jack hadn't talked him into returning to St. Bede's that night.

"What's our first lesson tomorrow?" asked Harry, checking his timetable.

"Latin," said Deakins. "Which is why I'm guiding Giles through the first Punic war."

"264 to 241 BC," said Giles.

"I bet you're enjoying that," said Harry.

"Yes, I am," said Giles, "and I just can't wait for the sequel, the second Punic war."

"218 to 201 BC," said Harry.

"It always amazes me how the Greeks and Romans seemed to know exactly when Christ would be born," said Giles.

"Ho, ho, ho," said Harry.

Deakins didn't laugh, but said, "And finally, we will have to consider the third Punic War, 149 to 146 BC."

"Do we really need to know about all three of them?" said Giles.

–◦–

St. Mary Redcliffe was packed with town and gown who'd come to celebrate an Advent service of eight readings and eight carols. The choir made their entrance through the nave, and advanced slowly down the aisle singing "O Come All Ye Faithful," then took their places in the choir stalls.

The headmaster read the first lesson. This was followed by "O Little Town of Bethlehem." The service sheet indicated that the soloist for the third verse would be Master Harry Clifton.

How silently, how silently, the wondrous gift is given, while God . . . Harry's mother sat proudly in the third row, while the old lady sitting next to her wanted to tell everyone in the congregation that they were listening to her grandson. The man seated on the other side of Maisie couldn't hear a word, but you would never have known that from the contented smile on his face. Uncle Stan was nowhere to be seen.

The captain of games read the second lesson, and when Giles returned to his place, Harry noticed that he was seated next to a distinguished-looking man with a head of silver hair, who he assumed must be Sir Walter Barrington. Giles had once told him that his grandfather lived in an even larger house than his, but Harry didn't think that could be possible. On the other side of Giles sat his mother and father. Mrs. Barrington smiled across at him, but Mr. Barrington didn't once look in his direction.

When the organ struck up the prelude for "We Three Kings," the congregation rose and sang lustily. The next lesson was read by Mr. Frobisher, after which came what Miss Monday anticipated would be the highlight of the service. The thousand-strong congregation didn't stir while Harry sang "Silent Night" with a clarity and confidence that caused even the headmaster to smile.

The library monitor read the next lesson. Harry had already coached him through St. Mark's words several times. Deakins had tried to get out of the chore, as he described it to Giles, but Mr. Frobisher had insisted; the fourth lesson was always read by the librarian. Deakins wasn't Giles, but he wasn't bad. Harry winked at him as he shuffled back to his seat next to his parents.

The choir then rose to sing "In Dulci Jubilo" while the congregation remained seated. Harry considered the carol to be among the most demanding in their repertoire, because of its unconventional harmonies.

Mr. Holcombe closed his eyes so that he could hear the senior choral scholar more clearly. Harry was singing "Now let all hearts be singing" when he thought he heard a slight, almost imperceptible, crack in the voice. He assumed Harry must have a cold. Miss Monday knew better. She'd heard those early signs so many times before. She prayed that she was mistaken, but knew her prayer would not be answered. Harry would get through the rest of the service with only a handful of people realizing what had happened, and he would even be able to carry on for a few more weeks, possibly months, but by Easter another child would be singing "Oh Rejoice That the Lord Has Arisen."

An old man who'd turned up only moments after the service had begun was among those who weren't in any doubt what had happened. Old Jack left just before the bishop gave his final blessing. He knew Harry wouldn't be able to visit him until the following Saturday, which would give him enough time to work out how to answer the inevitable question.

–◦–

"Might I have a private word with you, Clifton?" said Mr. Frobisher as the bell sounded for the end of prep. "Perhaps you'd join me in my study." Harry would never forget the last time he'd heard those words.

When Harry closed the study door, his housemaster beckoned him toward a seat by the fire, something he had never done before. "I just wanted to assure you, Harry"—another first—"that the fact you are no longer able to sing in the choir will not affect your bursary. We at St. Bede's are well aware that the contribution you have made to school life stretches far beyond the chapel."

"Thank you, sir," said Harry.

"However, we must now consider your future. The music master tells me that it will be some time before your voice fully recovers, which I'm afraid means that we must be realistic about your chances of being offered a choral scholarship to Bristol Grammar School."

"There is no chance," said Harry calmly.

"I have to agree with you," said Frobisher. "I'm relieved to find you understand the situation. But," he continued, "I would be happy to enter your name for an open scholarship to BGS. However," he added before Harry had time to respond, "in the circumstances, you might consider that you'd have a better chance of being offered a bursary at, say, Colston's School, or King's College Gloucester, both of which have far less demanding entrance examinations."

"No, thank you, sir," said Harry. "My first choice remains Bristol Grammar." He'd said the same thing to Old Jack just as firmly the previous Saturday, when his mentor had mumbled something about not burning your boats.

"So be it," said Mr. Frobisher, who had not expected any other response, but had still felt it was nothing less than his duty to come up with an alternative. "Now, let's turn this setback to our advantage."

"How do you suggest I do that, sir?"

"Well, now that you've been released from daily choir practice, you will have more time to prepare for your entrance exam."

"Yes, sir, but I still have my responsibilities as—"

"And I will do everything in my power to ensure that your duties as school captain are less onerous in future."

"Thank you, sir."

"By the way, Harry," said Frobisher as he rose from his chair, "I've just read your essay on Jane Austen, and I was fascinated by your suggestion that if Miss Austen had been able to go to university, she might never have written a novel, and even if she had, her work probably wouldn't have been so insightful."

"'Sometimes it's an advantage to be disadvantaged,'" said Harry.

"That doesn't sound like Jane Austen," said Mr. Frobisher.

"It isn't," replied Harry. "But it was said by someone else who didn't go to university," he added without explanation.

◄o►

Maisie glanced at her new watch and smiled. "I'll have to leave now, Harry, if I'm not going to be late for work."

"Of course, Mum," said Harry, leaping up from the table. "I'll walk with you to the tram stop."

"Harry, have you thought about what you'll do if you don't win that scholarship?" said his mother, finally asking a question she'd been avoiding for weeks.

"Constantly," said Harry as he opened the door for her. "But I won't be given much choice in the matter. I'll just have to go back to Merrywood, and when I turn fourteen I'll leave and look for a job."

10

"Do you feel ready to face the examiners, my boy?" asked Old Jack.

"As ready as I'm ever likely to be," replied Harry. "By the way, I took your advice, and checked over the examination papers for the past ten years. You were right, there's a definite pattern, with some of the same questions coming up at regular intervals."

"Good. And how's your Latin coming on? We can't afford to fail that, however well we do in your other papers."

Harry smiled when Old Jack said "we." "Thanks to Deakins I managed 69 percent in mocks last week, even if I did have Hannibal crossing the Andes."

"Only about six thousand miles out," chuckled Old Jack. "So what do you think will be your biggest problem?"

"The forty boys from St. Bede's who are also taking the exam, not to mention the two hundred and fifty from other schools."

"Forget them," said Old Jack. "If you do what you're capable of, they won't be a problem."

Harry remained silent.

"So, how's your voice coming along?" asked Old Jack, who always changed the subject whenever Harry fell silent.

"Nothing new to report," said Harry. "It could be weeks before I know if I'm a tenor, a baritone or a bass, and even then, there's no guarantee I'll be any good. One thing's for certain, BGS aren't going to offer me a choral scholarship while I'm like a horse with a broken leg."

"Snap out of it," said Old Jack. "It's not that bad."

"It's worse," said Harry. "If I was a horse, they'd shoot me and put me out of my misery."

Old Jack laughed. "So when are the exams?" he asked, even though he knew the answer.

"Thursday week. We start with general knowledge at nine o'clock, and there are five other papers during the day, ending with English at four."

"It's good that you finish with your favorite subject," said Jack.

"Let's hope so," said Harry. "But pray there's a question on Dickens, because there hasn't been one for the past three years, which is why I've been reading his books after lights out."

"Wellington wrote in his memoirs," said Old Jack, "that the worst moment of any campaign is waiting for the sun to rise on the morning of battle."

"I agree with the Iron Duke, which means I won't be getting much sleep for the next couple of weeks."

"All the more reason not to come and see me next Saturday, Harry. You ought to be making better use of your time. In any case, if I remember correctly, it's your birthday."

"How did you know that?"

"I confess that I didn't read it on the court page of *The Times*. But as it fell on the same day last year, I took a gamble and bought a small gift for you." He picked up a parcel wrapped in a page from one of last week's newspapers, and handed it to Harry.

"Thank you, sir," said Harry as he untied the string. He removed the newspaper, opened the small dark blue box and stared in disbelief at the man's Ingersoll watch he'd last seen in the display cabinet at Mr. Deakins's shop.

"Thank you," Harry repeated as he strapped the watch on his wrist. He couldn't take his eyes off it for some time, and could only wonder how Old Jack could possibly afford six shillings.

‹○›

Harry was wide awake long before the sun rose on the morning of the exams. He skipped breakfast in favor of going over some old general knowledge papers, checking capitals against countries from Germany to Brazil, dates of prime ministers from Walpole to Lloyd George, and of monarchs from King Alfred to George V. An hour later he felt ready to face the examiner.

Once again, he was seated in the front row, between Barrington and Deakins. Was this the last time, he wondered. When the clock on the tower struck ten, several masters marched down the rows of desks handing out the general knowledge paper to forty nervous boys. Well, thirty-nine nervous boys, and Deakins.

Harry read through the questions slowly. When he reached number 100, he allowed a smile to cross his face. He picked up his pen, dipped the nib in the inkwell and began to write. Forty minutes later he was back at question 100. He glanced at his watch; he still had another ten minutes in which to double-check his answers. He stopped for a moment at question 34 and reconsidered his original answer. Was it Oliver Cromwell or Thomas Cromwell who was sent to the Tower of London for treason? He recalled the fate of Cardinal Wolsey, and selected the man who'd taken his place as Lord Chancellor.

When the clock began to strike again, Harry had reached question 92. He quickly looked over his last eight answers before his paper was snatched away, the ink still drying on his final answer, Charles Lindbergh.

During the twenty-minute break, Harry, Giles and Deakins walked slowly around the cricket field where Giles had scored a century only a week before.

"Amo, amas, amat," said Deakins as he painstakingly took them through their conjugations without once referring to *Kennedy's Latin Primer*.

"Amamus, amatis, amant," repeated Harry as they made their way back toward the examination hall.

When Harry handed in his Latin paper an hour later, he felt confident he'd scored more than the required 60 percent, and even Giles looked pleased with himself. As the three of them strolled across to the refectory, Harry put an arm around Deakins's shoulder and said, "Thanks, old chum."

After Harry had read through the geography paper later that morning, he silently thanked his secret weapon. Old Jack had passed on so much knowledge over the years without ever making him feel that he'd been in a classroom.

Harry didn't pick up a knife or fork during lunch. Giles managed half a pork pie, while Deakins didn't stop eating.

History was the first paper that afternoon, and didn't cause him any anxiety. Henry VIII, Elizabeth, Raleigh, Drake, Napoleon, Nelson and Wellington all marched onto the battlefield, and Harry marched them back off again.

The mathematics paper was far easier than he had expected, and Giles even thought he might have scored another century.

During the final break, Harry returned to his study and glanced over an essay he'd written on *David Copperfield,* confident that he would excel in his favorite subject. He walked slowly back to the examination hall, repeating Mr. Holcombe's favorite word again and again. Concentrate.

He stared down at the final paper of the day, to find that this year belonged to Thomas Hardy and Lewis Carroll. He'd read *The Mayor of Casterbridge* and *Alice's Adventures in Wonderland,* but the Mad Hatter, Michael Henchard and the Cheshire Cat were not as familiar to him as Peggotty, Dr. Chillip and Barkis. His pen scratched slowly across the page, and when the clock chimed on the hour, he wasn't sure if he'd done enough. He walked out of the hall and into the afternoon sunshine, feeling a little depressed, although it was clear from the looks on the faces of his rivals that no one thought it had been an easy paper. That made him wonder if he was still in with a chance.

—◇—

There followed what Mr. Holcombe had often described as the worst part of any exam, those days of endless waiting before the results were formally posted on the school notice board; a time when boys end up doing something they will later regret, almost as if they want to be rusticated rather than learn their fate. One boy was caught drinking cider behind the bicycle shed, another smoking a Woodbine in the lavatory, while a third was seen leaving the local cinema after lights out.

Giles was out for a duck the following Saturday, his first of the season. While Deakins returned to the library, Harry went on long walks, going over every answer in his head again and again. It didn't improve matters.

On Sunday afternoon, Giles had a long net; on Monday, Deakins reluctantly handed over his responsibilities to the new library monitor, and on Tuesday Harry read *Far from the Madding Crowd* and cursed out loud. On Wednesday night, Giles and Harry talked into the small hours, while Deakins slept soundly.

◄○►

Long before the clock on the tower struck ten that Thursday morning, forty boys were already roaming around the quad, hands in pockets, heads bowed as they waited for the headmaster to make his appearance. Although every one of them knew that Dr. Oakshott wouldn't be a minute early or a minute late, by five to ten most eyes were staring across the quad waiting for the door of the headmaster's house to open. The rest were looking up at the clock on the great hall, willing the minute hand to move a little faster.

As the first chime sounded, the Reverend Samuel Oakshott opened his front door and stepped out onto the path. He was carrying a sheet of paper in one hand and four tin-tacks in the other. Not a man who left anything to chance. When he reached the end of the path, he opened the little wicket gate and walked across the quad at his usual pace, oblivious to all around him. The boys quickly stood aside, creating a corridor so the headmaster's progress would not be impeded. He came to a halt in front of the notice board as the tenth chime rang out. He posted the exam results on the board, and departed without a word.

Forty boys rushed forward, forming a scrum around the notice board. No one was surprised that Deakins headed the list, with 92 percent, and had been awarded the Peloquin Scholarship to Bristol Grammar School. Giles leaped in the air, making no attempt to disguise his relief when he saw 64 percent by his name.

They both turned to look for their friend. Harry was standing alone, far from the madding crowd.

MAISIE CLIFTON

1920–1936

11

When Arthur and me got married, the occasion couldn't have been described as pushing the boat out, but then, neither the Tancocks nor the Cliftons ever did have two brass farthings to rub together. The biggest expense turned out to be the choir, half a crown, and worth every penny. I'd always wanted to be a member of Miss Monday's choir, and although she told me my voice was good enough, I wasn't considered on account of the fact I couldn't read or write.

The reception, if you could call it that, was held at Arthur's parents' terraced house in Still House Lane: a barrel of beer, some peanut butter sandwiches and a dozen pork pies. My brother Stan even brought his own fish and chips. And to top it all, we had to leave early to catch the last bus to Weston-super-Mare for our honeymoon. Arthur booked us into a seafront guest house on the Friday evening, and as it rained for most of the weekend, we rarely left the bedroom.

It felt strange that the second time I had sex was also in Weston-super-Mare. I was shocked when I saw Arthur naked for the first time. A deep red, roughly stitched scar stretched tight across his stomach. Damn the Germans. He never said he'd been wounded during the war.

I wasn't surprised that Arthur became aroused the moment I pulled off my slip, but I must admit I'd expected him to take his boots off before we made love.

We checked out of the guest house on Sunday afternoon and

caught the last bus back to Bristol, as Arthur had to report to the dockyard by six o'clock on Monday morning.

After the wedding, Arthur moved into our house—just until we could afford a place of our own, he told my father, which usually meant until one of our parents passed away. In any case, both our families had lived on Still House Lane for as long as anyone could remember.

Arthur was delighted when I told him I was in the family way, because he wanted at least six babies. My worry was whether the first would be his, but, as only my mum and I knew the truth, there was no reason for Arthur to be suspicious.

Eight months later I gave birth to a boy, and thank God there was nothing to suggest that he wasn't Arthur's. We christened him Harold, which pleased my father, because it meant his name would survive for another generation.

From then on, I took it for granted that, like Mum and Gran, I would be stuck at home having a baby every other year. After all, Arthur came from a family of eight, and I was the fourth of five. But Harry turned out to be my only child.

◄○►

Arthur usually came straight home after work of an evening so he could spend some time with the baby before I put him to bed. When he didn't turn up that Friday night, I assumed he'd gone off to the pub with my brother. But when Stan staggered in just after midnight, blind drunk and flashing a wad of fivers, Arthur was nowhere to be seen. In fact, Stan gave me one of the fivers, which made me wonder if he'd robbed a bank. But when I asked him where Arthur was, he clammed up.

I didn't go to bed that night, just sat on the bottom step of the stairs waiting for my husband to come home. Arthur had never stayed out all night from the day we was married.

Although Stan had sobered up by the time he came down to the kitchen the following morning, he didn't say a word during breakfast. When I asked him again where Arthur was, he claimed he hadn't seen him since they'd clocked off work the previous evening. It's not difficult to tell when Stan's lying, because he won't look you in the eye. I was about to press him further when I heard a loud banging on the front door. My first thought was that it must be Arthur, so I rushed to answer it.

When I opened the door, two policemen burst into the house, ran into the kitchen, grabbed Stan, handcuffed him and told him he was being arrested for burglary. Now I knew where the wad of fivers had come from.

"I didn't steal anything," protested Stan. "Mr. Barrington gave me the money."

"A likely story, Tancock," said the first copper.

"But it's the God's honest truth, officer," he was saying as they dragged him off to the nick. This time I knew Stan wasn't lying.

I left Harry with my mum and ran all the way to the dockyard, hoping to find that Arthur had reported for the morning shift and would be able to tell me why Stan had been arrested. I tried not to think about the possibility that Arthur might also be locked up.

The man on the gate told me he hadn't seen Arthur all morning. But after he checked the rota, he looked puzzled, because Arthur hadn't clocked off the night before. All he had to say was, "Don't blame me. I wasn't on the gate last night."

It was only later that I wondered why he'd used the word "blame."

I went into the dockyard and asked some of Arthur's mates, but they all parroted the same line. "Haven't seen him since he clocked off last night." Then they quickly walked away. I was about to go off to the nick to see if Arthur had been arrested as well, when I saw an old man going past, head bowed.

I chased after him, quite expecting him to tell me to bugger off or claim he didn't know what I was talking about. But when I approached, he stopped, took off his cap and said, "Good morning." I was surprised by his good manners, which gave me the confidence to ask him if he'd seen Arthur that morning.

"No," he replied. "I last saw him yesterday afternoon when he was on the late shift with your brother. Perhaps you should ask him."

"I can't," I said. "He's been arrested and taken off to the nick."

"What have they charged him with?" asked Old Jack, looking puzzled.

"I don't know," I replied.

Old Jack shook his head. "I can't help you, Mrs. Clifton," he said. "But there are at least two people who know the whole story." He nodded toward the large red-brick building that Arthur always called "management."

I shivered when I saw a policeman coming out of the front door of the building, and when I looked back, Old Jack had disappeared.

I thought about going into "management," or Barrington House, to give it its proper name, but decided against it. After all, what would I say if I came face to face with Arthur's boss? In the end I began to walk aimlessly back home, trying to make sense of things.

—◦—

I watched Hugo Barrington when he gave his evidence. The same self-confidence, the same arrogance, the same half-truths spouted convincingly to the jury, just as he'd whispered them to me in the privacy of the bedroom. When he stepped down from the witness box, I knew Stan didn't have a snowball's chance in hell of getting off.

In the judge's summing-up, he described my brother as a common thief, who had taken advantage of his position to rob his employer. He ended by saying he had no choice but to send him down for three years.

I had sat through every day of the trial, hoping to pick up some snippet of information that might give me a clue as to what had happened to Arthur that day. But by the time the judge finally declared, "Court adjourned," I was none the wiser, although I was in no doubt that my brother wasn't telling the whole story. It would be some time before I found out why.

The only other person who attended the court every day was Old Jack Tar, but we didn't speak. In fact, I might never have seen him again if it hadn't been for Harry.

—◦—

It was some time before I was able to accept that Arthur would never be coming home.

Stan had only been away for a few days before I discovered the true meaning of the words "eke out." With one of the two bread-winners in the family banged up, and the other God knows where, we soon found ourselves quite literally on the breadline. Luckily there was an unwritten code that operated in Still House Lane: if someone was "away on holiday," the neighbors did whatever they could to help support his family.

The Reverend Watts dropped in regularly, and even returned some of the coins we'd put in his collection plate over the years. Miss Monday appeared irregularly and dispensed far more than good advice, always leaving with an empty basket. But nothing could compensate me for the loss of a husband, an innocent brother locked up in jail, and a son who no longer had a father.

Harry had recently taken his first step, but I was already fearful of hearing his first word. Would he even remember who used to sit at the head of the table, and ask why he was no longer there? It was Grandpa who came up with a solution as to what we should say if Harry started to ask questions. We all made a pact to stick to the same story; after all, Harry was hardly likely to come across Old Jack.

But at that time the Tancock family's most pressing problem was how to keep the wolf from our door, or, more important, the rent collector and the bailiff. Once I'd spent Stan's five pounds, pawned my mum's silver-plated tea strainer, my engagement ring and finally my wedding ring, I feared it couldn't be long before we were evicted.

But that was delayed for a few weeks by another knock on the door. This time it wasn't the police, but a man called Mr. Sparks, who told me he was Arthur's trade union representative, and that he'd come to see if I'd had any compensation from the company.

Once I'd settled Mr. Sparks down in the kitchen and poured him a cup of tea, I told him, "Not a brass farthing. They say he left without giving notice, so they aren't responsible for his actions. And I still don't know what really happened that day."

"Neither do I," said Mr. Sparks. "They've all clammed up, not just the management, but the workers as well. I can't get a word out of them. 'More than my life's worth,' one of them told me. But your husband's subs were fully paid up," he added, "so you're entitled to union compensation."

I just stood there, with no idea what he was going on about.

Mr. Sparks took a document out of his briefcase, placed it on the kitchen table and turned to the back page.

"Sign here," he said placing a forefinger on the dotted line.

After I had put an X where he was pointing, he took an envelope out of his pocket. "I'm sorry it's so little," he said as he handed it to me.

I didn't open the envelope until he had finished his cup of tea and left.

Seven pounds, nine shillings and sixpence turned out to be the value they'd put on Arthur's life. I sat alone at the kitchen table, and I think that was the moment I knew I'd never see my husband again.

That afternoon I went back to the pawn shop and redeemed my wedding ring from Mr. Cohen; it was the least I could do in memory of Arthur. The following morning I cleared the rent arrears, as well as the slate at the butcher, the baker and, yes, the candlestick maker. There was just enough left over to buy some secondhand clothes from the church jumble sale, mostly for Harry.

But it was less than a month before the chalk was once again scratching across the slate at the butcher, the baker and the candlestick maker, and it wasn't long after that I had to return to the pawn shop and hand my wedding ring back to Mr. Cohen.

When the rent collector came knocking on the door of number 27 and never received a reply, I suppose none of the family should have been surprised that the next caller would be the bailiff. That was when I decided the time had come for me to look for a job.

12

MAISIE'S ATTEMPTS TO find a job didn't turn out to be easy, not least because the government had recently issued a directive to all employers advising them to take on men who had served in the armed forces before considering any other candidates. This was in keeping with Lloyd George's promise that Britain's soldiers would return home to a land fit for heroes.

Although women over thirty had been given the vote at the last election after their sterling service in munitions factories during the war, they were pushed to the back of the queue when it came to peacetime jobs. Maisie decided that her best chance of finding employment was to apply for jobs men wouldn't consider, either because they felt they were too demeaning, or the pay was derisory. With that in mind, Maisie stood in line outside W.D. & H.O. Wills, the city's largest employer. When she reached the front of the queue, she asked the supervisor, "Is it true you're looking for packers in the cigarette factory?"

"Yes, but you're too young, luv," he told her.

"I'm twenty-two."

"You're too young," he repeated. "Come back in two or three years' time."

Maisie was back at Still House Lane in time to share a bowl of chicken broth and a slice of last week's bread with Harry and her mum.

The next day, she joined an even longer queue outside Harvey's, the wine merchants. When she reached the front, three hours later, she was told by a man wearing a starched white collar and a thin black tie that they were only taking on applicants with experience.

"So how do I get experience?" Maisie asked, trying not to sound desperate.

"By joining our apprentice scheme."

"Then I'll join," she told the starched collar.

"How old are you?"

"Twenty-two."

"You're too old."

Maisie repeated every word of the sixty-second interview to her mother over a thinner bowl of broth from the same pot along with a crust of bread from the same loaf.

"You could always try the docks," her mother suggested.

"What do you have in mind, Mum? Should I sign up to be a stevedore?"

Maisie's mum didn't laugh, but then Maisie couldn't remember the last time she had. "They've always got work for cleaners," she said. "And God knows that lot owe you."

Maisie was up and dressed long before the sun had risen the following morning and, as there wasn't enough breakfast to go round, she set out hungry on the long walk to the docks.

When she arrived, Maisie told the man on the gate she was looking for a cleaning job.

"Report to Mrs. Nettles," he said, nodding in the direction of the large red-brick building she'd so nearly entered once before. "She's in charge of hirin' and firin' cleaners." He clearly didn't remember her from her previous visit.

Maisie walked uneasily toward the building, but came to a halt a few paces before she reached the front door. She stood and watched as a succession of smartly dressed men wearing hats and coats and carrying umbrellas made their way through the double doors.

Maisie remained rooted to the spot, shivering in the cold morning air as she tried to find enough courage to follow them inside. She was just about to turn away when she spotted an older woman in overalls entering another door, at the side of the building. Maisie chased after her.

"What do you want?" asked the woman suspiciously once Maisie had caught up with her.

"I'm lookin' for a job."

"Good," she said. "We could do with some younguns. Report to Mrs. Nettles," she added, pointing toward a narrow door that might have been mistaken for a broom cupboard. Maisie walked boldly up to it and knocked.

"Come on in," said a tired voice.

Maisie opened the door to find a woman of about her mother's age sitting on the only chair, surrounded by buckets, mops and several large bars of soap.

"I was told to report to you if I was lookin' for a job."

"You was told right. That's if you're willing to work all the hours God gives, for damn all pay."

"What are the hours, and what's the pay?" asked Maisie.

"You start at three in the morning, and you have to be off the premises by seven, before their nibs turns up, when they expect to find their offices spick and span. Or you can start at seven of an evening and work through till midnight, whichever suits you. Pay's the same whatever you decide, sixpence an hour."

"I'll do both shifts," said Maisie.

"Good," the woman said, selecting a bucket and mop. "I'll see you back here at seven this evenin'," when I'll show you the ropes. My name's Vera Nettles. What's yours?"

"Maisie Clifton."

Mrs. Nettles dropped the bucket on the floor and propped the mop back up against the wall. She walked across to the door and opened it. "There's no work for you here, Mrs. Clifton," she said.

◄○►

Over the next month, Maisie tried to get a job in a shoe shop, but the manager didn't feel he could employ someone with holes in her shoes; a milliner's, where the interview was terminated the moment they discovered she couldn't add up; and a flower shop, which wouldn't consider taking on anyone who didn't have their own garden. Grandpa's allotment didn't count. In desperation, she applied for a job as a barmaid in a local pub, but the landlord said, "Sorry, luv, but your tits aren't big enough."

The following Sunday at Holy Nativity, Maisie knelt and asked God to give her a helping hand.

That hand turned out to be Miss Monday's, who told Maisie she had a friend who owned a tea shop on Broad Street and was looking for a waitress.

"But I don't have any experience," said Maisie.

"That may well prove to be an advantage," said Miss Monday. "Miss Tilly is most particular, and prefers to train her staff in her own way."

"Perhaps she'll think I'm too old, or too young."

"You are neither too old nor too young," said Miss Monday. "And be assured, I wouldn't recommend you if I didn't think you were up to it. But I must warn you, Maisie, that Miss Tilly is a stickler for time-keeping. Be at the tea shop before eight o'clock tomorrow. If you're late, that will not only be the first impression you make, but also the last."

Maisie was standing outside Tilly's Tea Shop at six o'clock the following morning, and didn't budge for the next two hours. At five minutes to eight a plump, middle-aged, smartly dressed woman, with her hair arranged in a neat bun and a pair of half-moon spectacles propped on the end of her nose, turned the "closed" sign on the door to "open," to allow a frozen Maisie to step inside.

"You've got the job, Mrs. Clifton," were her new boss's first words.

—◇—

Harry was left in the care of his grandmother whenever Maisie went to work. Although she was only paid nine pence an hour, she was allowed to keep half her tips, so that at the end of a good week she could take home as much as three pounds. There was also an unexpected bonus. Once the "open" sign had been turned back to "closed" at six o'clock in the evening, Miss Tilly would allow Maisie to take home any food that was left over. The word "stale" was never allowed to cross a customer's lips.

After six months, Miss Tilly was so pleased with Maisie's progress that she put her in charge of her own station of eight tables, and after another six months, several regulars would insist that Maisie served them. Miss Tilly solved the problem by increasing Maisie's allocation of tables to twelve, and raising her pay to a shilling an hour. With two pay packets coming in each week, Maisie was once again able to wear both her engagement ring and her wedding ring, and the silver-plated tea strainer was back in its place.

—◦—

If Maisie was honest about it, Stan being released from prison for good behavior after only eighteen months turned out to be a bit of a mixed blessing.

Harry, now aged three and a half, had to move back into his mother's room, and Maisie tried not to think about just how peaceful it had been while Stan was away.

Maisie was surprised when Stan got his old job back at the docks as if nothing had happened. This only convinced her that he knew far more about Arthur's disappearance than he let on, however much she pressed him. On one occasion when she became a little too persistent, he belted her one. Although the following morning Miss Tilly pretended not to notice the black eye, one or two of the customers did, so Maisie never raised the subject with her brother again. But whenever Harry asked him about his father, Stan stuck to the family line and said, "Your old man was killed in the war. I was standin' by his side when the bullet hit him."

—◦—

Maisie spent as much of her spare time with Harry as she could. She assumed that once he was old enough to attend Merrywood Elementary School, her life would become a lot easier. But taking Harry to school in the morning meant the added expense of a tram ride to make sure she was not late for work. She would then take a break in the afternoon so she could pick him up from school. Once Maisie had given him his tea, she would leave him in the care of his grandma and return to work.

Harry had only been at school for a few days when Maisie noticed some cane marks on his backside while she was giving him his weekly bath.

"Who did that?" she demanded.

"The headmaster."

"Why?"

"Can't tell you, Mum."

When Maisie saw six new red stripes even before the previous ones had faded, she questioned Harry again, but still he didn't let on. The third time the marks appeared, she put on her coat and set off for Merrywood Elementary with the intention of giving his teacher a piece of her mind.

Mr. Holcombe wasn't at all what Maisie had expected. To start with, he couldn't have been much older than she was, and he stood up when she entered the room—not at all like the teachers she remembered from her days at Merrywood.

"Why is my son being caned by the headmaster?" she demanded, even before Mr. Holcombe had a chance to offer her a seat.

"Because he keeps playing truant, Mrs. Clifton. He disappears soon after morning assembly, and gets back in time for football in the afternoon."

"So where is he spending the day?"

"At the docks would be my guess," said Mr. Holcombe. "Perhaps you might be able to tell me why."

"Because his uncle works there, and he's always telling Harry that school is a waste of time because sooner or later he'll end up joining him at Barrington's."

"I hope not," said Mr. Holcombe.

"Why do you say that?" asked Maisie. "It was good enough for his father."

"That may well be, but it won't be good enough for Harry."

"What do you mean?" Maisie asked indignantly.

"Harry is bright, Mrs. Clifton. Very bright. If only I could persuade him to attend class more regularly, there's no saying what he might achieve."

Maisie suddenly wondered if she would ever find out which of the two men was Harry's father.

"Some clever children don't discover how bright they are until after they've left school," continued Mr. Holcombe, "and then spend the rest of their lives regretting the wasted years. I want to make sure Harry does not fall into that category."

"What would you like me to do?" asked Maisie, finally sitting down.

"Encourage him to stay at school, and not slope off to the docks every day. Tell him how proud you'd be if he did well in class, and not only on the football field—which, just in case you didn't realize, Mrs. Clifton, isn't his forte."

"His forte?"

"I do apologize. But even Harry must have worked out by now that he's never going to make the school XI, let alone play for Bristol City."

"I'll do anything I can to help," promised Maisie.

"Thank you, Mrs. Clifton," said Mr. Holcombe as Maisie rose to leave. "If you felt able to encourage him, I've no doubt it will be far more effective in the long term than the headmaster's cane."

From that day, Maisie began to take a far greater interest in what Harry got up to at school. She enjoyed listening to his stories about Mr. Holcombe and what he'd taught him that day, and as the stripes didn't reappear, she assumed he must have stopped playing truant. And then one night just before going to bed, she checked on the sleeping child and found that the stripes were back, redder and deeper than before. She didn't need to go and see Mr. Holcombe, because he called in at the tea shop the following day.

"He managed to come to my class for a whole month," said Mr. Holcombe, "and then he disappeared again."

"But I don't know what more I can do," said Maisie helplessly. "I've already stopped his pocket money, and told him not to expect another penny from me unless he stays at school. The truth is, his uncle Stan has far more influence over him than I do."

"More's the pity," said Mr. Holcombe. "But I may have found a solution to our problem, Mrs. Clifton. However, it has no chance of succeeding without your full cooperation."

—◦—

Maisie assumed that although she was only twenty-six, she would never marry again. After all, widows with a child in tow were not much of a catch when there were so many single women available. The fact that she always wore her engagement and wedding rings probably cut down the number of propositions she received at the tea shop, although one or two still tried it on. She didn't include dear old Mr. Craddick, who just liked to hold her hand.

Mr. Atkins was one of Miss Tilly's regulars, and he liked to sit at one of the tables where Maisie was serving. He dropped in most mornings, always ordering a black coffee and a piece of fruit cake. To Maisie's surprise, after he'd paid his bill one morning, he invited her to the cinema.

"Greta Garbo in *Flesh and the Devil*," he said, trying to make it sound more tempting.

This wasn't the first time one of the customers had asked Maisie out, but it was the first time someone young and good-looking had shown any interest.

In the past, her stock response had succeeded in putting off the most persistent of suitors. "How kind of you, Mr. Atkins, but I like to spend any spare time I have with my son."

"Surely you could make an exception for just one evening?" he said, not giving up quite as easily as the others.

Maisie glanced quickly at his left hand: no sign of a wedding ring, or, even more damning, a pale circle revealing that one had been removed.

She heard herself saying, "How kind of you, Mr. Atkins," and agreed to meet him on Thursday evening, after she'd put Harry to bed.

"Call me Eddie," he said, leaving a sixpenny tip.

Maisie was impressed when Eddie turned up in a Flatnose Morris to drive her to the cinema. And to her surprise, all he got up to while they sat together in the back row was to watch the film. She wouldn't have complained if he had put an arm around her shoulder. In fact, she was considering how far she would let him go on their first date.

After the curtain came down, the organ lit up and they all rose to sing the National Anthem.

"Care for a drink?" asked Eddie as they made their way out of the cinema.

"I ought to be getting home before the trams pack up for the night."

"You don't have to worry about the last tram, Maisie, when you're with Eddie Atkins."

"All right then, just a quick one," she said as he guided her across the road to the Red Bull.

"So what do you do, Eddie?" Maisie asked as he placed a half pint of orange squash on the table in front of her.

"I'm in the entertainment business," he said, without going into any detail. Instead, he switched the subject back to Maisie. "I don't have to ask what you do."

After a second orange juice, he looked at his watch and said, "I've got an early start tomorrow, so I'd better get you home."

On the way back to Still House Lane, Maisie chatted about Harry, and how she was hoping he would join the choir at Holy Nativity. Eddie seemed genuinely interested, and when he brought the car to a halt outside No. 27, she waited for him to kiss her. But he just jumped out, opened the car door for her and accompanied Maisie to her front door.

Maisie sat at the kitchen table and told her mother everything that had happened, or not happened, that night. All Grandma had to say was, "What's his game?"

13

WHEN MAISIE SAW Mr. Holcombe walk into Holy Nativity accompanied by a smartly dressed man, she assumed that Harry must be in trouble again. She was surprised, because there hadn't been any red marks for over a year.

She braced herself as Mr. Holcombe headed toward her, but the moment he saw Maisie he simply gave her a shy smile before he and his companion slipped into the third pew on the other side of the aisle.

From time to time, Maisie glanced across to look at them, but she didn't recognize the other man, who was considerably older than Mr. Holcombe. She wondered if he might be the headmaster of Merrywood Elementary.

When the choir rose to sing the first anthem, Miss Monday glanced in the direction of the two men, before nodding to the organist to show that she was ready.

Maisie felt that Harry excelled himself that morning, but she was surprised when a few minutes later he rose to sing a second solo, and even more surprised when he performed a third. Everyone knew that Miss Monday never did anything unless there was a reason, but it still wasn't clear to Maisie what that reason might be.

After the Reverend Watts had blessed his flock at the end of the service, Maisie remained in her place and waited for Harry to appear, hoping he'd be able to tell her why he'd been asked to sing three solos. As she chatted anxiously to her mother, her eyes never left Mr. Holcombe, who was introducing the older man to Miss Monday and the Reverend Watts.

A moment later, the Reverend Watts led the two men into the vestry. Miss Monday marched down the aisle toward Maisie, a resolute look on her face, which every parishioner knew meant she was on a mission. "Can I have a private word with you, Mrs. Clifton?" she asked.

She didn't give Maisie a chance to reply, but simply turned and walked back down the aisle toward the vestry.

—◦—

Eddie Atkins hadn't shown his face in Tilly's for over a month, but then one morning he reappeared and took his usual seat at one of Maisie's tables. When she came over to serve him, he gave her a huge smile, as if he'd never been away.

"Good morning, Mr. Atkins," Maisie said as she opened her notepad. "What can I get for you?"

"My usual," said Eddie.

"It's been so long, Mr. Atkins," said Maisie. "You'll have to remind me."

"I'm sorry I haven't been in touch, Maisie," said Eddie, "but I had to go to America at rather short notice, and I only got back last night."

She wanted to believe him. Maisie had already admitted to her mother that she was a little disappointed she hadn't heard from Eddie after he'd taken her to the cinema. She'd enjoyed his company and felt the evening had gone rather well.

Another man had started visiting the tea shop regularly, and like Eddie he would only sit at one of Maisie's tables. Although she couldn't help noticing that he was showing considerable interest in her, she didn't give him any encouragement, because not only was he middle-aged but he was also wearing a wedding ring. He had a detached air about him, like a solicitor who is studying a client, and whenever he spoke to her he sounded a little pompous. Maisie could hear her mother asking, "What's his game?" But perhaps she'd misunderstood his intentions, because he never once tried to strike up a conversation with her.

Even Maisie couldn't resist a grin when, a week later, both of her suitors dropped in for a coffee on the same morning, and both asked if they could meet up with her later.

Eddie was first, and he got straight to the point. "Why don't I pick you up after work this evening, Maisie? There's something I'm rather keen to show you."

Maisie wanted to tell him she already had a date, just to make him realize she wasn't available whenever it suited him, but when she returned to his table a few minutes later with his bill, she found herself saying, "I'll see you after work then, Eddie."

She still had a smile on her face when the other customer said, "I wonder if I might have a word with you, Mrs. Clifton?"

Maisie wondered how he knew her name.

"Wouldn't you prefer to speak to the manageress, Mr. . . . ?"

"Frampton," he replied. "No, thank you, it's you I was hoping to speak to. Might I suggest we meet at the Royal Hotel during your afternoon break? It shouldn't take more than fifteen minutes of your time."

"Talk about buses never turning up when you need one," Maisie said to Miss Tilly, "and then two arrive at once." Miss Tilly told Maisie she thought she recognized Mr. Frampton, but couldn't place him.

When Maisie presented Mr. Frampton with his bill, she emphasized that she could only spare fifteen minutes because she had to be on time to pick up her son from school at four o'clock. He nodded as if that was something else he was aware of.

◄○►

Was it really in Harry's best interests to apply for a scholarship to St. Bede's?

Maisie wasn't sure who to discuss the problem with. Stan was bound to be against the idea, and wasn't likely to consider the other side of the argument. Miss Tilly was too close a friend of Miss Monday's to give a dispassionate view, and the Reverend Watts had already advised her to seek the Lord's guidance, which hadn't proved particularly reliable in the past. Mr. Frobisher had seemed such a nice man, but he'd made it clear that only she could make the final decision. Mr. Holcombe hadn't left her in any doubt how he felt.

Maisie didn't give Mr. Frampton another thought until she'd finished serving her last customer. She then exchanged a pinafore for her old coat.

Miss Tilly watched through the window as Maisie set off in the direction of the Royal Hotel. She felt a little anxious, but wasn't sure why.

Although Maisie had never been in the Royal before, she knew it had the reputation of being one of the best-run hotels in the West Country, and the chance to see it from the inside was one of the reasons she'd agreed to see Mr. Frampton.

She stood on the opposite pavement and watched as customers pushed their way through the revolving doors. She'd never seen anything quite like them, and only when she felt confident she'd got the hang of how they worked did she cross the road and step inside. She pushed a little too hard and found herself propelled into the foyer more quickly than she'd anticipated.

Maisie looked around and spotted Mr. Frampton sitting alone in a quiet alcove in the corner of the foyer. She walked across to join him. He immediately rose from his place, shook hands with her, and waited until she had taken the seat opposite him.

"Can I order you a coffee, Mrs. Clifton?" he asked, and before she could reply he added, "I should warn you, it's not in the same class as Tilly's."

"No, thank you, Mr. Frampton," said Maisie, whose only interest was to find out why he wanted to see her.

Mr. Frampton took his time lighting a cigarette, then inhaled deeply. "Mrs. Clifton," he began as he placed the cigarette on the ashtray, "you cannot have failed to notice that I have recently become a regular customer at Tilly's." Maisie nodded. "I have to confess that my only reason for visiting the café was you." Maisie had her well-prepared "amorous suitor" line ready for just as soon as he stopped talking. "In all the years I've been in the hotel trade," he continued, "I've never seen anyone do their job more efficiently than you. I only wish that every waitress in this hotel was of your caliber."

"I've been well trained," said Maisie.

"So have the other four waitresses in that tea shop, but none of them has your flair."

"I'm flattered, Mr. Frampton. But why are you telling—"

"I am the general manager of this hotel," he said, "and I'd like you to take charge of our coffee room, which is known as the Palm Court. As you can see—" he waved a hand expansively—"we have about a hundred covers, but less than a third of the places are regularly occupied. That's not exactly a worthwhile return on the company's investment. No doubt that would change if you were to take over. I believe I can make it worth your while."

Maisie didn't interrupt him.

"I can't see why your hours should differ greatly from those of your current employment. I'd be willing to pay you five pounds a week, and all the tips earned by the waitresses in the Palm Court would be split fifty-fifty with you. If you were able to build up the clientele, that could prove very remunerative. And then I—"

"But I couldn't think of leaving Miss Tilly," interrupted Maisie. "She's been so good to me over the past six years."

"I fully appreciate your feelings, Mrs. Clifton. Indeed, I would have been disappointed if that had not been your immediate response. Loyalty is a trait I greatly admire. However, you must not only consider your own future, but also your son's, should he take up the offer of a choral scholarship to St. Bede's."

Maisie was speechless.

◄○►

When Maisie finished work that evening, she found Eddie sitting in his car outside the tea shop waiting for her. She noticed that he didn't jump out to open the passenger door this time.

"So, where are you taking me?" she asked as she climbed in beside him.

"It's a surprise," said Eddie as he pressed the starter, "but I don't think you'll be disappointed."

He pushed the gear lever into first, and headed toward a part of the city that Maisie hadn't visited before. A few minutes later, he drove into a side alley and came to a halt outside a large oak door below a neon sign that announced in glowing red letters, EDDIE'S NIGHTCLUB.

"This is yours?" asked Maisie.

"Every square inch," said Eddie proudly. "Come inside and see for yourself." He leaped out of the car, opened the front door and led Maisie inside. "This used to be a granary," he explained as he took her down a narrow wooden staircase. "But now that ships can no longer sail this far up the river, the company's had to move, so I was able to pick up their lease for a very reasonable price."

Maisie entered a large, dimly lit room. It was some time before her eyes had adjusted well enough to take it all in. There were half a dozen men sitting on high leather stools drinking at the bar, and almost as many waitresses fluttering around them. The wall behind the bar consisted of a vast mirror, giving the impression the room was far larger than it actually was. At the center was a dance floor, surrounded by plush velvet banquettes that would just about seat two people. At the far end was a small stage with a piano, double bass, a set of drums and several music stands.

Eddie took a seat at the bar. Looking around the room he said, "This is why I've been spending so much time in America. Speakeasies like this are springing up all over New York and Chicago, and they're making a fortune." He lit a cigar. "And I promise you, there won't be anything else like this in Bristol, that's for sure."

"That's for sure," Maisie repeated as she joined him at the bar, but didn't attempt to climb up onto one of the high stools.

"What's your poison, doll?" said Eddie, in what he imagined to be an American accent.

"I don't drink," Maisie reminded him.

"That's one of the reasons I chose you."

"Chose me?"

"Sure. You'd be the ideal person to take charge of the cocktail waitresses. Not only would I pay you six pounds a week, but if the place takes off, the tips alone would be more than you could ever hope to earn at Tilly's."

"And would I be expected to dress like that?" asked Maisie, pointing to one of the waitresses who was wearing an off-the-shoulder red blouse and a tight-fitting black skirt that barely covered her knees. It amused Maisie that they were the same colors as the St. Bede's uniform.

"Why not? You're a great-lookin' broad, and the punters will pay good money to be served by someone like you. You'll get the odd proposition, of course, but I feel sure you can handle that."

"What's the point of a dance floor if it's a men-only club?"

"Another idea I picked up from the States," said Eddie. "If you want to dance with one of the cocktail waitresses, it'll cost you."

"And what else does that cost include?"

"That's up to them," said Eddie with a shrug of the shoulders. "So long as it doesn't take place on the premises, nothing to do with me," he added, laughing a little too loudly. Maisie didn't laugh. "So what do you think?" he asked.

"I think I'd better be getting home," said Maisie. "I didn't have time to let Harry know I'd be late."

"Whatever you say, honey," said Eddie. He draped an arm around her shoulder and led her out of the bar and back up the stairs.

As he drove her to Still House Lane, he told Maisie about his plans for the future. "I've already got my eye on a second site," he said excitedly, "so the sky's the limit."

"The sky's the limit," Maisie repeated, as they drew up outside No. 27.

Maisie jumped out of the car and walked quickly to the front door.

"So will you need a few days to think it over?" said Eddie, chasing after her.

"No, thank you, Eddie," said Maisie without hesitation. "I've already made up my mind," she added, taking a key out of her handbag.

Eddie grinned and put an arm around her. "I didn't think it would be a difficult decision for you to make."

Maisie removed the arm, smiled sweetly and said, "It's kind of you to consider me, honey, but I think I'll stick to serving coffee." She opened her front door before adding, "But thanks for asking."

"Anything you say, doll, but if you change your mind, my door is always open."

Maisie closed the door behind her.

14

MAISIE FINALLY SETTLED on the one person she felt she could seek advice from. She decided to turn up at the docks unannounced and hoped he'd be around when she knocked on his door.

She didn't tell either Stan or Harry whom she was visiting. One of them would try to stop her, while the other would feel she'd betrayed a confidence.

Maisie waited until her day off, and once she had dropped Harry at school, she took a tram to the dockyard. She had chosen her time carefully: late morning, when he was still likely to be in his office, while Stan would be fully occupied loading or unloading cargo at the other end of the dock.

Maisie told the man on the gate that she'd come to apply for a job as a cleaner. He pointed indifferently toward the red-brick building and still didn't remember her.

As she walked toward Barrington House, Maisie looked up at the windows on the fifth floor and wondered which office was his. She recalled her encounter with Mrs. Nettles, and the way she had been shown the door the moment she mentioned her name. Now Maisie not only had a job she enjoyed and where she was respected, but she'd had two other offers in the past few days. She didn't give Mrs. Nettles another thought as she walked straight past the building and continued along the quayside.

Maisie didn't slacken her pace until she could see his home. She found it hard to believe that anyone could possibly live in a railway carriage, and began to wonder if she'd made a dreadful mistake.

Had Harry's stories of a dining room, a bedroom and even a library, been exaggerated? "You can't stop now you've come this far, Maisie Clifton," she told herself, and knocked boldly on the carriage door.

"Come in, Mrs. Clifton," said a gentle voice.

Maisie opened the door to find an old man sitting in a comfortable seat, with books and other possessions scattered around him. She was surprised how clean the carriage was, and realized that, despite Stan's claims, it was she, and not Old Jack, who lived in third class. Stan had perpetuated a myth that had been ignored when viewed through the eyes of an unprejudiced child.

Old Jack immediately rose from his place and beckoned her toward the seat opposite. "You'll have come to see me about young Harry, no doubt."

"Yes, Mr. Tar," she replied.

"Let me guess," he said. "You can't make up your mind whether he should go to St. Bede's, or remain at Merrywood Elementary."

"How could you possibly know that?" asked Maisie.

"Because I've been considering the same problem for the past month," said Old Jack.

"So what do you think he should do?"

"I think that despite the many difficulties he will undoubtedly face at St. Bede's, if he doesn't take this opportunity, he could well spend the rest of his life regretting it."

"Perhaps he won't win a scholarship and the decision will be taken out of our hands."

"The decision was taken out of our hands," said Old Jack, "the moment Mr. Frobisher heard young Harry sing. But I have a feeling that wasn't the only reason you came to see me."

Maisie was beginning to understand why Harry admired this man so much. "You're quite right, Mr. Tar, I need your advice on another matter."

"Your son calls me Jack, except when he's cross with me, then he calls me Old Jack."

Maisie smiled. "I've been worried that even if he did win a scholarship, I wasn't earning enough for Harry to have all the little extras that the other boys at a school like St. Bede's take for granted. But fortunately I've just been offered another job, which would mean more money."

"And you're worried about how Miss Tilly will react when you tell her you're thinking of leaving?"

"You know Miss Tilly?"

"No, but Harry has spoken of her many times. She's clearly from the same mold as Miss Monday, and let me assure you, that's a limited edition. There's no need for you to concern yourself."

"I don't understand," said Maisie.

"Allow me to explain," said Old Jack. "Miss Monday has already invested a great deal of her time and expertise in making sure that Harry not only wins a scholarship to St. Bede's but, far more important, goes on to prove himself worthy of it. My bet is that she will have discussed every possible eventuality with her closest friend, who just happens to be Miss Tilly. So when you tell her about the new job, you may well find it doesn't come as a complete surprise."

"Thank you, Jack," said Maisie. "How lucky Harry is to have you as a friend. The father he never knew," she said softly.

"That is the nicest compliment I've received for a good many years," said Old Jack. "I'm only sorry that he lost his father in such tragic circumstances."

"Do you know how my husband died?"

"Yes, I do," replied Old Jack. Aware that he should never had raised the subject, he quickly added, "But only because Harry told me."

"What did he tell you?" asked Maisie anxiously.

"That his father was killed in the war."

"But you know that's not true," said Maisie.

"Yes, I do," said Old Jack. "And I suspect Harry also knows his father couldn't have died in the war."

"Then why doesn't he say so?"

"He probably thinks there's something you don't want to tell him."

"But I don't know the truth myself," admitted Maisie.

Old Jack didn't comment.

Maisie walked slowly home; one question answered, another still unresolved. Even so, she wasn't in any doubt that Old Jack could be added to the list of people who knew the truth about what had happened to her husband.

Old Jack turned out to be right about Miss Tilly, because when Maisie told her about Mr. Frampton's offer, she couldn't have been more supportive and understanding.

"We'll all miss you," she said, "and frankly the Royal is lucky to have you."

"How can I begin to thank you for all you've done for me over the years?" said Maisie.

"It's Harry who should be thanking you," said Miss Tilly, "and I suspect it will only be a matter of time before he realizes that."

—◇—

Maisie started her new job a month later, and it didn't take her long to discover why the Palm Court was never more than a third full.

The waitresses regarded their work simply as a job, unlike Miss Tilly, who considered it to be a vocation. They never bothered to remember the customers' names, or their favorite tables. Worse, the coffee was often cold by the time it was served, and the cakes were left to go stale until someone bought them. Maisie wasn't surprised they didn't get any tips; they didn't deserve them.

After another month, she began to realize just how much Miss Tilly had taught her.

After three months, Maisie had replaced five of the seven waitresses, without having to recruit anyone from Tilly's. She had also ordered smart new uniforms for all her staff, along with new plates, cups and saucers and, even more important, changed her coffee supplier and her cake-maker. That was something she was willing to steal from Miss Tilly.

"You're costing me a lot of money, Maisie," said Mr. Frampton when another stack of bills landed on his desk. "Try not to forget what I said about return on investment."

"Give me another six months, Mr. Frampton, and you'll see the results."

Although Maisie worked night and day, she always found time to drop Harry off at school in the morning and pick him up in the afternoon. But she warned Mr. Frampton that there would be one day when she wouldn't be on time for work.

When she told him why, he gave her the whole day off.

—◦—

Just before they left the house, Maisie checked herself in the mirror. She was dressed in her Sunday best but not going to church. She smiled down at her son, who looked so smart in his new red and black school uniform. Even so, she felt a little self-conscious as they waited at the tram stop.

"Two to Park Street," she told the clippie when the No. 11 pulled away. She was unable to hide her pride when she noticed him taking a closer look at Harry. It only convinced Maisie that she had made the right decision.

When they reached their stop, Harry refused to let his mum carry his suitcase. Maisie held on to his hand as they walked slowly up the hill toward the school, not sure which one of them was more nervous. She couldn't take her eyes off the hansom cabs and chauffeur-driven cars that were dropping off other boys for their first day of term. She only hoped that Harry would be able to find at least one friend among them. After all, some of the nannies were better dressed than she was.

Harry began to slow down as they got nearer the school gates. Maisie could sense his discomfort—or was it just fear of the unknown?

"I'll leave you now," she said, and bent down to kiss him. "Good luck, Harry. Make us all proud of you."

"Goodbye, Mum."

As she watched him walk away, Maisie noticed that someone else appeared to be taking an interest in Harry Clifton.

15

MAISIE WOULD NEVER forget the first time she had to turn away a customer.

"I'm sure there will be a table available in a few minutes, sir."

She prided herself on the fact that once a customer had paid the bill, her staff could clear the table, replace the cloth and have it re-laid and ready for the next guest within five minutes.

The Palm Court quickly became so popular that Maisie had to keep a couple of tables permanently reserved, just in case one of her regulars turned up unexpectedly.

She was a little embarrassed that some of her old customers from Tilly's had begun to migrate to the Palm Court, not least dear old Mr. Craddick, who remembered Harry from his paper round. She considered it an even greater compliment when Miss Tilly herself began to drop in for a morning coffee.

"Just checking on the opposition," she said. "By the way, Maisie, this coffee is superb."

"So it should be," Maisie replied. "It's yours."

Eddie Atkins also came in from time to time, and if the size of his cigars, not to mention his waistline, was anything to go by, the sky must still have been the limit. Although he was friendly, he never asked Maisie out, but he did regularly remind her that his door was always open.

Not that Maisie didn't have a string of admirers she occasionally allowed to take her out in the evening, maybe to dinner at a fashionable restaurant, sometimes a visit to the Old Vic or the cinema, especially if a Greta Garbo film was playing. But when they parted at the end of the evening, she allowed none of them more than a peck on the cheek before returning home. At least, not until she met Patrick Casey, who proved that the charm of the Irish was not just a cliché.

When Patrick first walked into the Palm Court, hers wasn't the only head that turned to take a closer look. He was a shade over six foot, with wavy dark hair and the build of an athlete. That would have been enough for most women, but it was the smile that captivated Maisie as, she suspected, it had many others.

Patrick told her he was in finance, but then Eddie had said he was in the entertainment business. His work brought him to Bristol once or twice a month, when Maisie would allow him to take her to dinner, the theater or the cinema, and occasionally she even broke her golden rule, and didn't take the last tram back to Still House Lane.

She wouldn't have been surprised to discover that Patrick had a wife and half a dozen offspring back at home in Cork, although he swore, hand on heart, that he was a bachelor.

—◇—

Whenever Mr. Holcombe dropped into the Palm Court, Maisie would guide him to a table in the far corner of the room that was partly obscured by a large pillar and was shunned by her regulars. But its privacy allowed her to bring him up to date on how Harry was getting on.

Today, he seemed more interested in the future than the past, and asked, "Have you decided what Harry will do once he leaves St. Bede's?"

"I haven't given it much thought," Maisie admitted. "After all, it's not for some time."

"It's soon enough," said Mr. Holcombe, "and I can't believe you'll want him to return to Merrywood Elementary."

"No, I don't," said Maisie firmly, "but what choice is there?"

"Harry says he'd like to go to Bristol Grammar School, but if he fails to win a scholarship, he's worried that you won't be able to afford the fees."

"That won't be a problem," Maisie assured him. "With my

present pay, combined with the tips, no one need know his mother is a waitress."

"Some waitress," said Mr. Holcombe, looking around the packed room. "I'm only surprised you haven't opened your own place."

Maisie laughed, and didn't give it another thought until she had an unexpected visit from Miss Tilly.

—◇—

Maisie attended Matins at St. Mary Redcliffe every Sunday so she could hear her son sing. Miss Monday had warned her that it wouldn't be much longer before Harry's voice broke, and she mustn't assume that a few weeks later he'd be singing tenor solos.

Maisie tried to concentrate on the canon's sermon that Sunday morning but found her mind drifting. She glanced across the aisle to see Mr. and Mrs. Barrington sitting with their son Giles and two young girls who she assumed must be their daughters, but whose names she didn't know. Maisie had been surprised when Harry told her that Giles Barrington was his closest friend. Nothing more than a coincidence of the alphabet had put them together in the first place, he'd said. She hoped it would never become necessary for her to tell him that Giles might be more than just a good friend.

—◇—

Maisie often wished she could do more to help Harry with his efforts to win a scholarship to Bristol Grammar School. Although Miss Tilly had taught her how to read a menu, add and subtract, and even write a few simple words, just the thought of what Harry must be putting himself through filled her with trepidation.

Miss Monday boosted Maisie's confidence by continually reminding her that Harry would never have got this far if she hadn't been willing to make so many sacrifices. "And in any case," she added, "you're every bit as clever as Harry, you just haven't been given the same opportunities."

Mr. Holcombe kept her informed on what he described as "the timing," and, as the date of the examination drew nearer, Maisie became just as nervous as the candidate. She realized the truth of one of Old Jack's remarks, that often the onlooker suffers even more than the participant.

The Palm Court room was now packed every day, but it didn't stop Maisie from initiating even more changes in a decade the press were describing as the "frivolous thirties."

In the morning, she had started offering her customers a variety of biscuits to go with their coffee, and in the afternoon, her tea menu was proving just as popular, especially after Harry told her that Mrs. Barrington had given him the choice of Indian or China tea. However, Mr. Frampton vetoed the suggestion that smoked salmon sandwiches should appear on the menu.

Every Sunday, Maisie would kneel on her little cushion; her one prayer was to the point. "Please God make sure Harry wins a scholarship. If he does, I'll never ask you for anything again."

With a week to go to the exams, Maisie found she couldn't sleep, and lay awake wondering how Harry was coping. So many customers wanted to pass on their best wishes to him, some because they had heard him singing in the church choir, others because he'd delivered their morning papers, or simply because their own children had been, were, or would at some time in the future be going through the same experience. It seemed to Maisie that half of Bristol was taking the exam.

On the morning of the examination, Maisie placed several regulars at the wrong table, gave Mr. Craddick coffee instead of his usual hot chocolate, and even presented two customers with someone else's bill. No one complained.

Harry told her he thought he'd done quite well, but he couldn't be certain if he'd done well enough. He mentioned someone called Thomas Hardy, but Maisie wasn't sure if he was a friend or one of the masters.

-◄o►-

When the long-case clock in the Palm Court room struck ten on that Thursday morning, Maisie knew the headmaster would be posting the exam results on the school notice board. But it was another twenty-two minutes before Mr. Holcombe walked into the room and headed straight for his usual table behind the pillar.

Maisie could not tell how Harry had done from the expression on the schoolmaster's face. She quickly crossed the room to join him and, for the first time in four years, sat down in the seat opposite a customer, although "collapsed" might be a more accurate description.

"Harry has passed with distinction," said Mr. Holcombe, "but I'm afraid he just missed out on a scholarship."

"What does that mean?" Maisie asked, trying to stop her hands from trembling.

"The top twelve candidates had marks of 80 percent or above, and were all awarded open scholarships. In fact, Harry's friend Deakins came top, with 92 percent. Harry achieved a very commendable 78 percent, and came seventeenth out of three hundred. Mr. Frobisher told me his English paper let him down."

"He should have read Hardy instead of Dickens," said a woman who'd never read a book.

"Harry will still be offered a place at BGS," said Mr. Holcombe, "but he won't receive the annual hundred pounds a year scholar's grant."

Maisie rose from her place. "Then I'll just have to work three shifts instead of two, won't I? Because he's not going back to Merrywood Elementary, Mr. Holcombe, I can tell you that."

—◇—

Over the next few days, Maisie was surprised by how many regulars offered their congratulations on Harry's magnificent achievement. She also discovered that one or two of her customers had children who had failed to pass the exam, in one case by a single percentage point. They would have to settle for their second choice. It made Maisie all the more determined that nothing would stop Harry reporting to Bristol Grammar School on the first day of term.

One strange thing she noticed during the next week was that her tips doubled. Dear old Mr. Craddick slipped her a five-pound note, saying, "For Harry. May he prove worthy of his mother."

When the thin white envelope dropped through the letterbox in Still House Lane, an event in itself, Harry opened the letter and read it to his mother. "Clifton, H." had been offered a place in the A stream for the Michaelmas term starting on September 15th. When he came to the last paragraph, which asked Mrs. Clifton to write and confirm whether the candidate wished to accept or reject the offer, he looked nervously at her.

"You must write back straight away, accepting the offer!" she said.

Harry threw his arms around her and whispered, "I only wish my father was alive."

Perhaps he is, thought Maisie.

⚬

A few days later, a second letter landed on the doormat. This one detailed a long list of items that had to be purchased before the first day of term. Maisie noticed that Harry seemed to require two of everything, in some cases three or more, and in one case, six: socks, gray calf length, plus garters.

"Pity you can't borrow a pair of my suspenders," she said. Harry blushed.

A third letter invited new pupils to select three extracurricular activities from a list ranging from the car club to the Combined Cadet Force—some of which involved an added charge of five pounds per activity. Harry chose the choir, for which there was no extra charge, as well as the theater club and the Arts Appreciation Society. The latter included a proviso that any visits to galleries outside Bristol would incur an extra cost.

Maisie wished there were a few more Mr. Craddicks around, but she never allowed Harry to suspect there was any reason for concern, even though Mr. Holcombe reminded her that her boy would be at Bristol Grammar School for the next five years. The first member of the family not to leave school before the age of fourteen, she told him.

Maisie braced herself for another visit to T. C. Marsh, Tailors of Distinction.

By the time Harry was fully kitted out and ready for the first day of term, Maisie had once again begun to walk to and from work, saving five pence a week on tram fares, or as she told her mother, "A pound a year, enough to pay for a new suit for Harry."

―◇―

Parents, Maisie had learned over the years, may be considered an unfortunate necessity by their offspring, but more often than not they are also an embarrassment.

On her first speech day at St. Bede's, Maisie had been the only mother not wearing a hat. After that, she had bought one from a secondhand shop and, however out of fashion it would become, it was going to have to last until Harry left Bristol Grammar School.

Harry had agreed that she should accompany him to school on the first day of term, but Maisie had already decided that he was old enough to catch a tram home in the evening. Her main anxiety was not about how Harry would get to and from school, but what to do with him in the evenings, now he was a day boy and would no longer be sleeping at school during term. She had no doubt that if he went back to sharing a room with his uncle Stan, it could only end in tears. She tried to put the problem out of her mind as she prepared for Harry's first day in his new school.

Hat in place, best, and only, overcoat recently cleaned, sensible black shoes with the only pair of silk stockings she possessed, Maisie felt ready to face the other parents. When she came down the stairs, Harry was already waiting for her by the door. He looked so smart in his new uniform of claret and black that she would have liked to parade him up and down Still House Lane so the neighbors would know that someone from the street was going to Bristol Grammar School.

As they had on his first day at St. Bede's, they caught the tram, but Harry asked Maisie if they could get off one stop before University Road. She was no longer allowed to hold his hand, although she did straighten his cap and tie more than once.

When Maisie first saw the noisy gathering of young men crowded around the school gates, she said, "I'd better be off or

123

I'll be late for work," which puzzled Harry, because he knew Mr. Frampton had given her the day off.

She gave her son a quick hug, but kept a wary eye on him as he made his way up the hill. The first person to greet him was Giles Barrington. Maisie was surprised to see him, as Harry had told her he would probably be going to Eton. They shook hands like a couple of grown men who had just closed an important deal.

Maisie could see Mr. and Mrs. Barrington standing at the back of the crowd. Was he making sure he avoided her? A few minutes later, Mr. and Mrs. Deakins joined them, accompanied by the Peloquin Memorial scholar. More handshakes, left-handed in Mr. Deakins's case.

As the parents began to take leave of their children, Maisie watched Mr. Barrington as he shook hands first with his son and then with Deakins, but turned away when Harry offered his hand. Mrs. Barrington looked embarrassed, and Maisie wondered if she might later ask why Hugo had ignored Giles's closest friend. If she did, Maisie felt certain he would not tell her the real reason. Maisie feared it couldn't be long before Harry asked why Mr. Barrington always snubbed him. As long as only three people knew the truth, she couldn't think of any reason why Harry would ever find out.

16

MISS TILLY HAD become such a regular at the Palm Court that she even had her own table.

She would usually arrive around four o'clock, and order a cup of tea (Earl Gray) and a cucumber sandwich. She always declined to take anything from the large assortment of cream cakes, jam tarts and chocolate éclairs, but would occasionally allow herself a buttered scone. When she popped by just before five one evening, unusually late for her, Maisie was relieved that her usual table was free.

"I wonder if I might sit somewhere a little more discreet today, Maisie. I need to have a quiet word with you."

"Of course, Miss Tilly," said Maisie, and led her to Mr. Holcombe's preferred table behind the pillar at the far end of the room. "I'm off in ten minutes," Maisie told her. "I'll join you then."

When her deputy, Susan, arrived to take over, Maisie explained that she would be joining Miss Tilly for a few minutes, but didn't expect to be served.

"Is the old duck unhappy about something?" Susan asked.

"That old duck taught me everything I know," said Maisie with a grin.

When five o'clock struck, Maisie walked across the room and took the seat opposite Miss Tilly. She rarely sat down with a customer, and on the few occasions she did, she had never felt at ease.

"Would you care for some tea, Maisie?"

"No, thank you, Miss Tilly."

"I quite understand. I'll try not to keep you too long, but before

I tell you my real purpose for wanting to see you, may I ask how Harry is getting on?"

"I wish he'd stop growing," said Maisie. "I seem to be letting down his trousers every few weeks. At this rate his long trousers will be short trousers before the end of the year."

Miss Tilly laughed. "What about his work?"

"His end-of-term report said—" Maisie paused, trying to recall the exact words—"'A most satisfactory start. Very promising.' He came top in English."

"Somewhat ironic," said Miss Tilly. "If I remember correctly, that was the subject that let him down in the entrance exam."

Maisie nodded, and tried not to think about the financial consequences of Harry not having read enough Thomas Hardy.

"You must be very proud of him," said Miss Tilly. "And when I went to St. Mary's on Sunday, I was delighted to see that he's back in the choir."

"Yes, but he now has to be satisfied with a place in the back row with the other baritones. His days as a soloist are over. But he's joined the theater club, and because there are no girls at BGS, he's playing Ursula in the school play."

"*Much Ado About Nothing*," said Miss Tilly. "Still, I mustn't waste any more of your time, so I'll come to the reason I wanted to see you." She took a sip of tea, as if she wanted to compose herself before she spoke again, and then it all came out in a rush.

"I'll be sixty next month, my dear, and for some time I have been considering retiring."

It had never crossed Maisie's mind that Miss Tilly wouldn't go on forever.

"Miss Monday and I have been thinking about moving down to Cornwall. We have our eye on a little cottage by the sea."

You mustn't leave Bristol, Maisie wanted to say. I love you both, and if you go, who will I turn to for advice?

"Matters came to a head last month," continued Miss Tilly, "when a local businessman made me an offer for the tea shop. It seems he wants to add it to his growing empire. And although I don't care for the idea of Tilly's being part of a chain, his offer was far too tempting to turn down out of hand." Maisie only had one question, but she didn't interrupt while Miss Tilly was in full flow. "Since then, I've been giving the matter a great deal of thought, and I decided that if you were able to come up with the same amount he has offered, I would rather you took over the business than I hand it over to a stranger."

"How much did he offer?"

"Five hundred pounds."

Maisie sighed. "I'm flattered you even thought of me," she said at last, "but the truth is, I don't have five hundred pennies to my name, let alone five hundred pounds."

"I was afraid you might say that," said Miss Tilly. "But if you could find a backer, I feel sure they would consider the business a good investment. After all, I made a profit of one hundred and twelve pounds and ten shillings last year, which didn't include my salary. I would have let you have it for less than five hundred pounds, but we've found a delightful little cottage in St. Mawes, and the owners won't consider a penny less than three hundred. Miss Monday and I could just about survive on our savings for a year or two, but as neither of us has a pension to fall back on, the extra two hundred pounds will make all the difference."

Maisie was just about to tell Miss Tilly how sorry she was but it was out of the question, when Patrick Casey strolled into the room and sat down at his usual table.

—◦—

It wasn't until after they'd made love that Maisie told Patrick about Miss Tilly's offer. He sat up in bed, lit a cigarette and inhaled deeply.

"Raising that amount of capital shouldn't prove too difficult. After all, it's hardly Brunel trying to raise the money to build Clifton Suspension Bridge."

"No, but it is Mrs. Clifton trying to raise five hundred pounds when she hasn't got two halfpennies to rub together."

"True, but you'd be able to show a cash flow and a proven income stream, not to mention the tea shop's goodwill. Mind you, I'll need to look at the books for the past five years and make sure you've been told the whole story."

"Miss Tilly would never try to deceive anyone."

"You'll also have to check that there isn't a rent review due in the near future," Patrick said, ignoring her protestations, "and double-check that her accountant hasn't come up with penalty clauses the moment you start making a profit."

"Miss Tilly wouldn't do something like that," said Maisie.

"You're so trusting, Maisie. What you have to remember is, this won't be in the hands of Miss Tilly, but a lawyer who feels he's got to earn his fee, and an accountant looking for a payday in case you don't retain him."

"You've clearly never met Miss Tilly."

"Your faith in the old lady is touching, Maisie, but my job is to protect people like you, and a hundred and twelve pounds ten shillings profit a year wouldn't be enough for you to live on, remembering you'll be expected to make regular repayments to your investor."

"Miss Tilly assured me that the profit didn't include her salary."

"That might well be the case, but you don't know what that salary is. You'll need at least another two hundred and fifty pounds a year if you're to survive, otherwise not only will you be out of pocket, but Harry will be out of the grammar school."

"I can't wait for you to meet Miss Tilly."

"And what about tips? At the Royal you get 50 percent of all the tips, which comes to at least another two hundred pounds a year, which at the moment isn't taxed, although I've no doubt some future government will catch on to that."

"Perhaps I should tell Miss Tilly that it's too great a risk. After all, as you keep reminding me, I have a guaranteed income at the Royal, with no risks attached."

"True, but if Miss Tilly is half as good as you say she is, this could be an opportunity that might not arise again."

"Make your mind up, Patrick," said Maisie, trying not to sound exasperated.

"I will, the moment I've seen the books."

"You will, the moment you meet Miss Tilly," Maisie said, "because then you'll understand the real meaning of goodwill."

"I can't wait to meet this paragon of virtue."

"Does that mean you'll represent me?"

"Yes," he said, stubbing out his cigarette.

"And how much will you be charging this penniless widow, Mr. Casey?"

"Turn the light out."

—◦—

"Are you sure this is a risk worth taking," asked Mr. Frampton, "when you have so much to lose?"

"My financial adviser thinks so," replied Maisie. "He's assured me that not only do all the figures add up, but once I've paid off the loan, I should be showing a profit within five years."

"But those are the years Harry will be at Bristol Grammar."

"I'm well aware of that, Mr. Frampton, but Mr. Casey has secured a substantial salary for me as part of the bargain, and after I've split the tips with my staff, I should be earning roughly the same amount I'm currently taking home. More important, in five years' time I'll own a real asset, and from then on, all the profits will be mine," she said, trying to recall Patrick's exact words.

"It's clear to me that you've made up your mind," said Mr. Frampton. "But let me warn you, Maisie, there's a great deal of difference between being an employee, when you know you'll be taking home a wage packet every week, and being an employer, when it will be your responsibility to put your money into several wage packets every Friday night. Frankly, Maisie, you are the best at what you do, but are you really sure you want to switch from being a player to joining the management?"

"Mr. Casey will be there to advise me."

"Casey's a capable fellow, I'll give you that, but he also has to look after more important clients right across the country. It will be you who has to run the business from day to day. If anything were to go wrong, he won't always be around to hold your hand."

"But I may not be given an opportunity like this again in my lifetime." Another of Patrick's pronouncements.

"So be it, Maisie," said Frampton. "And don't be in any doubt how much we'll all miss you at the Royal. The only reason you're not irreplaceable is because you trained your deputy so well."

"Susan won't let you down, Mr. Frampton."

"I'm sure she won't. But she'll never be Maisie Clifton. Let me be the first to wish you every success in your new venture, and if things don't work out as planned, there will always be a job for you here at the Royal."

Mr. Frampton rose from behind his desk and shook hands with Maisie, just as he'd done six years before.

17

A MONTH LATER, Maisie signed six documents in the presence of Mr. Prendergast, the manager of the National Provincial Bank on Corn Street. But not until Patrick had taken her through each page, line by line, now happy to admit how wrong he'd been to doubt Miss Tilly. If everyone behaved as honorably as she did, he told her, he'd be out of a job.

Maisie handed Miss Tilly a check for £500 on March 19th, 1934, receiving a huge hug and a tea shop in return. A week later, Miss Tilly and Miss Monday left for Cornwall.

When Maisie opened her doors for business the following day, she retained the name "Tilly's." Patrick had advised her never to underestimate the goodwill of Tilly's name above the door ("founded in 1898") and that she should not even think of changing it until Miss Tilly was of blessed memory and perhaps not even then. "Regulars don't like change, especially sudden ones, so don't rush them into anything."

Maisie did, however, spot a few changes that could be made without offending any of the regulars. She felt a new set of table-cloths wouldn't go amiss, and the chairs and even the tables were beginning to look, well, quaint. And hadn't Miss Tilly noticed the carpet was wearing a bit thin?

"Pace yourself," Patrick warned her on one of his monthly visits. "Remember that it's far easier to spend money than to earn it, and don't be surprised if a few of the old biddies disappear and you don't make quite as much as you'd anticipated in the first few months."

Patrick turned out to be right. The number of covers dropped in the first month, and then again in the second, proving just how popular Miss Tilly had been. Had they fallen again in the third, Patrick would have been advising Maisie about cash flow and overdraft limits, but it bottomed—another of Patrick's expressions—and even began to climb the following month, though not sharply.

—◇—

At the end of her first year, Maisie had broken even, but she hadn't made enough to pay back any of the bank's loan.

"Don't fret, my dear," Miss Tilly told her on one of her rare visits to Bristol. "It was years before I made a profit." Maisie didn't have years.

The second year began well, with some of her regulars from the Palm Court returning to their old stamping ground. Eddie Atkins had put on so much weight, and his cigars were so much larger, that Maisie could only assume the entertainment business was thriving. Mr. Craddick appeared at eleven o'clock every morning, dressed in a raincoat, umbrella in hand, whatever the weather. Mr. Holcombe dropped in from time to time, always wanting updates on how Harry was getting on, and she never allowed him to pay the bill. Patrick's first stop whenever he returned to Bristol was always Tilly's.

During her second year, Maisie had to replace one supplier who didn't seem to know the difference between fresh and stale, and one waitress who wasn't convinced that the customer was always right. Several young women applied for the job, as it was becoming more acceptable for women to go to work. Maisie settled on a young lady called Karen, who had a mop of curly fair hair, big blue eyes and what the fashion magazines were describing as an hourglass figure. Maisie had a feeling that Karen might attract some new customers who were a little younger than most of her regulars.

Selecting a new cake supplier proved a more difficult task. And although several companies tendered for the contract, Maisie was very demanding. However, when Bob Burrows of Burrows' Bakery (founded 1935) turned up on her doorstep and told her that Tilly's would be his first customer, she put him on a month's trial.

Bob turned out to be hard-working and reliable, and even more important, his goods were always so fresh and tempting that her customers would often say, "Well, perhaps just one more." His cream buns and fruit scones were particularly popular, but it was his chocolate brownies, the new fad, that seemed to disappear from the cakestand long before midday. Although Maisie regularly pressed him, Bob kept telling her that he just couldn't make any more.

One morning, after Bob had dropped off his wares, Maisie thought he looked a little forlorn, so she sat him down and poured him a cup of coffee. He confessed to her that he was suffering from the same cash-flow problems she'd experienced in her first year. But he was confident things would soon look up as he'd recently been taken on by two new shops, although he stressed how much he owed to Maisie for giving him his first break.

As the weeks passed, these morning coffee breaks became something of a ritual. Even so, Maisie couldn't have been more surprised when Bob asked her out on a date, as she considered theirs to be a professional relationship. He had bought tickets for *Glamorous Night,* a new musical that was playing at the Hippodrome, which Maisie had hoped Patrick might take her to. She thanked Bob, but said she didn't want to spoil their relationship. She would have liked to add that there were already two men in her life, a fifteen-year-old who was worrying about his acne, and an Irishman who only visited Bristol once a month and didn't seem to realize she was in love with him.

Bob didn't take no for an answer, and a month later Maisie was even more embarrassed when he presented her with a marcasite brooch. She kissed him on the cheek, and wondered how he'd found out it was her birthday. That evening she placed the brooch in a drawer, and might have forgotten all about it if other gifts hadn't followed at regular intervals.

Patrick seemed amused by his rival's persistence, and over dinner one night he reminded Maisie that she was a good-looking woman with prospects.

Maisie didn't laugh. "It's got to stop," she said.

"Then why don't you find another supplier?"

"Because good ones are a lot harder to find than lovers. In any case, Bob's reliable, his cakes are the best in town and his prices are lower than any of his competitors."

"And he's in love with you," said Patrick.

"Don't tease, Patrick. It's got to stop."

"I'll tell you something far more important that's got to stop," said Patrick, bending down and opening his briefcase.

"May I remind you," said Maisie, "that we're meant to be having a romantic candlelit dinner together, not talking business."

"I'm afraid this can't wait," he said, placing a sheaf of papers on the table. "These are your accounts for the past three months, and they don't make happy reading."

"But I thought you said things have been looking up."

"So they have. You've even managed to keep your outgoings within the limit recommended by the bank, but, inexplicably, your income has dropped during the same period."

"How's that possible?" said Maisie. "We did a record number of covers last month."

"That's why I decided to check carefully through all your bills and receipts for the past month. They just don't add up. I've come to the sad conclusion, Maisie, that one of your waitresses must have her hand in the till. It's common enough in the catering trade; it usually turns out to be the barman or the head waiter but once it starts, there's no way of stopping it until you find the person responsible and sack them. If you don't identify the culprit fairly soon, you're going to have another year without showing a profit, and you won't be able to pay back one penny of the bank loan, let alone start reducing your overdraft."

"What do you advise?"

"You'll have to keep a closer eye on all your staff in future, until one of them gives herself away."

"How will I know which one it is?"

"There are several signs to look out for," said Patrick. "Someone who's living beyond their means, perhaps wearing a new coat or an expensive piece of jewelry, or taking a holiday they wouldn't normally be able to afford. She'll probably tell you she's got a new boyfriend, but—"

"Oh, hell," said Maisie. "I think I know who it might be."

"Who?"

"Karen. She's only been with me a few months, and recently she's been going up to London on her weekends off. Last Monday she turned up at work wearing a new scarf and a pair of leather gloves that made me feel quite envious."

"Don't jump to any conclusions," said Patrick, "but keep a close eye on her. Either she's pocketing the tips or she's got her hands in the till, or both. And one thing I can promise you, it won't stop. In most cases the thief becomes more and more confident until they're finally caught. You need to stop it, and stop it quickly, before she puts you out of business."

◆◇◆

Maisie hated having to spy on her staff. After all, she'd chosen most of the younger ones herself, while the older ones had been at Tilly's for years.

She kept an especially close eye on Karen, but there weren't any obvious signs that she was stealing. But then, as Patrick had warned her, thieves are more cunning than honest people, and there was no way Maisie could keep an eye on her all the time.

And then the problem solved itself. Karen handed in her notice, announcing that she was engaged and would be joining her fiancé in London at the end of the month. Maisie thought her engagement ring was quite exquisite, although she could only wonder who'd paid for it. But she dismissed the thought, relieved she would now have one less problem to worry about.

But when Patrick returned to Bristol a few weeks later, he warned Maisie that her monthly income had dropped again, so it couldn't have been Karen.

"Is it time to call in the police?" Maisie asked.

"Not yet. The last thing you need are any false accusations or rumors that will only cause ill-feeling among your staff. The police may well flush out the thief, but before they do you could lose some of your best staff, who won't like being under suspicion.

135

And you can also be sure that some of the customers will find out, and you don't need that."

"How much longer can I afford to go on like this?"

"Let's give it another month. If we haven't found out who it is by then, you'll have to call in the police." He gave her a huge smile. "Now let's stop talking business and try to remember that we're meant to be celebrating your birthday."

"That was two months ago," she said. "And if it hadn't been for Bob, you wouldn't even have known."

Patrick opened his briefcase once again, but this time he produced a royal blue box with Swan's familiar logo on it. He passed it across to Maisie, who took her time opening it, to find a pair of black leather gloves and a woolen scarf in the traditional Burberry pattern.

"So you're the one who's been robbing me blind," said Maisie as she threw her arms around him.

Patrick didn't respond.

"What's the matter?" asked Maisie.

"I have another piece of news." Maisie looked into his eyes, and wondered what else could possibly be going wrong at Tilly's. "I've been promoted. I'm to be the new deputy manager of our head office in Dublin. I'll be tied to my desk most of the time, so somebody else will be taking my place over here. I will still be able to visit you, but not that often."

Maisie lay in his arms and cried all night. She had thought she wouldn't want to get married again, until the man she loved was no longer available.

She turned up late for work the following morning to find Bob waiting on the doorstep. Once she'd opened the front door, he began to unload the morning delivery from his van.

"I'll be with you in a moment," said Maisie as she disappeared into the staff washroom.

She'd said her last goodbyes to Patrick as he boarded a train at Temple Meads, when she'd burst into tears again. She must have looked a sight and didn't want the regulars to think anything was wrong. "Never bring your personal problems to work," Miss

Tilly had often reminded her staff. "The customers have enough problems of their own without having to worry about yours."

Maisie looked in the mirror: her makeup was a mess. "Damn," she said out loud when she realized she'd left her handbag on the counter. As she walked back into the shop to retrieve it, she suddenly felt sick. Bob was standing with his back to her, one hand in the till. She watched as he stuffed a handful of notes and coins into a trouser pocket, closed the till quietly and then went back to his van to pick up another tray of cakes.

Maisie knew exactly what Patrick would have advised. She walked into the café and stood by the till as Bob strolled back through the door. He was not carrying a tray, but a small red leather box. He gave her a huge smile and fell on one knee.

"You will leave the premises right now, Bob Burrows," Maisie said, in a tone that surprised even her. "If I ever see you anywhere near my tea shop again, I will call the police."

She expected a stream of explanations or expletives, but Bob simply stood up, put the money he'd stolen back on the counter and left without a word. Maisie collapsed onto the nearest chair just as the first member of staff arrived.

"Good morning, Mrs. Clifton. Nice weather for the time of year."

18

WHENEVER A THIN brown envelope dropped through the letterbox at No. 27, Maisie assumed it was from Bristol Grammar School, and would probably be another bill for Harry's tuition fees, plus any "extras," as the Bristol Municipal Charities liked to describe them.

She always called into the bank on the way home to deposit the day's takings in the business account and her share of the tips in a separate account, described as "Harry's," hoping that at the end of each quarter she would have enough to cover the next bill from BGS.

Maisie ripped open the envelope, and, although she couldn't read every word of the letter, recognized the signature and, above it, the figures £37 10s. It was going to be a close-run thing, but after Mr. Holcombe had read Harry's latest report to her, she had to agree with him: it was proving to be a good investment.

"Mind you," Mr. Holcombe had warned her, "the outgoings aren't going to be any less when the time comes for him to leave school."

"Why not?" Maisie asked. "He shouldn't find it hard to get a job after all that education, and then he can start paying his own bills."

Mr. Holcombe shook his head sadly, as if one of his less attentive pupils had failed to grasp a point. "I'm rather hoping that when he leaves Bristol, he'll want to go up to Oxford and read English."

"And how long will that take?" asked Maisie.

"Three, possibly four years."

"He should have read an awful lot of English by then."

"Certainly enough to get a job."

Maisie laughed. "Perhaps he'll end up a schoolmaster like you."

"He's not like me," said Mr. Holcombe. "If I had to guess, he'll end up as a writer."

"Can you make a living as a writer?"

"Certainly, if you're successful. But if that doesn't work out, you could be right—he might end up a schoolmaster like me."

"I'd like that," Maisie said, missing the irony.

She placed the envelope in her bag. When she called into the bank after work that afternoon, she would have to make sure there was at least £37 10s in Harry's account before she could consider writing out a check for the full amount. Only the bank makes money when you're overdrawn, Patrick had told her. The school had occasionally given her two or three weeks' grace in the past, but Patrick had explained that, like the tea shop, they would also have to balance their books at the end of each term.

Maisie didn't have long to wait for her tram, and once she had taken her seat, her thoughts returned to Patrick. She would never admit to anyone, even her mother, how much she missed him.

Her thoughts were interrupted by a fire engine overtaking the tram. Some of the passengers stared out of the window to follow its progress. Once it was out of sight, Maisie turned her attention to Tilly's. Since she'd sacked Bob Burrows, the bank manager had reported that the tea shop had begun to make a steady profit each month, and might even break Miss Tilly's record of £112 10s by the end of the year, which would allow Maisie to start paying back some of the £500 loan. There might even be enough left over to buy a new pair of shoes for Harry.

Maisie got off the tram at the end of Victoria Street. As she made her way across Bedminster Bridge, she checked her watch, Harry's first present, and once again thought about her son. Seven thirty-two: she would have more than enough time to open the tea shop and be ready to serve her first customer by eight. It always pleased her to find a little queue waiting on the pavement as she turned the "closed" sign to "open."

Just before she reached the High Street, another fire engine shot past, and she could now see a plume of black smoke rising high into the sky. But it wasn't until she turned into Broad Street that her heart began to beat faster. The three fire engines and a police car were parked in a semi-circle outside Tilly's.

Maisie began to run.

"No, no, it can't be Tilly's," she shouted, and then she spotted several members of her staff standing in a group on the other side of the road. One of them was crying. Maisie was only a few yards from where the front door used to be when a policeman stepped in her path and prevented her from going any further.

"But I'm the owner!" she protested as she stared in disbelief at the smoking embers of what had once been the most popular tea shop in the city. Her eyes watered and she began to cough as the thick black smoke enveloped her. She stared at the charred remains of the once gleaming counter, while a layer of ash covered the floor where the chairs and tables with their spotless white tablecloths had stood when she'd locked up the previous evening.

"I'm very sorry, madam," said the policeman, "but for your own safety I must ask you to join your staff on the other side of the road."

Maisie turned her back on Tilly's and reluctantly began to cross the road. Before she reached the other side, she saw him standing on the edge of the crowd. The moment their eyes met, he turned and walked away.

—◇—

Detective Inspector Blakemore opened his notebook and looked across the table at the suspect.

"Can you tell me where you were at around three o'clock this morning, Mrs. Clifton?"

"I was at home in bed," Maisie replied.

"Is there anyone who can verify that?"

"If by that, Detective Inspector, you mean was anyone in bed with me at the time, the answer is no. Why do you ask?"

The policeman made a note, which gave him a little more time to think. Then he said, "I'm trying to find out if anyone else was involved."

"Involved in what?" asked Maisie.

"Arson," he replied, watching her carefully.

"But who would want to burn down Tilly's?" Maisie demanded.

"I was rather hoping you might be able to assist me on that point," said Blakemore. He paused, hoping Mrs. Clifton would add something that she would later regret. But she said nothing.

Detective Inspector Blakemore couldn't make up his mind if Mrs. Clifton was a very cool customer, or simply naive. He knew one person who would be able to answer that question.

◄○►

Mr. Frampton rose from behind his desk, shook hands with Maisie and motioned her toward a chair.

"I was so sorry to hear about the fire at Tilly's," he said. "Thank God no one was hurt." Maisie hadn't been thanking God a lot lately. "I do hope the building and contents were comprehensively insured," he added.

"Oh, yes," said Maisie. "Thanks to Mr. Casey it was well covered, but unfortunately the insurance company is refusing to pay out a penny until the police can confirm that I was not involved."

"I can't believe the police think you're a suspect," said Frampton.

"With my financial problems," said Maisie, "who can blame them?"

"It will only be a matter of time before they work out that's a ridiculous suggestion."

"I don't have any time," said Maisie. "Which is why I've come to see you. I've got to find a job, and when we last met in this room, I recall you saying that if I ever wanted to come back to the Royal . . ."

"And I meant it," interrupted Mr. Frampton. "But I can't give you your old position back, because Susan's doing an excellent job, and I've recently taken on three of Tilly's staff, so I don't have any vacancies in the Palm Court. The only position I have available at the moment is hardly worthy—"

"I'll consider anything, Mr. Frampton," said Maisie, "and I mean anything."

"Some of our customers have been telling us that they would like something to eat after the hotel restaurant has closed for the night," said Mr. Frampton. "I've been considering introducing a limited service of coffee and sandwiches after ten o'clock, which would be available until the breakfast room opens at six a.m. I could only offer you three pounds a week to begin with, although of course all the tips would be yours. Naturally I'd understand if you felt—"

"I'll take it."

"When would you be able to start?"

"Tonight."

—◦—

When the next brown envelope landed on the mat at No. 27, Maisie stuffed it in her bag, unopened, and wondered how long it would be before she received a second, perhaps a third, and then finally a thick white envelope containing a letter not from the bursar, but the headmaster, requesting that Mrs. Clifton withdraw her son from the school at the end of term. She dreaded the moment when Harry would have to read that letter to her.

In September Harry was expecting to enter the sixth form, and he couldn't hide the excitement in his eyes whenever he talked about "going up" to Oxford and reading English at the feet of Alan Quilter, one of the most prominent scholars of the day. Maisie couldn't bear the thought of having to tell him that would no longer be possible.

Her first few nights at the Royal had been very quiet, and things didn't get much busier during the following month. She hated being idle, and when the cleaning staff arrived at five in the morning they would often discover there was nothing for them to do in the Palm Court room. Even on her busiest night Maisie didn't have more than half a dozen customers, and several of those had been turfed out of the hotel bar just after midnight and seemed more interested in propositioning her than in ordering coffee and a ham sandwich.

Most of her customers were commercial travelers who only booked in for one night, so her chances of building up a regular clientele didn't look promising, and the tips were certainly not going to take care of the brown envelope that remained unopened in her handbag.

Maisie knew that if Harry was to remain at Bristol Grammar School and have the slightest chance of going up to Oxford, there was only one person she could turn to for help. She would beg if necessary.

19

"What makes you think Mr. Hugo would be willing to help?" asked Old Jack, leaning back in his seat. "He's never shown any sign of caring about Harry in the past. On the contrary . . ."

"Because if there's one person on earth who ought to feel some responsibility for Harry's future, it's that man." Maisie immediately regretted her words.

Old Jack was silent for a moment before he asked, "Is there something you're not telling me, Maisie?"

"No," she replied, a little too quickly. She hated lying, especially to Old Jack, but she was determined that this was one secret she would take to her grave.

"Have you given any thought to when and where you will confront Mr. Hugo?"

"I know exactly what I'm going to do. He rarely leaves his office before six in the evening, and by then most of the other staff in the building have already left for the night. I know his office is on the fifth floor, I know it's the third door on the left. I know—"

"But do you know about Miss Potts?" interrupted Old Jack. "Even if you did manage to get past reception and somehow made it to the fifth floor unnoticed, there's no way of avoiding her."

"Miss Potts? I've never heard of her."

"She's been Mr. Hugo's private secretary for the past fifteen years. I can tell you from personal experience, you don't need a guard dog if you've got Miss Potts as a secretary."

"Then I'll just have to wait until she goes home."

"Miss Potts never goes home before the boss, and she's

always behind her desk thirty minutes before he arrives in the morning."

"But I'll have even less chance of getting into the Manor House," said Maisie, "where they have a guard dog too. He's called Jenkins."

"Then you'll have to find a time and place when Mr. Hugo will be on his own, can't escape and can't rely on Miss Potts or Jenkins to come to his rescue."

"Is there such a time and place?" asked Maisie.

"Oh yes," said Old Jack. "But you'll have to get your timing right."

◄○►

Maisie waited until it was dark before she slipped out of Old Jack's railway carriage. She tiptoed across the gravel path, eased open the back door, climbed in, and shut it behind her. Resigned to a long wait, she settled herself down on the comfortable leather seat. She had a clear view of the building through a side window. Maisie waited patiently for each light to go out. Old Jack had warned her that his would be among the last.

She used the time to go over the questions she planned to ask him. Questions she'd rehearsed for several days before trying them out on Old Jack that afternoon. He'd made several suggestions, which she'd happily agreed to.

Just after six, a Rolls-Royce drew up and parked outside the front of the building. A chauffeur got out and stationed himself alongside. A few moments later Sir Walter Barrington, the chairman of the company, marched out of the front door, climbed into the back of the car and was whisked away.

More and more lights went out, until finally only one was still aglow, like a single star on the top of a Christmas tree. Suddenly Maisie heard feet crunching across the gravel. She slipped off the seat and crouched down on the floor. She could hear two men, deep in conversation, heading toward her. Her plan didn't include two men, and she was about to leap out of the other side and try to disappear into the night when they came to a halt.

"... But despite that," said a voice she recognized, "I'd be

145

obliged if my involvement could remain strictly between the two of us."

"Of course, sir, you can rely on me," said another voice she'd heard before, although she couldn't remember where.

"Let's keep in touch, old fellow," said the first voice. "I have no doubt I'll be calling on the bank's services again."

Maisie heard one set of footsteps moving away. She froze when the car door opened.

He got in, took his place behind the wheel and pulled the door closed. Doesn't have a chauffeur, prefers to drive the Bugatti himself, fancies himself behind the wheel—all priceless pieces of information supplied by Old Jack.

He switched on the ignition and the vehicle shuddered into life. He revved the engine several times before crunching the gear lever into first. The man on the gate saluted as Mr. Barrington drove out onto the main road and headed toward the city, just as he did every night, on his way back to the Manor House.

"Don't let him know you're in the back until he's reached the city center," Old Jack had advised. "He won't risk stopping there, because he'll be afraid someone might see you together and recognize him. But once he reaches the outskirts of the city, he won't hesitate to chuck you out. You'll have ten to fifteen minutes at most."

"That's all I'll need," Maisie had told him.

Maisie waited until he'd driven past the cathedral and across College Green, which was always busy at that time of night. But just as she was about to sit up and tap him on the shoulder, the car began to slow down and then came to a halt. The door opened, he got out, the door closed. Maisie peered between the front seats and was horrified to see that he had parked outside the Royal Hotel.

A dozen thoughts flashed through her mind. Should she jump out before it was too late? Why was he visiting the Royal? Was it a coincidence that it was on her day off? How long did he plan to be there? She decided to stay put, fearing she would be spotted if she got out in such a public place. Besides, this could well be her last chance to confront him face to face before the bill had to be paid.

The answer to one of her questions turned out to be twenty minutes, but long before he got back into the driver's seat and drove off, Maisie was in a cold sweat. She had no idea her heart could beat that fast. She waited until he had gone about half a mile before she sat up and tapped him on the shoulder.

He looked shocked as he turned round, which was followed by a look of recognition, and then realization. "What do you want?" he demanded, recovering slightly.

"I have a feeling you know exactly what I want," said Maisie. "My only interest is Harry, and making sure his school fees are paid for the next two years."

"Give me one good reason why I should pay your son's school fees."

"Because he's your son," Maisie replied calmly.

"And what makes you so sure of that?"

"I watched you when you first saw him at St. Bede's," said Maisie, "and every Sunday at St. Mary's when he sang in the choir. I saw the look in your eyes then, and I saw it again when you refused to shake hands with him on the first day of term."

"That's not proof," said Barrington, sounding a little more confident. "It's nothing more than a woman's intuition."

"Then perhaps the time has come to let another woman know what you get up to on a works outing."

"What makes you think she'd believe you?"

"Nothing more than a woman's intuition," said Maisie. This silenced him, and gave her the confidence to continue. "Mrs. Barrington might also be interested to know why you went to so much trouble to have my brother arrested the day after Arthur disappeared."

"A coincidence, nothing more."

"And is it also just a coincidence that my husband has never been seen since?"

"I had nothing to do with Clifton's death!" shouted Barrington as he swerved across the road, narrowly missing an oncoming vehicle.

Maisie sat bolt upright, stunned by what she'd heard. "So it was you who was responsible for my husband's death."

"You have no proof of that," he said defiantly.

"I don't need any more proof. But in spite of all the damage you've done to my family over the years, I'll still give you an easy way out. You take care of Harry's education while he's still at Bristol Grammar School, and I won't bother you again."

It was some time before Barrington responded. He eventually said, "I'll need a few days to work out the best way to handle the payments."

"The company's charitable trust could easily take care of such a small amount," said Maisie. "After all, your father is chairman of the governors."

This time he didn't have a ready response. Was he wondering how she'd come across that piece of information? He wasn't the first person to underestimate Old Jack. Maisie opened her handbag, pulled out the thin brown envelope and placed it on the seat beside him.

The car swung into an unlit alley. Barrington jumped out and opened the back door. Maisie stepped out, feeling that the confrontation couldn't have gone much better. As her feet touched the ground, he grabbed her by the shoulders and shook her violently.

"Now you listen to me, Maisie Clifton, and listen carefully," he said, a look of fury in his eyes. "If you ever threaten me again, I'll not only see that your brother is sacked, but I'll make sure he never works in this city again. And if you're ever foolish enough to even hint to my wife that I'm that boy's father, I'll have you arrested, and it won't be a prison you'll end up in, but a mental asylum."

He let go of her, clenched a fist and then punched her full in the face. She collapsed onto the ground and curled up into a ball, expecting him to kick her again and again. When nothing happened, she looked up to see him standing over her. He was tearing the thin brown envelope into little pieces and scattering them like confetti over a bride.

Without another word, he jumped back into the car and sped away.

‒◦‒

When the white envelope came through the letterbox, Maisie knew she was beaten. She would have to tell Harry the truth when he got back from school that afternoon. But first she had to drop into the bank, deposit her meager tips from the previous evening, and tell Mr. Prendergast there would be no more bills from BGS, as her son would be leaving at the end of term.

She decided to walk to the bank and save a penny on the tram fare. On the way, she thought about all the people she'd let down. Would Miss Tilly and Miss Monday ever forgive her? Several of her staff, particularly some of the older ones, hadn't been able to find another job. Then there were her parents, who had always watched over Harry so that she could go to work; Old Jack, who couldn't have done more to help her son; and most of all, Harry himself, who in the words of Mr. Holcombe, was about to be crowned with the laurels of victory.

When she reached the bank, she joined the longest queue, as she was in no hurry to be served.

"Good morning, Mrs. Clifton," said the teller cheerfully when she eventually reached the front of the line.

"Good morning," Maisie replied before placing four shillings and sixpence on the counter.

The teller checked the amount carefully, then placed the coins in different trays below the counter. He next wrote out a slip to confirm the sum Mrs. Clifton had deposited, and handed it to her. Maisie stood to one side to allow the next customer to take her place while she put the slip in her bag.

"Mrs. Clifton," said the teller.

"Yes?" she said, looking back up.

"The manager was hoping to have a word with you."

"I quite understand," she said. Maisie didn't need him to tell her there wasn't enough money in her account to cover the latest invoice from the school. In fact, it would be a relief to let Mr. Prendergast know there would be no further bills for extracurricular activities.

The young man led her silently across the banking hall and down a long corridor. When he reached the manager's office, he knocked gently on the door, opened it and said, "Mrs. Clifton, sir."

"Ah, yes," said Mr. Prendergast. "I do need to have a word with you, Mrs. Clifton. Please come in." Where had she heard that voice before?

"Mrs. Clifton," he continued once she was seated, "I am sorry to have to inform you that we have been unable to honor your most recent check for thirty-seven pounds ten shillings, made payable to Bristol Municipal Charities. Were you to present it again, I fear there are still insufficient funds in your account to cover the full amount. Unless, of course, you anticipate depositing any further funds in the near future?"

"No," said Maisie, taking the white envelope from her bag and placing it on the desk in front of him. "Perhaps you would be kind enough to let the BMC know that, given time, I will pay off any other expenses that have arisen during Harry's last term."

"I'm very sorry, Mrs. Clifton," said Mr. Prendergast. "I only wish I could help in some way." He picked up the white envelope. "May I open this?" he asked.

"Yes, of course," said Maisie, who until that moment had tried to avoid finding out just how much she still owed the school.

Mr. Prendergast picked up a thin silver paperknife from his desk and slit open the envelope. He extracted a check from the Bristol and West of England Insurance Company to the value of six hundred pounds, made payable to Mrs. Maisie Clifton.

HUGO BARRINGTON

1921–1936

20

I wouldn't even have remembered her name, if she hadn't later accused me of killing her husband.

It all began when my father insisted I accompany the workers on their annual outing to Weston-super-Mare. "Good for their morale to see the chairman's son taking an interest," he said.

I wasn't convinced, and quite frankly considered the whole exercise a waste of time, but once my father has made up his mind about anything, there is no point arguing. And it would have been a waste of time if Maisie—such a common name—hadn't come along for the ride. Even I was surprised to find how eager she was to jump into bed with the boss's son. I assumed that once we were back in Bristol, I'd never hear from her again. Perhaps I wouldn't have, if she hadn't married Arthur Clifton.

—◇—

I was sitting at my desk going over the tender for the *Maple Leaf,* checking and rechecking the figures, hoping to find some way the company might save a little money, but however hard I tried, the bottom line didn't make good reading. It didn't help that it had been my decision to tender for the contract.

My opposite number at Myson had driven a hard bargain, and after several delays I hadn't budgeted for, we were running five months behind schedule, with penalty clauses that would be triggered should we fail to complete the build by December 15th. What had originally looked like a dream contract that would show a handsome profit, was turning into a nightmare in which we would wake up on December 15th with heavy losses.

My father had been against Barrington's taking on the contract in the first place and had made his views clear. "We should stick to what we're good at," he repeated from the chair at every board meeting. "For the past hundred years, Barrington's Shipping Line has transported goods to and from the far corners of the earth, leaving our rivals in Belfast, Liverpool and Newcastle to build ships."

I knew I wouldn't be able to sway him, so I spent my time trying to persuade the younger members of the board that we had missed out on several opportunities in recent years, while others had snapped up lucrative contracts that could easily have come our way. I finally convinced them, by a slim majority, to dip a toe in the water and sign up with Myson to build them a cargo vessel to add to their fast-growing fleet.

"If we do a good job and deliver the *Maple Leaf* on time," I told the board, "more contracts are sure to follow."

"Let's hope we don't live to regret it," was my father's only comment after he'd lost the vote at the board meeting.

I was already regretting it. Although the Barrington Line was predicting record profits for 1921, it was beginning to look as if its new subsidiary, Barrington Shipbuilding, would be the only red entry on the annual balance sheet. Some members of the board were already distancing themselves from the decision, reminding everyone that they had voted with my father.

I had only recently been appointed managing director of the company and I could just imagine what was being said behind my back. "Chip off the old block" clearly wasn't on anyone's lips. One director had already resigned and couldn't have made his views more clear when he departed, warning my father, "The boy lacks judgment. Be careful he doesn't end up bankrupting the company."

But I hadn't given up. I remained convinced that as long as we finished the job on time, we could still break even, and possibly make a small profit. So much depended on what happened during the next few weeks. I'd already given the order to work round the clock in three eight-hour shifts, and promised the workforce handsome bonuses if they managed to complete the contract on time. After all, there were enough men hanging around outside the gates, desperate for work.

—◦—

I was just about to tell my secretary I was going home, when he burst into my office unannounced.

He was a short, squat man, with heavy shoulders and bulging muscles, the build of a stevedore. My first thought was to wonder how he had managed to get past Miss Potts, who followed in his wake looking unusually flustered. "I couldn't stop him," she said, stating the obvious. "Shall I call the watchman?"

I looked into the man's eyes and said, "No."

Miss Potts remained by the door while we sized each other up, like a mongoose and a snake, each wondering who would strike first. Then the man reluctantly removed his cap and started jabbering. It was some time before I could understand what he was saying.

"My best mate's goin' to die! Arthur Clifton's goin' to die unless you do somethin' about it."

I told him to calm down and explain what the problem was, when my works manager came charging into the room.

"I'm sorry you've been troubled by Tancock, sir," he said once he'd caught his breath, "but I can assure you it's all under control. Nothin' for you to worry about."

"What is all under control?" I asked.

"Tancock here claims that his mate Clifton was workin' inside the hull when the shift changed, and the new shift somehow managed to seal him inside."

"Come and see for yourself!" shouted Tancock. "You can hear him tappin'!"

"Could that be possible, Haskins?" I asked.

"Anything's possible, sir, but it's more likely Clifton's buggered off for the day and is already in the pub."

"Then why hasn't he signed off at the gate?" demanded Tancock.

"Nothing unusual in that, sir," said Haskins, not looking at him. "Signin' on's what matters, not signin' off."

155

"If you don't come and see for yourself," said Tancock, "you'll go to your grave with his blood on your hands." This outburst silenced even Haskins.

"Miss Potts, I'm going down to number one dock," I said. "I shouldn't be too long."

The squat little man ran out of my office without another word.

"Haskins, join me in my car," I said. "We can discuss what ought to be done on the way."

"Nothin' needs to be done, sir," he insisted. "It's all stuff and nonsense."

It wasn't until we were alone in the car that I put it bluntly to my ganger. "Is there any chance that Clifton really might be sealed up in the hull?"

"No chance, sir," said Haskins firmly. "I'm only sorry to be wastin' your time."

"But the man seems pretty certain," I said.

"Like he's always certain about what'll win the three thirty at Chepstow."

I didn't laugh.

"Clifton's shift ended at six," Haskins continued, taking on a more serious tone. "He must've known that the welders would be moving in and would expect to finish the job before the next shift reported for duty at two in the mornin'."

"What was Clifton doing down in the hull in the first place?"

"Making the final checks before the welders got to work."

"Is it possible he didn't realize his shift had ended?"

"You can hear the end-of-shift horn in the middle of Bristol," said Haskins as we drove past Tancock, who was running like a man possessed.

"Even if you were deep inside the hull?"

"I suppose it's just possible he might not have heard it if he was in the double bottom, but I've never come across a docker who didn't know what time his shift ends."

"As long as he has a watch," I said, looking to see if Haskins was wearing one. He wasn't. "If Clifton really is still down there, do we have the equipment to get him out?"

"We've got enough acetylene torches to burn through the hull and remove a complete section. Problem is, it'd take hours, and if Clifton's down there, there wouldn't be much chance of him still bein' alive by the time we reached him. On top of that, it would take the men another fortnight, perhaps longer, to replace the whole section. And as you keep remindin' me, guv, you've got everyone on bonuses to save time, not waste it."

The night shift was well into its second hour by the time I brought my car to a halt by the side of the ship. There must have been over a hundred men on board, working flat out, hammering, welding and sealing in the rivets. As I climbed the gangway, I could see Tancock running toward the ship. When he caught up with me a few moments later he had to bend double, his hands on his thighs, while he recovered.

"So, what do you expect me to do, Tancock?" I asked once he'd caught his breath.

"Stop them all workin', guv, just for a few minutes, then you'll hear him tappin'."

I nodded my approval.

Haskins shrugged his shoulders, clearly unable to believe I would even consider giving such an order. It took him several minutes to get everyone to down tools and for the workers to fall silent. Every man on the ship, as well as the dockside, stood still and listened intently, but other than the occasional squawk from a passing gull or a smoker's cough, I heard nothing.

"Like I said, sir, it's been a waste of everyone's time," said Haskins. "By now Clifton will be sippin' his third pint at the Pig and Whistle."

Someone dropped a hammer, and the sound echoed around the docks. Then for a moment, just a moment, I thought I heard a different sound, regular and soft.

"That's him!" shouted Tancock.

And then, as suddenly as it had started, the noise stopped.

"Did anyone else hear anything?" I shouted.

"I didn't hear nothin'," said Haskins, looking around at the men, almost daring them to defy him.

Some of them stared back at him, while one or two picked up their hammers menacingly, as if they were waiting for someone to lead them over the top.

I felt like a captain who was being given one last chance to quell a mutiny. Either way I couldn't win. If I told the men to go back to work, the rumors would spread until every man in the dockyard believed I was personally responsible for Clifton's death. It would be weeks, months, possibly even years before I could recover my authority. But if I gave the order to break open the hull, any hope of making a profit on the contract would be scuppered, and with it my chances of ever becoming chairman of the board. I just stood there, hoping the continued silence would convince the men that Tancock was wrong. As each second of silence passed, my confidence grew.

"It seems no one heard nothin', sir," Haskins said a few moments later. "Can I have your permission to put the men back to work?"

They didn't move a muscle, just continued to glare defiantly at me. Haskins stared back at them, and one or two eventually lowered their eyes.

I turned to the ganger and gave the order to get back to work. In the moment's silence that followed, I could have sworn I heard a tap. I glanced at Tancock, but then the sound was drowned out by a thousand other noises as the men went resentfully back to work.

"Tancock, why don't you bugger off down the pub and see if your mate's there," said Haskins. "And when you find him, give him a tickin' off for wastin' everybody's time."

"And if he isn't," I said, "call by his house and ask his wife if she's seen him." I realized my mistake the moment I'd spoken, and quickly added, "That is, assuming he has a wife."

"Yes, guv, he does," said Tancock. "She's my sister."

"If you still can't find him, report back to me."

"It'll be too late by then," said Tancock as he turned and walked off, his shoulders slumped.

"I'll be in my office should you need me, Haskins," I said, before walking down the gangway. I drove back to Barrington House, hoping never to see Tancock again.

I returned to my desk, but was unable to concentrate on the letters Miss Potts had left for me to sign. I could still hear that tapping in my head, repeating itself again and again, like a popular melody that plays continually in your mind and even stops you from sleeping. I knew that if Clifton didn't report for work the next morning, I would never be rid of it.

During the next hour, I began to feel more confident that Tancock must have found his mate and would now be regretting making such a fool of himself.

It was one of the rare occasions when Miss Potts left the office before me, and I was just locking the top drawer of my desk before going home, when I heard footsteps running up the stairs. It could only be one man.

I looked up, and the man I'd hoped never to see again was standing in the doorway, pent-up fury blazing in his eyes.

"You killed my best mate, you bastard," he said, shaking a fist. "You may as well have murdered him with your bare hands!"

"Now, steady on, Tancock, old chap," I said. "For all we know, Clifton may still be alive."

"He's gone to his grave just so you could finish your bloody job on time. No man will ever sail on that ship once they find out the truth."

"Men die in shipbuilding accidents every day," I said lamely.

Tancock took a pace toward me. He was so angry that for a moment I thought he was going to hit me, but he just stood there, feet apart, fists clenched, glaring at me. "When I've told the police what I know, you'll have to admit you could've saved his life with a single word. But because you were only interested in how much money you would make, I'm going to make sure that no man on these docks will ever work for you again."

I knew if the police did become involved, half of Bristol would think Clifton was still inside that hull and the union would demand it was opened up. If that happened, I wasn't in any doubt what they'd find.

I rose slowly from my chair and walked across to the safe on the far side of the room. I entered the code, turned the key, pulled open the door and extracted a thick white envelope before returning to my desk. I picked up a silver letter opener, slit open the envelope and took out a five-pound note. I even wondered whether Tancock had ever seen one before. I placed it on the blotting pad in front of him and watched his piggy eyes grow larger by the second.

"Nothing is going to bring back your friend," I said, placing a second note on top of the first. His eyes never left the money. "And anyway, who knows, he might just have done a bunk for a few days. That wouldn't be considered unusual in his line of work." I placed a third note on top of the second. "And when he comes back, your mates will never let you forget it." A fourth note was followed by a fifth. "And you wouldn't want to be charged with wasting the police's time, would you? That's a serious offense for which you can go to jail." Two more notes. "And of course you'd also lose your job." He looked up at me, his anger visibly turning to fear. Three more notes. "I could hardly be expected to employ a man who was accusing me of murder." I placed the last two notes on top of the pile. The envelope was empty.

Tancock turned away. I took out my wallet and added one more five-pound note, three pounds and ten shillings to the pile: £68 10s in all. His eyes returned to the notes. "There's plenty more where that came from," I said, hoping I sounded convincing.

Tancock walked slowly toward my desk and, without looking at me, gathered up the notes, stuffed them into his pocket and left without a word.

I went to the window and watched as he walked out of the building and headed slowly for the dock gate.

I left the safe wide open, scattered some of its contents on the floor, dropped the empty envelope on my desk and left my office without locking up. I was the last person to leave the building.

21

"DETECTIVE INSPECTOR BLAKEMORE, sir," said Miss Potts, then stood aside to allow the policeman to enter the managing director's office.

Hugo Barrington studied the inspector carefully as he entered the room. He couldn't have been much more than the regulation minimum height of five feet nine inches, and he was a few pounds overweight, but still looked fit. He was carrying a raincoat that had probably been bought when he was still a constable, and wore a brown felt hat of a more recent vintage, indicating that he hadn't been an inspector all that long.

The two men shook hands, and once he was seated, Blakemore took a notebook and pen out of an inside jacket pocket. "As you know, sir, I am following up inquiries concerning an alleged theft that took place on these premises last night." Barrington didn't like the word "alleged." "Could I begin by asking when you first discovered that the money was missing?"

"Yes, of course, inspector," said Barrington, trying to sound as helpful as possible. "I arrived at the docks around seven o'clock this morning and drove straight to the sheds to check how the night shift had got on."

"Is that something you do every morning?"

"No, only from time to time," said Hugo, puzzled by the question.

"And how long did you spend there?"

"Twenty, perhaps thirty minutes. Then I came up to my office."

"So you would have been in your office at around seven twenty, seven thirty at the latest."

"Yes, that sounds about right."

"And was your secretary already here by then?"

"Yes, she was. I rarely manage to get in before her. She's a formidable lady," he added with a smile.

"Quite," said the detective inspector. "So it was Miss Potts who told you the safe had been broken into?"

"Yes. She said that when she came in this morning, she'd found the safe door open and some of its contents scattered on the floor, so she immediately rang the police."

"She didn't ring you first, sir?"

"No, inspector. I would have been in my car on the way to work at that time."

"So, you say your secretary arrived before you this morning. And did you leave before her last night, sir?"

"I don't recall," said Barrington. "But it would be most unusual for me to leave after her."

"Yes, Miss Potts has confirmed that," said the detective inspector. "But she also said—" he glanced down at his notebook—" 'I left before Mr. Barrington last night, as a problem had arisen which needed his attention.'" Blakemore looked up. "Are you able to tell me what that problem was, sir?"

"When you run a company as large as this," said Hugo, "problems arise all the time."

"So you don't remember what particular problem arose yesterday evening?"

"No, inspector, I do not."

"When you arrived in your office this morning and found the safe door open, what was the first thing you did?"

"I checked to see what was missing."

"And what did you discover?"

"All my cash had been taken."

"How can you be sure it had *all* been taken?"

"Because I found this open envelope on my desk," Hugo said, handing it over.

"And how much should there have been in the envelope, sir?"

"Sixty-eight pounds and ten shillings."

"You seem very certain of that."

"Yes, I am," said Hugo. "Why should that surprise you?"

"It's simply that Miss Potts told me there was only sixty pounds in the safe, all in five-pound notes. Perhaps you could tell me, sir, where the other eight pounds and ten shillings came from?"

Hugo didn't answer immediately. "I do sometimes keep a little loose change in my desk drawer, inspector," he said finally.

"That's quite a large sum to describe as 'a little loose change.' However, allow me to return to the safe for a moment. When you entered your office this morning, the first thing you noticed was that the safe door was open."

"That is correct, inspector."

"Do you have a key for the safe?"

"Yes, of course."

"Are you the only person who knows the code and is in possession of a key, sir?"

"No, Miss Potts also has access to the safe."

"Can you confirm that the safe was locked when you went home last night?"

"Yes, it always is."

"Then we must assume that the burglary was carried out by a professional."

"What makes you say that, inspector?" asked Barrington.

"But if he was a professional," said Blakemore, ignoring the question, "what puzzles me is why he left the safe door open."

"I'm not sure I'm following you, inspector."

"I'll explain, sir. Professional burglars tend to leave everything just as they found it, so that their crime won't be found out immediately. It allows them more time to dispose of the stolen goods."

"More time," repeated Hugo.

"A professional would have closed the safe door and taken the envelope with him, making it more likely that it would be some time before you discovered anything was missing. In my experience, some people don't open their safes for days, even weeks. Only an amateur would have left your office in such disarray."

"Then perhaps it was an amateur?"

"Then how did he manage to open the safe, sir?"

"Maybe he somehow got hold of Miss Potts's key?"

"And the code as well? But Miss Potts assures me that she takes her safe key home every night, as I understand you do, sir." Hugo said nothing. "May I be allowed to look inside the safe?"

"Yes, of course."

"What is that?" asked the inspector, pointing to a tin box on the bottom shelf of the safe.

"It's my coin collection, inspector. A hobby of mine."

"Would you be kind enough to open it, sir?"

"Is that really necessary?" asked Hugo impatiently.

"Yes, I'm afraid it is, sir."

Hugo reluctantly opened the box, to reveal a hoard of gold coins he had collected over many years.

"Now, here's another mystery," said the inspector. "Our thief takes sixty pounds from the safe, and eight pounds ten shillings from your desk drawer, but leaves behind a box of gold coins that must be worth considerably more. And then there's the problem of the envelope."

"The envelope?" said Hugo.

"Yes, sir, the envelope you say contained the money."

"But I found it on my desk this morning."

"I don't doubt that, sir, but you will notice that it has been slit neatly open."

"Probably with my letter opener," said Hugo, holding it up triumphantly.

"Quite possibly, sir, but in my experience, burglars have a tendency to rip open envelopes, not slit them neatly with a letter opener as if they already knew what was inside."

"But Miss Potts told me that you'd found the thief," said Hugo, trying not to sound exasperated.

"No, sir. We have found the money, but I'm not convinced that we've found the guilty party."

"But you found some of the money in his possession?"

"Yes, we did, sir."

"Then what more do you want?"

"To be certain we've got the right man."

"And who is the man you've charged?"

"I didn't say I'd charged him, sir," said the inspector as he turned a page in his notebook. "A Mr. Stanley Tancock, who turns out to be one of your stevedores. Name ring a bell, sir?"

"Can't say it does," said Hugo. "But if he works in the yard, he would certainly have known where my office was."

"I am in no doubt, sir, that Tancock knew where your office was, because he says he came to see you around seven yesterday evening to tell you that his brother-in-law, a Mr. Arthur Clifton, was trapped in the hull of a ship being built in the yard, and if you didn't give the order to get him out, he would die."

"Ah, yes, I remember now. I did go over to the yard yesterday afternoon as my ganger will confirm, but it turned out to be a false alarm and a waste of everyone's time. Clearly he just wanted to find out where the safe was, so he could come back later and rob me."

"He admits that he came back to your office a second time," said Blakemore, turning another page of his notes, "when he claims you offered him sixty-eight pounds and ten shillings if he would keep his mouth shut about Clifton."

"I've never heard such an outrageous suggestion."

"Then let us consider the alternative for a moment, sir. Let us suppose that Tancock did come back to your office with the intention of robbing you some time between seven o'clock and seven thirty yesterday evening. Having somehow managed to get into the building unobserved he reaches the fifth floor, makes his way to your office, and with either your key or Miss Potts's unlocks the safe, enters the code, removes the envelope, slits it neatly open and takes out the money, but doesn't bother with a box of gold coins. He leaves the safe door open, spreads some of its contents on the floor and places the neatly opened envelope on your desk, and then, like the Scarlet Pimpernel, disappears into thin air."

"It needn't have been between seven and seven thirty in the evening," said Hugo defiantly. "It could have been any time before eight this morning."

"I think not, sir," said Blakemore. "You see, Tancock has an alibi between eight and eleven o'clock last night."

"No doubt this so-called 'alibi' is some mate of his," said Barrington.

"Thirty-one of them, at the last count," said the detective inspector. "It seems that having stolen your money, he turned up at the Pig and Whistle public house at around eight o'clock, and not only were the drinks on him, but he also cleared his slate. He paid the landlord with a new five-pound note, which I have in my possession."

The detective removed his wallet, took out the note and placed it on Barrington's desk.

"The landlord also added that Tancock left the pub at around eleven, and was so drunk that two of his friends had to accompany him to his home in Still House Lane, where we found him this morning. I am bound to say, sir, that if it was Tancock who robbed you, we have a master criminal on our hands and I'd be proud to be the man who puts him behind bars. Which I suspect is exactly what you had in mind, sir," he added, looking directly at Barrington, "when you *gave* him the money."

"And why on earth would I do that?" said Hugo, trying to keep his voice even.

"Because if Stanley Tancock was arrested and sent to jail, no one would take his story about Arthur Clifton seriously. Incidentally, Clifton hasn't been seen since yesterday afternoon. So I shall be recommending to my superiors that the hull be opened up without further delay so that we can discover if it was a false alarm and Tancock was wasting everyone's time."

—◇—

Hugo Barrington checked in the mirror and straightened his bow tie. He hadn't told his father about the Arthur Clifton incident or the visit from Detective Inspector Blakemore. The less the old man knew the better. All he'd said was that some money had been stolen from his office and one of the stevedores had been arrested.

Once he'd put on his dinner jacket, Hugo sat on the end of the bed and waited for his wife to finish dressing. He hated being late, but he knew that no amount of badgering would make Elizabeth move any faster. He'd checked on Giles and his baby sister Emma, who were both fast asleep.

Hugo had wanted two sons, an heir and a spare. Emma was an inconvenience, which meant he'd have to try again. His father had been a second child and lost his older brother fighting the Boers in South Africa. Hugo's older brother had been killed at Ypres, along with half his regiment. So, in time, Hugo could expect to succeed his father as chairman of the company and, when his father died, to inherit the title and the family fortune.

So he and Elizabeth would have to try again. Not that making love to his wife was a pleasure anymore. In fact, he couldn't remember if it ever had been. Recently he'd been looking for distractions elsewhere.

"Yours is a marriage made in heaven," his mother used to say. His father was more practical. He had felt that bringing together his elder son and the only daughter of Lord Harvey was more of a merger than a marriage. When Hugo's brother was killed on the Western Front, his fiancée was passed on to Hugo. No longer a merger, more of a takeover. Hugo wasn't surprised to discover on his wedding night that Elizabeth was a virgin; his second virgin, in fact.

Elizabeth finally emerged from the dressing room, apologizing, as she always did, for keeping him waiting. The journey from the Manor House to Barrington Hall was only a couple of miles, and all the land in between the two houses belonged to the family. By the time Hugo and Elizabeth entered his parents' drawing room at a few minutes past eight, Lord Harvey was already on his second sherry. Hugo glanced around the room at the other guests. There was only one couple he didn't recognize.

His father immediately took him across and introduced him to Colonel Danvers, the recently appointed chief constable of the county. Hugo decided not to mention his meeting that morning with Detective Inspector Blakemore to the colonel, but just before they sat down for dinner, he took his father on one side to bring him up to date on the theft, never once mentioning the name of Arthur Clifton.

Over a dinner of game soup, succulent lamb and green beans, followed by crème brûlée, the conversation ranged from the Prince of Wales's visit to Cardiff and his less than helpful remarks about sympathizing with the mine workers, to Lloyd George's latest import tariffs and the effect they would have on the shipping industry, and George Bernard Shaw's *Heartbreak House,* which had recently opened to mixed reviews at the Old Vic Theater, before returning to the Prince of Wales and the vexed question of how to find him a suitable wife.

When the servants had cleared the table after dessert, the ladies retired to the drawing room to enjoy coffee, while the butler offered the gentlemen brandy or port.

"Shipped by me and imported by you," said Sir Walter, raising a glass to Lord Harvey while the butler circled the table offering cigars to the guests. Once Lord Harvey's Romeo y Julieta had been lit to his satisfaction, he turned to his son-in-law and said, "Your father tells me that some blighter broke into your office and stole a large amount of cash."

"Yes, that's correct," Hugo replied. "But I'm pleased to say they've caught the thief. Sadly he turned out to be one of our stevedores."

"Is that right, Danvers?" asked Sir Walter. "You've caught the man?"

"I did hear something about it," responded the chief constable, "but I wasn't told that anybody had been charged yet."

"Why not?" demanded Lord Harvey.

"Because the man is saying that I *gave* him the money," Hugo interjected. "In fact, when the detective inspector questioned me this morning, I began to wonder which one of us was the criminal, and which the injured party."

"I'm sorry to hear you feel that way," said Colonel Danvers. "May I ask who the officer in charge of the investigation was?"

"Detective Inspector Blakemore," said Hugo, before adding, "I got the impression he might have a grudge against our family."

"When you employ as many people as we do," said Sir Walter, placing his glass back on the table, "there's bound to be the odd person who bears a grudge."

"I must admit," said Danvers, "that Blakemore's not known for his tact. But I'll look into the matter, and if I feel he's overstepped the mark I'll assign someone else to the case."

22

Schooldays are the happiest days of your life, claimed R.C. Sherriff, but that had not been Hugo Barrington's experience. Although he had a feeling that Giles would, as his father put it, "make a better fist of things."

Hugo tried to forget what had happened on his first day at school, some twenty-four years ago. He'd been driven to St. Bede's in a hansom carriage, accompanied by his father, mother and elder brother Nicholas, who had just been appointed school captain. Hugo had burst into tears when another new bug had innocently asked, "Is it true your grandfather was a docker?" Sir Walter was proud his father had "pulled himself up by his bootstraps," but with eight-year-olds, first impressions stick. "Grandpa was a docker! Grandpa was a docker! Cry baby! Cry baby!" chanted the rest of the dorm.

Today his son Giles would be driven to St. Bede's in Sir Walter Barrington's Rolls-Royce. Hugo had wanted to take his son to school in his own car, but his father wouldn't hear of it. "Three generations of Barringtons have been educated at St. Bede's and Eton. My heir must arrive in style."

Hugo didn't point out to his father that Giles hadn't, as yet, been offered a place at Eton, and that it was even possible the boy might have ideas of his own as to where he would like to be educated. "Heaven forbid," he could hear his father saying. "Ideas smack of rebellion and rebellions must be put down."

Giles hadn't spoken since they'd left the house, although his mother hadn't stopped fussing over her only son for the past hour. Emma had started to sob when she was told she couldn't accompany them, while Grace—another girl; he wouldn't bother to try again—just clung on to Nanny's hand and waved from the top step as they drove away.

Hugo had other things than the family's female line on his mind as the car maneuvered its way slowly through the country lanes toward the city. Was he about to see Harry Clifton for the first time? Would he recognize him as the other son he'd wanted but would never have, or would he be left in no doubt the moment he saw the boy that he couldn't be his kinsman?

Hugo would have to be careful to avoid Clifton's mother. Would he even recognize her? He'd recently discovered that she was working as a waitress in the Palm Court room at the Royal Hotel, which he used to frequent whenever he had business meetings in the city. Now he would have to confine himself to the occasional visit in the evening, and then only if he was certain she'd left for the day.

Maisie's brother, Stan Tancock, had been released from prison after serving eighteen months of his three-year sentence. Hugo never did find out what had happened to Detective Inspector Blakemore but he never saw the man again following his father's dinner party. A young detective sergeant gave evidence at Tancock's trial, and he clearly wasn't in any doubt who the guilty party was.

Once Tancock was safely behind bars, speculation about what had happened to Arthur Clifton quickly dried up. In a business where death is commonplace, Arthur Clifton became just another statistic. However, when Lady Harvey launched the *Maple Leaf* six months later, Hugo couldn't help thinking that *Davy Jones's Locker* would have been a more appropriate name for the vessel.

When the final figures were presented to the board, Barrington's ended up showing a loss of £13,712 on the project. Hugo didn't suggest that they tender for any more shipbuilding contracts in the future, and Sir Walter never referred to the subject again. In the years that followed, Barrington's returned to its traditional business as a shipping line, and continued to go from strength to strength.

After Stan had been carted off to the local prison, Hugo had assumed that would be the last he heard of him. But shortly before Tancock was due to be released, the deputy governor of HMP Bristol rang Miss Potts and asked for an appointment. When they met, the deputy governor pleaded with Barrington to give Tancock his old job back, otherwise he would have little hope of ever being employed again. At first, Hugo was delighted to hear this piece of news, but after giving the matter some thought, changed his mind and dispatched Phil Haskins, his chief ganger, to visit Tancock in prison and tell him he could have his job back on one condition: he was never to mention the name of Arthur Clifton again. If he did, he could collect his cards and look for work elsewhere. Tancock had accepted the offer gratefully, and as the years passed it became clear that he had kept his side of the bargain.

The Rolls-Royce drew up outside the front gate of St. Bede's and the chauffeur leaped out to open the backdoor. Several pairs of eyes turned to look in their direction, some with admiration, others with envy.

Giles clearly didn't enjoy the attention and quickly walked away, disowning the chauffeur as well as his parents. His mother chased after him, bent down and pulled his socks up, before giving his fingernails one last inspection. Hugo spent his time looking into the faces of countless children, wondering if he would instantly recognize someone he'd never seen before.

And then he saw a boy walking up the hill, unaccompanied by a mother or father. He looked past the boy to see a woman watching him, a woman he could never forget. Both of them must have been wondering if he had one son or two reporting for their first day at St. Bede's.

⟨○⟩

When Giles caught chicken pox and had to spend a few days in the sanatorium, his father realized this might be his chance to prove that Harry Clifton wasn't his son. He didn't tell Elizabeth he was going to visit Giles while he was in the san, as he didn't want her around when he asked Matron a seemingly innocuous question.

Once he'd dealt with the morning post, Hugo told Miss Potts that he would be popping into St. Bede's to see his son and she shouldn't expect him back for at least a couple of hours. He drove into the city and parked outside Frobisher House. He remembered only too well where the san was, as he'd had to visit it regularly when he was at St. Bede's.

Giles was sitting up in bed having his temperature taken when his father strode into the room. The boy's face lit up the moment he saw him.

Matron was standing by the bed, checking her patient's temperature. "Down to ninety-nine. We'll have you back in time for the first lesson on Monday morning, young man," she declared as she shook the thermometer. "I'll leave you now, Mr. Barrington, so you can spend a little time with your son."

"Thank you, Matron," said Hugo. "I wonder if I might have a word with you before I leave?"

"Of course, Mr. Barrington. You'll find me in my office."

"You don't look too bad to me, Giles," said Hugo once Matron had left the room.

"I'm fine, Papa. In fact, I was rather hoping Matron would let me out on Saturday morning so I can play football."

"I'll have a word with her before I go."

"Thank you, Papa."

"So, how's the work coming along?"

"Not bad," said Giles. "But that's only because I share a study with the two brightest boys in my class."

"And who are they?" asked his father, dreading the reply.

"There's Deakins, he's the cleverest boy in the school. In fact, the other boys won't even talk to him because they think he's a swot. But my best friend is Harry Clifton. He's very clever too, but not as clever as Deakins. You've probably heard him singing in the choir. I know you'll like him."

"But isn't Clifton the son of a stevedore?" Hugo said.

"Yes, and just like Grandpa he doesn't hide the fact. But how did you know that, Papa?"

"I think Clifton used to work for the company," Hugo said, immediately regretting his words.

"It must have been before your time, Papa," said Giles, "because his father was killed in the war."

"Who told you that?" said Hugo.

"Harry's mother. She's a waitress at the Royal Hotel. We went to tea there on his birthday."

Hugo would have liked to have asked when Clifton's birthday was, but feared it might be one question too many. Instead, he said, "Your mother sends her love. I think she and Emma plan to visit you later this week."

"Yuk. That's all I need," said Giles. "Chicken pox and a visit from my dreadful sister."

"She's not that bad," said his father, laughing.

"She's worse," said Giles. "And Grace doesn't look as if she's going to be any better. Do they have to come on holiday with us, Papa?"

"Yes, of course they do."

"I was wondering if Harry Clifton could join us in Tuscany this summer. He's never been abroad."

"No," said Hugo a little too firmly. "Holidays are strictly for the family, not to be shared with strangers."

"But he's not a stranger," said Giles. "He's my best friend."

"No," Hugo repeated, "and that's an end of the matter." Giles looked disappointed. "So what would you like for your birthday, my boy?" Hugo asked, quickly changing the subject.

"The latest radio," said Giles without hesitation. "It's called a Roberts Reliable."

"Are you allowed to have radios at school?"

"Yes," said Giles, "but you can only play them at weekends. If you're caught listening after lights out or during the week, they get confiscated."

"I'll see what I can do. Will you be coming home on your birthday?"

"Yes, but only for tea. I have to be back at school in time for prep."

"Then I'll try and drop in," said Hugo. "I'll be off now. I want a word with Matron before I leave."

"Don't forget to ask her if she'll let me out on Saturday morning," Giles reminded him as his father left the room to carry out the real purpose of his visit.

"I'm so glad you were able to drop by, Mr. Barrington. It will perk Giles up no end," said Matron as he walked into her office. "But as you can see, he's almost fully recovered."

"Yes, and he's hoping you'll let him out on Saturday morning so he can play in a football match."

"I'm sure that will be possible," said Matron. "But you said there was something else you wanted to talk about?"

"Yes, Matron. As you know, Giles is color-blind. I just wanted to ask if it was causing him any difficulties."

"Not that I'm aware of," said Matron. "If it is, it certainly doesn't stop him hitting a red ball across a green field until it reaches a white boundary."

Barrington laughed before he delivered his next well-prepared line. "When I was at St. Bede's, I used to be teased because I was the only boy who suffered from color-blindness."

"Let me assure you," said Matron, "no one teases Giles. And in any case, his best friend is also color-blind."

—◦—

Hugo drove back to his office thinking that something had to be done before the situation got out of control. He decided to have another word with Colonel Danvers.

Once he was back behind his desk, he told Miss Potts he didn't want to be disturbed. He waited until she'd closed the door before he picked up the telephone. A few moments later the chief constable was on the line.

"It's Hugo Barrington, Colonel."

"How are you, my boy?" asked the chief constable.

"I'm well, sir. I was wondering if you could advise me on a private matter."

"Fire away, old fellow."

"I'm looking for a new head of security, and I wondered if you might be able to point me in the right direction."

"As a matter of fact I do know a man who might fit the bill, but I'm not sure if he's still available. I'll find out and give you a call back."

The chief constable was as good as his word, and phoned back the following morning. "The man I had in mind has a part-time job at the moment, but he's looking for something more permanent."

"What can you tell me about him?" asked Hugo.

"He was being groomed for higher things in the force, but he had to leave when he was badly injured trying to apprehend a robber during a raid on the Midland Bank. You probably remember the story. It even hit the national press. In my opinion, he'd be the ideal candidate to head your security team, and frankly you'd be lucky to get him. If you're still interested, I could drop you a line with his details."

⦿

Barrington rang Derek Mitchell from his home, as he didn't want Miss Potts to find out what he was up to. He agreed to meet the former policeman at the Royal Hotel at six o'clock on Monday evening, after Mrs. Clifton would have left for the day and the Palm Court would be empty.

Hugo arrived a few minutes early and headed straight for a table at the far end of the room that he wouldn't normally have considered. He took a seat behind the pillar, where he knew his meeting with Mitchell would not be seen or overheard. While he waited, he went over a list of questions in his mind that needed answering if he was going to put his trust in a complete stranger.

At three minutes to six, a tall, well-built man of military bearing pushed his way through the revolving doors. His dark navy blazer, gray flannels, short hair and highly polished shoes all suggested a life of discipline.

Hugo stood and raised a hand as if he was summoning a waiter. Mitchell walked slowly across the room, making no attempt to disguise a slight limp, an injury which, according to Danvers, was the reason Mitchell had been invalided out of the police service.

Hugo recalled the last occasion he'd come face to face with a police officer, but this time he would be asking the questions.

"Good evening, sir."

"Good evening, Mitchell," said Hugo as they shook hands. Once Mitchell had sat down, Hugo took a closer look at his broken nose and cauliflower ears, and also recalled from Colonel Danvers's notes that he used to play in the second row for Bristol.

"Let me say from the outset, Mitchell," said Hugo, not wasting any time, "that what I want to discuss with you is of a highly confidential nature, and must be kept strictly between the two of us." Mitchell nodded. "It is so confidential, in fact, that even Colonel Danvers has no idea of the real reason I needed to see you, as I am certainly not looking for someone to head up my security operation."

Mitchell's face remained inscrutable as he waited to hear what Hugo had in mind.

"I am looking for someone to act as a private detective. His sole purpose will be to report to me each month on the activities of a woman who lives in this city, and in fact works in this hotel."

"I understand, sir."

"I want to know everything she gets up to, whether professional or personal, however insignificant it might seem. She must never, I repeat, never, become aware of your interest in her. So before I reveal her name, do you consider yourself capable of carrying out such an assignment?"

"These things are never easy," said Mitchell, "but they're not impossible. As a young detective sergeant, I worked on an undercover operation which resulted in a particularly loathsome individual ending up behind bars for sixteen years. If he were to walk into this hotel now, I'm confident he wouldn't recognize me."

Hugo smiled for the first time. "Before I go any further," he continued, "I need to know if you would be willing to take on such an assignment?"

"That would depend on several things, sir."

"Such as?"

"Would it be a full-time position, because I currently have a night security job, working for a bank."

"Hand in your notice tomorrow," said Hugo. "I don't want you to be working for anyone else."

"And what are the hours?"

"At your discretion."

"And my salary?"

"I will pay you eight pounds a week, a month in advance, and will also cover any legitimate expenses."

Mitchell nodded. "May I suggest you make any payments in cash, sir, so that nothing can be traced back to you?"

"That seems sensible," said Hugo, who'd already made that decision.

"And would you want the monthly reports to be in writing, or in person?"

"In person. I want as little committed to paper as possible."

"Then we should always meet at a different location and never on the same day of the week. That way it would be unlikely that anyone would come across us more than once."

"I have no problem with that," said Hugo.

"When would you want me to start, sir?"

"You started half an hour ago," said Barrington. He removed a slip of paper and an envelope containing £32 from an inside pocket and handed them to Mitchell.

Mitchell studied the name and address written on the piece of paper for a few moments before handing it back to his new boss. "I'll also need your private number, sir, and details of when and where you can be contacted."

"At my office any evening between five and six," said Hugo. "You must never contact me at home unless it's an emergency," he added as he took out a pen.

"Just tell me the numbers, sir, don't write them down."

23

"WERE YOU THINKING of attending Master Giles's birthday party?" asked Miss Potts.

Hugo looked at his diary. *Giles, 12th birthday, 3 p.m., Manor House* was written in bold letters at the top of the page.

"Do I have time to pick up a present on the way home?"

Miss Potts left the room, and returned a moment later carrying a large parcel wrapped in shiny red paper and tied with a ribbon.

"What's inside?" asked Hugo.

"The latest Roberts radio; the one he asked for when you visited him in the san last month."

"Thank you, Miss Potts," said Hugo. He checked his watch. "I'd better leave now if I'm going to be in time to see him cut the cake."

Miss Potts placed a thick file in his briefcase and before he could ask, she said, "Your background notes for tomorrow morning's board meeting. You can go over them after Master Giles has returned to St. Bede's. That way there will be no need for you to come back this evening."

"Thank you, Miss Potts," said Hugo. "You think of everything."

As he drove through the city on his way home, Hugo couldn't help noticing how many more cars there seemed to be on the highway than there had been a year ago. Pedestrians were becoming more wary of casually crossing the road since the government had increased the speed limit to 30 miles per hour. A horse reared up as Hugo shot past a hansom cab. He wondered how much longer they could hope to survive now that the city council had authorized its first taxi cab.

Once he had driven out of the city, Hugo sped up, not wanting to be late for his son's party. How quickly the boy was growing. He was already taller than his mother. Would he end up taller than his father?

When Giles left St. Bede's and took up his place at Eton in a year's time, Hugo felt confident that his friendship with the Clifton boy would soon be forgotten, although he realized there were other difficulties that needed to be addressed before then.

He slowed down as he passed through the gates of his estate. He always enjoyed the long drive through the avenue of oaks up to the Manor House. Jenkins was standing on the top step as Hugo got out of the car. He held open the front door and said, "Mrs. Barrington is in the drawing room, sir, with Master Giles and two of his school friends."

As he walked into the hall, Emma came running down the stairs and threw her arms around her father.

"What's in the parcel?" she demanded.

"A birthday present for your brother."

"Yes, but what is it?"

"You'll have to wait and see, young lady," said her father with a smile before he handed his briefcase to the butler. "Would you put that in my study, Jenkins," he said as Emma grabbed him by the hand and began to tug him toward the drawing room.

Hugo's smile evaporated the moment he opened the door and saw who was sitting on the sofa.

Giles leaped up and ran toward his father, who handed him the parcel and said, "Happy birthday, my boy."

"Thank you, Papa," he said, before introducing his friends.

Hugo shook Deakins's hand, but when Harry offered his, he just said, "Good afternoon, Clifton," and sat down in his favorite chair.

Hugo watched with interest as Giles undid the ribbon on his parcel and they both saw the present for the first time. Even his son's unbridled delight with his new radio didn't bring a smile to

Hugo's lips. He had a question that he needed to ask Clifton, but it mustn't appear as if the boy's reply was of any significance.

He remained silent while the three boys took turns tuning into the two stations and listening intently to the strange voices and music that came out of the speaker. This was regularly followed by laughter or applause.

Mrs. Barrington chatted to Harry about a recent concert of the *Messiah* she'd attended, adding how much she'd enjoyed his rendition of "I Know That My Redeemer Liveth."

"Thank you, Mrs. Barrington," said Harry.

"Are you hoping to go on to Bristol Grammar School after you leave St. Bede's, Clifton?" asked Hugo, spotting an opening.

"Only if I win a scholarship, sir," he replied.

"But why is that important?" asked Mrs. Barrington. "Surely you will be offered a place, like any other boy?"

"Because my mother wouldn't be able to afford the fees, Mrs. Barrington. She's a waitress at the Royal Hotel."

"But wouldn't your father—"

"He's dead," said Harry. "He was killed in the war."

"I'm sorry," said Mrs. Barrington. "I didn't realize."

At that moment the door opened and the under-butler entered the room carrying a large cake on a silver tray. After Giles had succeeded in blowing out all twelve candles with one puff, everyone applauded.

"And when's your birthday, Clifton?" asked Hugo.

"It was last month, sir," Harry replied.

After Giles had cut the cake, Hugo stood up and left the room without another word.

He went straight to his study, but found he couldn't concentrate on his papers for the next day's board meeting. Clifton's reply meant he would have to seek advice from a lawyer who specialized in the law of heredity.

After an hour or so he heard voices in the hall, then the front door closing and the sound of a car driving away. A few minutes later there was a knock on his study door, and Elizabeth walked in.

"What made you leave us so abruptly?" she asked. "And why didn't you come and say goodbye, when you must have known Giles and his guests were leaving?"

"I have a very tricky board meeting tomorrow morning," he said without looking up.

"That's no reason not to say goodbye to your son, especially on his birthday."

"I've got a lot on my mind," he said, still looking down at his notes.

"Surely nothing is so important that you need to be rude to guests. You were more offhand with Harry Clifton than you would be with one of the servants."

Hugo looked up for the first time. "That's possibly because I consider Clifton inferior to our servants." Elizabeth looked shocked. "Did you know that his father was a dock laborer and his mother is a waitress? I'm not sure that's the sort of boy Giles should be mixing with."

"Giles clearly thinks otherwise, and whatever his background, Harry's a charming boy. I can't understand why you're so against him. You didn't treat Deakins that way, and his father's a newsagent."

"He's also an open scholar."

"And Harry is the school's prize choral scholar, as every churchgoing citizen in Bristol knows. Next time you come across him, I hope you'll be a little more civil." Without another word, Elizabeth left the room, closing the door firmly behind her.

—◇—

Sir Walter Barrington remained in his place at the head of the boardroom table as his son entered the room.

"I'm becoming increasingly concerned about the government's proposed legislation on import tariffs," said Hugo as he took a seat on the right of his father, "and the effect it might have on our balance sheet."

"That's why we have a lawyer on the board," said Sir Walter, "so that he can advise us on such matters."

"But I've calculated that it could cost us twenty thousand pounds a year if it becomes law. Don't you think we ought to seek a second opinion?"

"I suppose I could have a word with Sir James Amhurst when I'm next in London."

"I'm traveling up to London on Tuesday for the Association of British Ship Owners' annual dinner," said Hugo. "As he's the industry's legal adviser, perhaps I should have a word with him."

"Only if you're convinced it's necessary," said Sir Walter. "And don't forget that Amhurst charges by the hour, even at dinner."

‹o›

The Association of British Ship Owners' dinner was held at the Grosvenor House, and was attended by over a thousand members and their guests.

Hugo had earlier phoned the association's secretary and asked if he could be seated next to Sir James Amhurst. The secretary raised an eyebrow, but agreed to rearrange the guests on the top table. After all, old Joshua Barrington had been a founder member of the association.

After the Bishop of Newcastle had said grace, Hugo made no attempt to interrupt the eminent silk while he was deep in conversation with the man on his right. However, when the lawyer finally turned his attention to the stranger they'd put on his left, Hugo didn't waste any time in getting to the point.

"My father, Sir Walter Barrington," he began, capturing his quarry's attention, "is rather concerned about the import tariff bill that is going through the House of Commons, and the effects it might have on the industry. He wonders if he could consult you on the subject when he's next in London."

"By all means, dear boy," said Sir James. "Just ask his secretary to give my clerk a call and I'll make sure I'm free when he's next in town."

"Thank you, sir," said Hugo. "On a lighter note, I wondered if you'd ever read anything by Agatha Christie?"

"Can't say I have," said Sir James. "Is she any good?"

"I'm much enjoying her latest book, *Where There's a Will*," said Hugo, "but I'm not sure if the plot would stand up in a court of law."

"What's the lady suggesting?" asked Amhurst as a sliver of over-cooked beef served on a cold plate was placed in front of him.

"According to Miss Christie, the eldest son of an hereditary knight automatically inherits his father's title, even if the child is illegitimate."

"Ah, now that is indeed an interesting legal conundrum," said Sir James. "In fact, the Law Lords have quite recently reviewed such a case. Benson *v.* Carstairs, if I remember correctly. It's often referred to by the press as 'the bastard's amendment.'"

"And what conclusion did their lordships come to?" asked Hugo, trying not to sound too interested.

"If no loophole could be found in the original will, they came out in favor of the first born, even if the young man in question was illegitimate." Another answer Hugo hadn't wanted to hear. "However," Sir James continued, "their lordships decided to cover their backsides, and added a codicil that each case should be treated on its own merits, and then only after it had been reviewed by the Garter King of Arms. Typical of the Law Lords," he added before picking up his knife and fork and attacking the beef. "Too frightened to set a precedent, but quite happy to pass the buck."

When Sir James returned his attention to the man on his right, Hugo thought about the implications of Harry Clifton discovering that he might have the right to inherit not only the Barrington shipping line, but also the family estate. Having to admit he had sired an illegitimate son would be bad enough, but the idea of Harry Clifton inheriting the family title after his death and becoming Sir Harry did not bear thinking about. He would be willing to do anything in his power to make sure that wouldn't be the outcome.

24

HUGO BARRINGTON WAS having breakfast when he read the letter from the headmaster of St. Bede's, outlining the details of an appeal the school was launching to raise a thousand pounds to build a new cricket pavilion for the First XI. He opened his checkbook and had written the figures "100" when he was distracted by the sound of a car coming to a halt on the gravel outside.

Hugo walked across to the window to see who could possibly be visiting him so early on a Saturday morning. He was puzzled when he saw his son step out of the back of a taxi carrying a suitcase, as he'd been looking forward to watching him open the batting for the school that afternoon in the final match of the season against Avonhurst.

Jenkins appeared just in time to open the front door as Giles reached the top step. "Good morning, Master Giles," he said, as if he'd been expecting him.

Hugo walked quickly out of the breakfast room to find his son standing in the hall, head bowed, suitcase by his side. "What are you doing at home?" he asked. "Isn't there another week to go before the end of term?"

"I've been rusticated," said Giles simply.

"Rusticated?" repeated his father. "And what have you done to merit that, may I ask?"

Giles looked up at Jenkins, who stood silently by the front door. "I'll take Master Giles's suitcase up to his bedroom," the butler said, before picking up the bag and proceeding slowly up the stairs.

"Follow me," said Hugo once the butler was out of sight.

Neither of them spoke again until Hugo had closed the study door behind him. "What have you done to cause the school to take such a drastic measure?" demanded his father as he sank back into his chair.

"I was caught stealing from the tuck shop," said Giles, who had been left standing in the middle of the room.

"Is there some simple explanation? A misunderstanding, perhaps?"

"No, there isn't, sir," said Giles, fighting back tears.

"Do you have anything to say in your defense?"

"No, sir." Giles hesitated. "Except . . ."

"Except what?"

"I always gave the sweets away, Papa. I never kept them for myself."

"To Clifton, no doubt."

"And to Deakins as well," said Giles.

"Was it Clifton who put you up to it in the first place?"

"No, it was not," responded Giles firmly. "In fact, once he found out what I'd been up to, Harry always took the sweets I gave him and Deakins back to the tuck shop. He even took the blame when Mr. Frobisher accused him of stealing them."

A long silence followed before his father said, "So you've been rusticated, not actually expelled?"

Giles nodded.

"Do you think they will allow you to go back next term?"

"I doubt it," said Giles.

"What makes you so sure of that?"

"Because I've never seen the headmaster so angry."

"Not half as angry as your mother will be when she finds out."

"Please don't tell her, Papa," pleaded Giles, bursting into tears.

"And how do you expect me to explain to her why you're home a week early and might not even be returning to St. Bede's next term?"

Giles made no attempt to respond, but continued to sob quietly.

"And Heaven knows what your grandparents will say," his father added, "when I have to tell them why you won't be going to Eton after all."

Another long silence followed.

"Go to your room, and don't even think about coming back down until I say so."

"Yes, sir," said Giles. He turned to leave.

"And whatever you do, don't discuss this with anyone, especially not in front of the servants."

"Yes, Papa," said Giles, who ran out of the room, nearly colliding with Jenkins as he shot past him on the stairs.

Hugo leaned forward in his chair, trying to think if there might be some way to turn the situation around before he had to face an inevitable call from the headmaster. He placed his elbows on the desk and his head in his hands, but it was some time before his eyes focused on the check.

A smile crossed his lips as he added an extra nought before signing it.

25

MITCHELL WAS SEATED in the far corner of the waiting room, reading the *Bristol Evening Post*, when Hugo walked across and sat down beside him. It was so drafty that Hugo kept his hands in his pockets.

"The subject," said Mitchell, still looking at his newspaper, "is trying to raise five hundred pounds for a business venture."

"What sort of business venture could she possibly be interested in?"

"Tilly's tea shop," replied Mitchell. "It seems the subject worked there before she moved to the Palm Court room at the Royal. Miss Tilly has recently had an offer of five hundred pounds for the business from a Mr. Edward Atkins. Miss Tilly doesn't care for Atkins and has made it clear to the subject that if she were able to raise the same amount, she would prefer her to take over the business."

"Where could she possibly hope to get hold of that much money?"

"Perhaps from someone who wished to have financial control over her, which might at a later date prove advantageous?"

Hugo remained silent. Mitchell's eyes never left his paper.

"Has she approached anyone to try and raise the money?" Hugo eventually asked.

"She's currently taking advice from a Mr. Patrick Casey, who represents Dillon and Co., a finance company based in Dublin. They specialize in raising loans for private clients."

"How do I get in touch with Casey?"

"I wouldn't advise that," said Mitchell.

"Why not?"

"He visits Bristol about once a month, and always stays at the Royal."

"We wouldn't have to meet at the Royal."

"He has struck up a close personal relationship with the subject. Whenever he's in town he takes her to dinner or the theater, and recently she's been seen returning with him to the hotel, where they spend the night together in room 371."

"Fascinating," said Hugo. "Anything else?"

"It may also interest you to know that the subject banks with the National Provincial, 49 Corn Street. The manager is a Mr. Prendergast. Her current account is showing a balance of twelve pounds and nine shillings."

Hugo would like to have asked how Mitchell had come across that particular piece of information, but satisfied himself with saying, "Excellent. The moment you come up with anything else, however insignificant, ring me." He took a bulky envelope from his overcoat pocket and slipped it across to Mitchell.

"The train now arriving at platform nine is the seven twenty-two from Taunton."

Mitchell pocketed the envelope, folded his newspaper and walked out of the waiting room. He'd never once looked at his employer.

⎯◦⎯

Hugo had been unable to hide his anger when he discovered the real reason Giles had failed to be offered a place at Eton. He'd phoned the headmaster, who refused to take his calls, his prospective housemaster, who sympathized but offered no hope of redemption, and even the provost, who said he'd call back, but didn't. Although Elizabeth and the girls had no idea what had caused Hugo to so regularly lose his temper of late, and for no apparent reason, they continued to bear the brunt of Giles's misdemeanors with equanimity.

Hugo reluctantly accompanied Giles to Bristol Grammar School on his first day of term, although he wouldn't allow either Emma

190

or Grace to join them, despite Emma bursting into tears and sulking.

When Hugo brought the car to a halt in College Street, the first person he saw standing outside the school gates was Harry Clifton. Even before he pulled on the brake, Giles had leaped out and run across to greet his friend.

Hugo avoided mingling with the other parents, whom Elizabeth seemed quite happy to chat to, and when he inadvertently came across Clifton, he made a point of not shaking hands with him.

On the journey back to the Manor House, Elizabeth asked her husband why he treated Giles's best friend with such disdain. Hugo reminded his wife that their son should have gone to Eton, where he would have mixed with other gentlemen and not with the sons of local tradesmen and, in Clifton's case, far worse. Elizabeth retreated into the comparative safety of silence, as she had so often done recently.

26

"LOCAL TEA SHOP burned to the ground! Arson suspected!" hollered the paperboy standing on the corner of the Broad.

Hugo threw on the brakes, leaped out of his car and handed the lad a ha'penny. He began reading the front page as he walked back to his car.

> Tilly's Tea Shop, a Bristol landmark, much frequented by local citizens, was razed to the ground in the early hours of the morning. Police have arrested a local man in his early thirties and charged him with arson. Miss Tilly, who now lives in Cornwall . . .

Hugo smiled when he saw the photograph of Maisie Clifton and her staff standing on the pavement, grimly surveying the burned-out remains of Tilly's. The gods were clearly on his side.

He climbed back into his car, placed the newspaper on the passenger seat and continued on his journey to Bristol Zoo. He would need to make an early appointment to see Mr. Prendergast.

Mitchell had advised him that if he hoped to keep the fact that he was the subject's backer confidential, any meetings with Prendergast should be held in Barrington's offices, and preferably after Miss Potts had gone home for the night. Hugo didn't attempt to explain to Mitchell that he wasn't sure if Miss Potts did go home at night. He was looking forward to the meeting with Prendergast, when he would administer the last rites, but there was someone else he needed to see before he could do that.

—◦—

Mitchell was feeding Rosie when he arrived.

Hugo walked slowly across, leaned on the railing and pretended to take an interest in the Indian elephant that Bristol Zoo had recently acquired from Uttar Pradesh, and was already attracting a large number of visitors. Mitchell tossed up a lump of bread, which Rosie caught in her trunk and transferred to her mouth in one fluid movement.

"The subject has returned to work at the Royal Hotel," said Mitchell as if he was addressing the elephant. "She's doing the late shift in the Palm Court from ten at night until six the following morning. She's paid three pounds a week, plus whatever she can make in tips, which, as there are so few customers at that time of night, doesn't add up to much." He threw another crust at the elephant, and continued, "A Bob Burrows has been arrested and charged with arson. Burrows was her patisserie supplier before the subject sacked him. He's made a full confession, even admitting that he had planned to propose to the subject and had purchased an engagement ring, but she'd spurned him; or at least that's his story."

A smile crossed Hugo's lips. "And who's in charge of the case?" he asked.

"A Detective Inspector Blakemore," said Mitchell. Hugo's smile was replaced by a frown. "Although Blakemore initially thought the subject might be an accomplice of Burrows," continued Mitchell, "he has since informed the Bristol and West of England Insurance Company that she is no longer a suspect."

"That's a pity," said Hugo, the frown still in place.

"Not necessarily," said Mitchell. "The insurance company will be issuing Mrs. Clifton with a check for six hundred pounds in full and final settlement of her claim." Hugo smiled.

"I wonder if she's told her son," said Hugo, almost to himself.

If Mitchell heard the comment, he ignored it. "The only other piece of information that might be of some interest to you," he continued, "is that Mr. Patrick Casey booked into the Royal Hotel on Friday night, and took the subject to the Plimsoll Line for dinner. They returned to the hotel afterward, when she accompanied him to his room, No. 371, and didn't leave until just after seven o'clock the following morning."

A long silence followed, always the sign that Mitchell had come to the end of his monthly report. Hugo removed an envelope from an inside pocket and slipped it to Mitchell, who didn't acknowledge the transaction as he threw his last piece of bread to a contented Rosie.

⚬

"Mr. Prendergast to see you," said Miss Potts, standing aside to allow the banker to enter the managing director's office.

"It's good of you to come all this way," said Hugo. "I'm sure you'll appreciate why I didn't want to discuss such a highly confidential matter at the bank."

"I quite understand," said Prendergast, who had opened his Gladstone bag and extracted a thick file even before he'd sat down. He passed a single sheet of paper across the desk to Mr. Barrington.

Hugo checked the bottom line, before settling back in his chair.

"Just to recap, if I may," said Prendergast. "You put up a capital sum of five hundred pounds, which allowed Mrs. Clifton to purchase the business known as Tilly's, a tea shop on Broad Street. The agreed contract was for the full amount, plus compound interest at five percent per annum, to be paid back to the principal within a period of five years.

"Although Tilly's managed to declare a small trading profit in Mrs. Clifton's first year and again in her second, there was never a large enough surplus for her either to pay the interest or to return any part of the capital sum, so at the time of the fire, Mrs. Clifton owed you £572 16 shillings. To this sum I must add bank charges of £20, making a grand total of £592 16 shillings. This, of course, will be well covered by the insurance payout, which means that while your investment is secure, Mrs. Clifton will be left with virtually nothing."

"How unfortunate," said Hugo. "May I ask why the final sum doesn't appear to include any charge for services rendered by Mr. Casey?" he added after studying the figures more closely.

"Because Mr. Casey has informed the bank that he will not be submitting any bills for his services."

Hugo frowned. "At least that is one piece of good news for the poor woman."

"Indeed. None the less, I fear she will no longer be able to cover her son's fees at Bristol Grammar School for next term."

"How sad," said Hugo. "So will the boy have to be removed?"

"I'm sorry to say that's the inevitable conclusion," said Mr. Prendergast. "It is a great shame, because she dotes on the child, and I believe she would sacrifice almost anything to keep him there."

"A great shame," repeated Hugo as he closed the file and rose from his chair. "I won't keep you any longer, Mr. Prendergast," he added. "I have an appointment in the city in about half an hour. Perhaps I can give you a lift?"

"That is most kind of you, Mr. Barrington, but it won't be necessary. I drove myself over here."

"What do you drive?" Hugo asked as he picked up his briefcase and headed toward the door.

"A Morris Oxford," said Prendergast, quickly stuffing some papers back into his Gladstone bag and following Hugo out of the office.

"The people's car," said Hugo. "I'm told that, like you, Mr. Prendergast, it's very reliable." Both men laughed as they walked down the stairs together. "Sad business, Mrs. Clifton," said Hugo as they stepped out of the building. "But then, I'm not altogether sure I approve of women getting involved in business. It's not the natural way of things."

"I quite agree," said Prendergast, as the two men came to a halt by Barrington's car. "Mind you," he added, "you could not have done more for the poor woman."

"It's kind of you to say so, Prendergast," said Hugo. "But despite that, I'd be obliged if my involvement could remain strictly between the two of us."

"Of course, sir," said Prendergast as the two men shook hands, "you can rely on me."

"Let's keep in touch, old fellow," said Hugo as he climbed into his car. "I have no doubt I'll be calling on the bank's services again." Prendergast smiled.

As Hugo drove toward the city, his thoughts returned to Maisie Clifton. He had dealt her a blow from which she was unlikely to recover, but he now intended to deliver the knockout punch.

He drove into Bristol wondering where she was at that moment. Probably sitting her son down to explain to him why he would have to leave BGS at the end of the summer term. Had she even for one fleeting moment imagined that Harry might be able to continue his studies as if nothing had happened? Hugo decided that he wouldn't raise the subject with Giles until the boy told him the sad news that his friend Harry would not be returning to BGS to join him in the sixth form.

Even the thought of his own son having to go to Bristol Grammar School still made him pulse with anger, but he had never let Elizabeth or his father know the real reason Giles had failed to get a place at Eton.

Once he'd driven past the cathedral, he continued across College Green before turning into the entrance of the Royal Hotel. He was a few minutes early for his appointment, but he was confident the manager would not keep him waiting. He pushed his way through the revolving doors and strolled across the lobby, not needing to be told where Mr. Frampton's office was.

The manager's secretary leaped up the moment Hugo entered the room. "I'll let Mr. Frampton know you're here," she said, almost running into the adjoining office. The manager appeared a moment later.

"What a pleasure to see you, Mr. Barrington," he said, ushering him into his office. "I do hope you and Mrs. Barrington are both well." Hugo nodded and took a seat opposite the hotel manager, but didn't shake hands.

"When you asked to see me, I took the liberty of checking over the arrangements for your company's annual dinner," said Frampton. "Just over three hundred guests will be attending, I understand?"

"I have no interest how many guests are attending," said Hugo. "That isn't the reason I came to see you, Frampton. I wish to discuss a private matter that I find most distasteful."

"I'm very sorry to hear that," said Frampton, sitting bolt upright.

"One of our non-executive directors was staying at the hotel on Thursday night, and the following day he made a most serious allegation that I feel it is my duty to bring to your attention."

"Yes, of course," said Frampton, rubbing his sweating palms on his trousers. "The last thing we would want to do is annoy one of our most valued customers."

"I'm glad to hear it," said Hugo. "The gentleman in question checked into the hotel after the restaurant had closed and went into the Palm Court in the hope of being provided with some light refreshment."

"A service I myself instituted," said Frampton, allowing himself a strained smile.

"He gave his order to a young lady who appeared to be in charge," continued Hugo, ignoring the comment.

"Yes, that would be our Mrs. Clifton."

"I've no idea who it was," said Hugo. "However, as she was serving him with a cup of coffee and some sandwiches, another gentleman entered the Palm Court, made an order and asked if it could be sent up to his room. The only thing my friend recalls about the man was that he had a slight Irish accent. My friend then signed his bill and retired for the night. He rose early the following morning, as he wished to have breakfast and go over his papers before the board meeting. When he came out of his room he observed the same woman, still dressed in her hotel uniform, leaving room 371. She then walked to the end of the corridor, climbed through the window and out onto the fire escape."

"I'm absolutely appalled, sir. I . . ."

"The board member concerned has requested that whenever he comes to Bristol in the future, he should be booked into another hotel. Now, I don't wish to appear prudish, Frampton, but the Royal has always been somewhere I've been happy to bring my wife and children."

"Be assured, Mr. Barrington, the person concerned will be dismissed immediately, and not supplied with a reference. May I add how grateful I am that you have brought this matter to my attention."

Hugo rose from his place. "Of course, I wouldn't want any reference made to me or the company should you feel it necessary to dismiss the lady in question."

"You can be assured of my discretion," said Frampton.

Hugo smiled for the first time. "On a happier note, may I say how much we're all looking forward to the annual dinner, which no doubt will be up to your usual high standard. Next year we'll be celebrating the company's centenary, so I feel sure my father will want to push the boat out." Both men laughed a little too loudly.

"You can rely on us, Mr. Barrington," said Frampton as he followed his client out of the office.

"And one more thing, Frampton," said Hugo, as they walked across the foyer. "I'd rather you didn't say anything to Sir Walter about this. My father can be a little old-fashioned when it comes to such matters, so I think it's best kept between ourselves."

"I couldn't agree more, Mr. Barrington," said Frampton. "You can be assured I shall deal with the matter personally."

As Hugo pushed his way back through the revolving doors, he couldn't help wondering just how many hours Mitchell must have spent at the Royal before he was able to supply him with such a priceless piece of information.

He jumped back into his car, switched on the engine and continued on his journey home. He was still thinking about Maisie Clifton when he felt a tap on his shoulder. He experienced a moment of blind panic as he turned around and saw who was sitting on the back seat. He even wondered if somehow she'd found out about his meeting with Frampton.

"What do you want?" he demanded, not slowing down for fear that someone might see them together.

As he listened to her demands, he could only wonder how she was so well informed. Once she'd finished, he readily agreed to her terms, knowing that it would be the easiest way of getting her out of the car.

Mrs. Clifton placed a thin brown envelope on the passenger seat next to him. "I'll wait to hear from you," she said.

Hugo put the envelope in an inside pocket. He only slowed down when he came to an unlit alley, but didn't stop until he was certain no one else could see them. He leaped out of the car and opened the back door. When he saw the look on her face, it was clear she felt she'd more than achieved her purpose.

Hugo allowed her a moment of triumph, before he grabbed her by the shoulders and shook her as if he was trying to remove an obstinate apple from a tree. Once he'd left her in no doubt what would happen if she ever bothered him again, he punched her in the face with all his strength. She collapsed to the ground curled up into a ball, and didn't stop shaking. Hugo thought about kicking her in the stomach but didn't want to risk being witnessed by a passerby. He drove away without giving her another thought.

OLD JACK TAR

1925–1936

27

On a balmy Thursday afternoon in the Northern Transvaal, I killed eleven men, and a grateful nation awarded me the Victoria Cross for service above and beyond the call of duty. I haven't had a peaceful night's sleep since.

If I'd killed one Englishman in my homeland, a judge would have sentenced me to hang by the neck until I was dead. Instead, I have been sentenced to life imprisonment, because I still see the faces of those eleven wretched young men every day, like an image on a coin that never fades. I've often considered suicide, but that would be the coward's way out.

In the citation, gazetted in *The Times,* it was stated that my actions had been responsible for saving the lives of two officers, five non-commissioned officers and seventeen private soldiers of the Royal Gloucesters. One of those officers, Lieutenant Walter Barrington, has made it possible for me to serve my sentence with some dignity.

Within weeks of the action I was shipped back to England, and a few months later I was honorably discharged following what would now be described as a mental breakdown. After six months in an army hospital, I was released back into the world. I changed my name, avoided my hometown of Wells in Somerset, and set off for Bristol. Unlike the prodigal son, I refused to travel a few miles into the next county where I would have been able to enjoy the tranquillity of my father's home.

During the day, I would roam the streets of Bristol, rummaging around in dustbins for scraps, while at night my bedroom was a park, my resting place a bench, my blanket a newspaper, my morning call the first bird to announce a new dawn. When it was too cold or wet, I retreated to the waiting room of a local railway station, where I slept below the bench and rose before the first train shunted in the next morning. As the nights became longer, I signed up as a non-paying guest of the Salvation Army on Little George Street, where kind ladies supplied me with thick bread and thin soup before I fell asleep on a horse-hair mattress below a single blanket. Luxury.

As the years passed I hoped that my former companions-in-arms and brother officers would assume I was dead. I had no desire for them to find out that this was the prison I'd chosen to carry out my life sentence in. And it might have stayed thus, had a Rolls-Royce not screeched to a halt in the middle of the road. The back door swung open and out leaped a man I hadn't seen for years.

"Captain Tarrant!" he cried as he advanced toward me. I looked away, hoping he'd think he'd made a mistake. But I remembered only too well that Walter Barrington was not a man who suffered from self-doubt. He grabbed me by the shoulders and stared at me for some time before he said, "How can this be possible, old fellow?"

The more I tried to convince him I did not need his help, the more determined he became to be my savior. I finally gave in, but not before he had agreed to my terms and conditions.

At first he begged me to join him and his wife at the Manor House, but I'd survived too long without a roof over my head to regard such comfort as anything other than a burden. He even offered me a seat on the board of the shipping company that bore his name.

"What use could I possibly be to you?" I asked.

"Your very presence, Jack, would be an inspiration to us all."

I thanked him, but explained that I had not yet completed my sentence for the murder of eleven men. Still he didn't give in.

I finally agreed to take the job of night watchman at the docks, with three pounds a week pay and accommodation provided: an abandoned Pullman railway carriage now became my prison cell.

I suppose I might have continued my life sentence until the day I died, had I not come into contact with Master Harry Clifton.

Harry would claim, years later, that I had shaped his whole life. In truth, it was he who saved mine.

The first time I came across young Harry, he couldn't have been more than four or five. "Come on in, lad," I called to him when I spotted him crawling toward the carriage on his hands and knees. But he immediately leaped up and ran away.

The following Saturday he got as far as looking in through the window. I tried again. "Why don't you come in, my boy? I'm not going to bite you," I said, trying to reassure him. This time he took up my offer and opened the door, but after exchanging a few words, he ran away again. Was I that frightening a figure?

The next Saturday, he not only opened the door, but stood, feet apart, in the doorway, staring at me defiantly. We chatted for over an hour, about everything from Bristol City FC to why snakes shed their skins and who built Clifton Suspension Bridge, before he said, "I'll have to be off now, Mr. Tar, my mum's expecting me home for tea." This time he walked away, but looked back several times.

After that, Harry came to visit me every Saturday until he went to Merrywood Elementary School, when he started turning up most mornings. It took me some time to convince the boy that he should stay at school and learn to read and write. Frankly I wouldn't have managed even that without the help of Miss Monday, Mr. Holcombe and Harry's spirited mother. It took a formidable team to get Harry Clifton to realize his potential, and I knew we had succeeded when once again he could only find the time to visit me on Saturday mornings because he was preparing to enter for a choral scholarship to St. Bede's.

Once Harry had started at his new school, I didn't expect to see him again until the Christmas holidays. But to my surprise, I found him standing outside my door just before eleven o'clock on the first Friday night of term.

He told me he'd left St. Bede's because a prefect was bullying him—damned if I can recall the cad's name—and he was going to run away to sea. If he had, I suspect the boy would have ended up an admiral. But happily he listened to my advice and was back at school in time for breakfast the following morning.

Because he always used to come to the docks with Stan Tancock, it was some time before I realized Harry was Arthur Clifton's boy. He once asked me if I'd known his father, and I told him yes, and that he was a good and decent man with a fine war record. He then asked me if I knew how he died. I said I didn't. The only time I ever lied to the boy. It was not for me to ignore the wishes of his mother.

—◁◦▷—

I was standing on the dockside when the shift changed. No one ever gave me a second glance, almost as if I wasn't there, and I knew that some of them thought I wasn't *all* there. I did nothing to dispel this, as it allowed me to serve my sentence in anonymity.

Arthur Clifton had been a good ganger, one of the best, and he took his job seriously, unlike his best mate, Stan Tancock, whose first port of call on the way home was always the Pig and Whistle. That was on the nights he managed to get home.

I watched Clifton as he disappeared inside the hull of the *Maple Leaf* to make some final checks before the welders moved in to seal the double bottom. It was the raucous sound of the shift horn that must have distracted everyone; one shift coming off, another coming on, and the welders needed to get started promptly if they were going to finish the job by the end of their shift and earn their bonus. No one gave a second thought to whether Clifton had climbed back out of the double bottom, myself included.

We all assumed that he must have heard the blast on the horn and was among the hundreds of dockers trooping through the gates, making their way home. Unlike his brother-in-law, Clifton rarely stopped for a pint at the Pig and Whistle, preferring to go straight to Still House Lane and be with his wife and child. In those days, I didn't know his wife or child, and perhaps I never would have if Arthur Clifton had returned home that night.

The second shift was working flat out when I heard Tancock shouting at the top of his voice. I saw him pointing to the ship's hull. But Haskins, the chief ganger, simply brushed him aside as if he were a tiresome wasp.

Once Tancock realized he was getting nowhere with Haskins, he charged down the gangway and began to run along the quayside in the direction of Barrington House. When Haskins realized where Tancock was headed, he chased after him and had nearly caught up with him by the time he barged through the swing doors into the shipping line's headquarters.

To my surprise, a few minutes later Tancock came running back out of the building, and I was even more surprised when Haskins and the managing director followed close behind. I couldn't imagine what would have convinced Mr. Hugo to leave his office after such a brief conversation with Stan Tancock.

I found out the reason soon enough, because the moment Mr. Hugo arrived on the dock, he gave orders for the entire shift to lay down their tools, stop working and remain silent, as if it were Remembrance Sunday. And indeed, a minute later, Haskins ordered them all back to work.

That was when it first occurred to me that Arthur Clifton might still be inside the double bottom. But surely no man could be so callous as to walk away if he'd thought, even for a moment, that someone might be trapped alive in a steel grave of their own making.

When the welders went back to work, Mr. Hugo spoke to Tancock again before Tancock trooped off through the dockyard gates and out of sight. I looked back to see if Haskins was pursuing him again, but he was clearly more interested in pushing his men to their limits to recover lost time, like a galley master driving his slaves. A moment later, Mr. Hugo walked down the gangway, climbed back into his car and drove off to Barrington House.

The next time I looked out of my carriage window I saw Tancock running back through the gates and once again charging toward Barrington House. This time he didn't reappear for at least half an hour, and when he did, he was no longer red-cheeked and pulsating with rage, but appeared far calmer. I decided he must have found Clifton and was simply letting Mr. Hugo know.

I looked up at Mr. Hugo's office and saw him standing by the window watching Tancock as he left the yard. He didn't move away from the window until he was out of sight. A few minutes later Mr. Hugo came out of the building, walked across to his car and drove away.

I wouldn't have given the matter another thought if Arthur Clifton had clocked in for the morning shift, but he didn't, nor did he ever again.

The following morning, a Detective Inspector Blakemore paid me a visit in my carriage. You can often judge the character of a person by the way he treats his fellow men. Blakemore was one of those rare people who could see beyond his nose.

"You say that you saw Stanley Tancock leaving Barrington House between seven and seven thirty yesterday evening?"

"Yes, I did," I told him.

"Did he appear to be in a hurry, or anxious, or attempting to slip away unnoticed?"

"On the contrary," I said. "I remember thinking at the time he looked remarkably carefree given the circumstances."

"Given the circumstances?" repeated Blakemore.

"Only an hour or so earlier, he'd been protesting that his mate Arthur Clifton was trapped in the double bottom of the *Maple Leaf,* and they were doing nothing to help him."

Blakemore wrote down my words in his notebook.

"Do you have any idea where Tancock went after that?"

"No," I replied. "When I last saw him he was walking out of the gates with an arm around one of his mates."

"Thank you, sir," said the detective inspector. "That's been most helpful." It had been a long time since anyone had called me sir. "Would you be willing, at your own convenience, to come down to the station and make a written statement?"

"I'd prefer not to, inspector," I told him, "for personal reasons. But I'd be quite happy to write out a statement that you could collect at any time that suits you."

"That's good of you, sir."

The detective inspector opened his briefcase, dug out a police statement sheet and handed it to me. He then raised his hat and said, "Thank you, sir, I'll be in touch." But I never saw him again.

Six weeks later, Stan Tancock was sentenced to three years' imprisonment for theft, with Mr. Hugo acting as the prosecution's principal witness. I attended every day of the trial, and there wasn't any doubt in my mind which one of them was the guilty party.

28

"TRY NOT TO forget that you saved my life."

"I've spent the last twenty-six years trying to forget," Old Jack reminded him.

"But you were also responsible for saving the lives of twenty-four of your fellow West Countrymen. You remain a hero in this city and you seem to be totally unaware of the fact. So I'm bound to ask, Jack, how much longer you intend to go on torturing yourself?"

"Until I can no longer see the eleven men I killed as clearly as I can see you now."

"But you were doing no more than your duty," protested Sir Walter.

"That's how I saw it at the time," admitted Jack.

"So what changed?"

"If I could answer that question," replied Jack, "we wouldn't be having this conversation."

"But you're still capable of doing so much for your fellow men. Take that young friend of yours, for example. You tell me he keeps playing truant, but if he was to discover that you are Captain Jack Tarrant of the Royal Gloucestershire Regiment, winner of the Victoria Cross, don't you think he might listen to you with even more respect?"

"He might also run away again," replied Jack. "In any case, I have other plans for young Harry Clifton."

"Clifton, Clifton . . ." said Sir Walter. "Why is that name familiar?"

"Harry's father was trapped in the double bottom of the *Maple Leaf,* and no one came to his—"

"That's not what I heard," said Sir Walter, his tone changing. "I was told that Clifton left his wife because she was, not to put too fine a point on it, a loose woman."

"Then you were misled," said Jack, "because I can tell you that Mrs. Clifton is a delightful and intelligent woman, and any man who was lucky enough to be married to her would never want to leave her."

Sir Walter looked genuinely shocked, and it was some time before he spoke again. "Surely you don't believe that cock-and-bull story about Clifton being trapped in the double bottom?" he asked quietly.

"I'm afraid I do, Walter. You see, I witnessed the whole episode."

"Then why didn't you say something about it at the time?"

"I did. When I was interviewed by Detective Inspector Blakemore the following day, I told him everything I'd seen, and at his request I made a written statement."

"Then why wasn't your statement produced in evidence at Tancock's trial?" asked Sir Walter.

"Because I never saw Blakemore again. And when I turned up at the police station, I was told he was no longer in charge of the case and his replacement refused to see me."

"I had Blakemore taken off the case," said Sir Walter. "The damn man was as good as accusing Hugo of giving the money to Tancock, so there wouldn't be an investigation into the Clifton affair." Old Jack remained silent. "Let's not talk of this anymore," said Sir Walter. "I know my son is far from perfect, but I refuse to believe—"

"Or perhaps you don't want to believe," said Old Jack.

"Jack, whose side are you on?"

"On the side of justice. As you used to be when we first met."

"And I still am," said Sir Walter. But he fell silent for some time before adding, "I want you to make me a promise, Jack. If you ever find out anything about Hugo that you believe would harm the family's reputation, you won't hesitate to tell me."

"You have my word on it."

"And you have my word, old friend, that I would not hesitate to hand Hugo over to the police if I thought for one moment that he had broken the law."

"Let's hope nothing else arises that would make that necessary," said Old Jack.

"I agree, old friend. Let's talk of more palatable things. Is there anything you are in need of at the moment? I could still . . ."

"Do you have any old clothes that are surplus to requirements?"

Sir Walter raised an eyebrow. "Dare I ask?"

"No, you daren't," said Old Jack. "But I have to visit a particular gentleman, and I'll need to be appropriately dressed."

◄○►

Old Jack had grown so thin over the years that Sir Walter's clothes hung off him like flax on a distaff, and, like Sir Andrew Aguecheek, he was several inches taller than his old friend, so he had to let down the turn-ups on the trousers and even then they barely reached his ankles. But he felt that the tweed suit, checked shirt and striped tie would serve its purpose for this particular meeting.

As Jack walked out of the dockyard for the first time in years, a few familiar faces turned to give the smartly dressed stranger a second look.

When the school bell rang at four o'clock, Old Jack stepped back into the shadows while the noisy, boisterous nippers poured out through the gates of Merrywood Elementary as if they were escaping from prison.

Mrs. Clifton had been waiting there for the past ten minutes, and when Harry saw his mum, he reluctantly allowed her to take him by the hand. A damn fine-looking woman, Old Jack thought as he watched the two of them walking away, Harry, as always, jumping up and down, endlessly chattering, displaying as much energy as Stephenson's *Rocket*.

Old Jack waited until they were out of sight before he crossed the road and walked into the school yard. If he'd been dressed in his old clothes, he would have been stopped by someone in authority long before he reached the front door. He looked up and down the corridor, and spotted a master coming toward him.

"I'm sorry to trouble you," said Old Jack, "but I'm looking for Mr. Holcombe."

"Third door on the left, old fellow," the man said, pointing down the corridor.

When Old Jack came to a halt outside Mr. Holcombe's classroom he gave a gentle tap on the door.

"Come in."

Old Jack opened the door to find a young man, his long black gown covered in chalk dust, seated at a table in front of rows of empty desks, marking exercise books. "I'm sorry to disturb you," said Old Jack, "I'm looking for Mr. Holcombe."

"Then you need look no further," said the schoolmaster, putting down his pen.

"My name is Tar," he said as he stepped forward, "but my friends call me Jack."

Holcombe's face lit up. "I do believe you're the man Harry Clifton goes off to visit most mornings."

"I fear I am," admitted Old Jack. "I apologize."

"No need," said Holcombe. "I only wish I had the same influence over him that you do."

"That's why I came to see you, Mr. Holcombe. I'm convinced that Harry's an exceptional child and should be given every chance to make the best of his talents."

"I couldn't agree with you more," said Holcombe. "And I suspect he has one talent even you don't know about."

"And what might that be?"

"He has the voice of an angel."

"Harry's no angel," said Old Jack with a grin.

"I quite agree, but it may turn out to be our best chance of breaking down his defenses."

"What do you have in mind?" asked Old Jack.

"There's a possibility he might just be tempted to join the choir at Holy Nativity. So if you were able to convince him to come to school more often, I know I can teach him to read and write."

"Why's that so important for a church choir?"

"It's compulsory at Holy Nativity, and Miss Monday, the choir mistress, refuses to make any exceptions to the rule."

"Then I'll just have to make sure the boy attends your lessons, won't I?" said Old Jack.

"You could do more than that. On the days he doesn't come to school, you could teach him yourself."

"But I'm not qualified to teach anyone."

"Harry Clifton is not impressed by qualifications, and we both know that he listens to you. Perhaps we could work as a team."

"But if Harry were to find out what we were up to, neither of us would ever see him again."

"How well you know him," said the schoolmaster with a sigh. "We'll just have to make sure he doesn't find out."

"That may prove something of a challenge," said Old Jack, "but I'm willing to give it a try."

"Thank you, sir," said Mr. Holcombe. The schoolmaster paused before adding, "I wonder if I might be allowed to shake hands with you." Old Jack looked surprised as the schoolmaster thrust out his hand. Old Jack shook it warmly. "And may I say it has been an honor to meet you, Captain Tarrant."

Old Jack looked horrified. "How could you possibly . . ."

"My father has a picture of you that still hangs on the wall in our front room."

"But why?" asked Old Jack.

"You saved his life, sir."

◄○►

Harry's visits to Old Jack became less frequent during the next few weeks, until the only time they met was on a Saturday morning. Old Jack knew that Mr. Holcombe must have succeeded in his plan when Harry asked him if he would come to Holy Nativity the following Sunday to hear him sing.

On Sunday morning, Old Jack rose early, used Sir Walter's private cloakroom on the fifth floor of Barrington House to have a shower, a recent invention, and even trimmed his beard, before putting on the other suit Sir Walter had given him.

Arriving at Holy Nativity just before the service began, he

slipped into the back row and took a seat at the end of the pew. He spotted Mrs. Clifton in the third row, sitting between what could only have been her mother and father. As for Miss Monday, he could have picked her out in a congregation of a thousand.

Mr. Holcombe had not been exaggerating about the quality of Harry's voice. It was as good as anything he could remember from his days at Wells Cathedral. As soon as the boy opened his mouth to sing "Lead Me, Lord," Old Jack was left in no doubt that his protégé had an exceptional gift.

Once the Reverend Watts had given his final blessing, Old Jack slipped back out of the church and quickly made his way to the docks. He would have to wait until the following Saturday before he could tell the boy how much he'd enjoyed his singing.

As he walked back, Old Jack recalled Sir Walter's reproach. "You could do so much more for Harry if you would only give up this self-denial." He thought carefully about Sir Walter's words but he wasn't yet ready to remove the shackles of guilt. He did, however, know a man who could change Harry's life, a man who had been with him on that dreadful day, a man he hadn't spoken to for more than twenty-five years. A man who taught at a school that supplied St. Mary Redcliffe with choristers. Unfortunately Merrywood Elementary was not a natural recruiting ground for its annual choral scholarship, so the man would have to be guided in the right direction.

Old Jack's only fear was that Lieutenant Frobisher might not remember him.

29

OLD JACK WAITED until Hugo had left Barrington House, but it was another half an hour before the lights finally went out in Miss Potts's room.

Jack stepped out of the railway carriage and began to walk slowly toward Barrington House, aware that he had only half an hour before the cleaning ladies came on duty. He slipped into the unlit building and climbed the stairs to the fifth floor; after twenty-five years of Sir Walter turning a blind eye, like a cat he could find his way to the door marked "Managing Director" in the dark.

He sat down at Hugo's desk. He switched on the light; if anyone noticed it was on, they would simply assume Miss Potts was working late. He thumbed through the telephone directory until he came to the "St.'s": Andrew's, Bartholomew's, Beatrice's, Bede's.

He picked up a telephone for the first time in his life, not quite sure what to do next. A voice came on the line. "Number please?"

"TEM 8612," said Jack, his forefinger resting just below the number.

"Thank you, sir." As he waited, Old Jack became more nervous by the minute. What would he say if someone else came on the line? He'd just put the phone down. He took a piece of paper out of his pocket, unfolded it and laid it out on the desk in front of him. Next, he heard a ringing tone, followed by a click, then a man's voice. "Frobisher House."

"Is that Noel Frobisher?" he asked, recalling the tradition that each house at St. Bede's was named after the housemaster of the day. He looked down at his script; each line had been carefully prepared and endlessly rehearsed.

"Speaking," said Frobisher, clearly surprised to hear a voice he didn't recognize addressing him by his Christian name. A long silence followed. "Is there anyone there?" Frobisher asked, sounding a little irritated.

"Yes, it's Captain Jack Tarrant."

There was an even longer silence, before Frobisher eventually said, "Good evening, sir."

"Forgive me for calling at this late hour, old fellow, but I need to seek your advice."

"Not at all, sir. It's a great privilege to speak to you after all these years."

"Kind of you to say so," said Old Jack. "I'll try not to waste too much of your time, but I need to know if St. Bede's still supplies St. Mary Redcliffe with trebles for its choir?"

"We do indeed, sir. Despite so many changes in this modern world, that's one tradition that remains constant."

"And in my day," said Old Jack, "the school awarded a choral scholarship each year to a treble who showed exceptional talent."

"We still do, sir. In fact, we will be considering applications for the position in the next few weeks."

"From any school in the county?"

"Yes, from any school that can produce a treble of outstanding quality. But they must also have a solid academic grounding."

"Well, if that's the case," said Old Jack, "I would like to submit a candidate for your consideration."

"Of course, sir. Which school is the boy attending at the moment?"

"Merrywood Elementary."

Another long silence followed. "I have to admit that it would be the first time we've had an applicant from that particular school. Do you by any chance know the name of its music master?"

"It doesn't have a music master," said Old Jack, "but you should get in touch with the boy's teacher, Mr. Holcombe, who will introduce you to his choir mistress."

"May I ask the boy's name?" said Frobisher.

"Harry Clifton. If you want to hear him sing, I recommend you attend Matins at Holy Nativity Church this Sunday."

"Will you be there, sir?"

"No," said Old Jack.

"How do I get in touch with you once I've heard the boy sing?" asked Frobisher.

"You don't," said Old Jack firmly, and put the phone down. As he folded up his script and placed it back in his pocket, he could have sworn he heard footsteps crunching across the gravel outside. He quickly switched off the light, slipped out of Mr. Hugo's office and into the corridor.

He heard a door open, and voices on the stairs. The last thing he needed was to be found on the fifth floor, which was strictly out of bounds to anyone other than the company's executives and Miss Potts. He wouldn't want to embarrass Sir Walter.

He began to walk quickly down the stairs. He'd reached the third floor when he saw Mrs. Nettles heading toward him, a mop in one hand, a bucket in the other, a woman he didn't recognize by her side.

"Good evening, Mrs. Nettles," said Old Jack. "And what a fine evening it is to be doing my rounds."

"Evenin', Old Jack," she replied as she ambled past him. Once he had turned the corner, he stopped and listened attentively. "That's Old Jack," he heard Mrs. Nettles say. "The so-called night watchman. He's completely crackers, but quite harmless. So if you come across him, just ignore him . . ." Old Jack chuckled as her voice faded with each step she took.

He strolled back toward the railway carriage, wondering how long it would be before Harry came to seek his advice on whether he should enter his name for a choral scholarship to St. Bede's.

30

HARRY KNOCKED ON the carriage door, strolled in and took the seat opposite Old Jack in first class.

During term time at St. Bede's, Harry had only been able to see Old Jack regularly on Saturday mornings. Jack had returned the compliment by attending Matins at St. Mary Redcliffe, where from the back pew he enjoyed watching Mr. Frobisher and Mr. Holcombe beam with pride at his protégé.

In the school holidays, Old Jack could never be sure exactly when Harry was going to turn up because he treated the railway carriage like a second home. Whenever he returned to St. Bede's at the beginning of a new term, Old Jack missed the boy's company. He was touched when Mrs. Clifton described him as the father Harry never had. In truth, Harry was the son he'd always wanted.

"Finished your paper round early?" said Old Jack, rubbing his eyes and blinking, when Harry strolled into the carriage that Saturday morning.

"No, you just dozed off, old man," said Harry, passing him a copy of the previous day's *Times*.

"And you're getting cheekier by the day, young man," Old Jack said with a grin. "So, how's the paper round working out?"

"Good. I think I'm going to be able to save enough money to buy my mum a watch."

"A sensible present, considering your mother's new job. But can you afford it?"

"I've already saved four shillings," said Harry. "I reckon I'll have about six by the end of the holidays."

"Have you chosen the watch you want?"

"Yes. It's in Mr. Deakins's display cabinet, but it won't be there for much longer," said Harry, grinning.

Deakins. A name Old Jack could never forget. "How much is it?" he asked.

"No idea," said Harry. "I'm not going to ask Mr. Deakins until the day before I go back to school."

Old Jack wasn't sure how to tell the boy that six shillings wasn't going to be enough to buy a watch, so he changed the subject. "I hope the paper round isn't stopping you from studying. I'm sure I don't have to remind you that the exams are getting closer by the day."

"You're worse than the Frob," said Harry, "but you'll be pleased to learn that I'm spending two hours every morning in the library with Deakins, and another two most afternoons."

"*Most* afternoons?"

"Well, Giles and I do occasionally go to the flicks, and as Gloucestershire are playing Yorkshire at the county ground next week, it will be a chance to see Herbert Sutcliffe batting."

"You'll miss Giles when he goes to Eton," said Old Jack.

"He's still working on his father to let him join me and Deakins at BGS."

"Deakins and me," said Old Jack. "And be warned, if Mr. Hugo has made up his mind, it will take more than Giles to shift him."

"Mr. Barrington doesn't like me," said Harry, taking Old Jack by surprise.

"What makes you say that?"

"He treats me differently from the other boys at St. Bede's. It's as if I'm not good enough to be a friend of his son."

"You're going to have to face that problem all your life, Harry," said Old Jack. "The English are the biggest snobs on earth, and most of the time without reason. The lesser the talent, the bigger the snob, in my experience. It's the only way the so-called upper classes can hope to survive. Be warned, my boy, they don't care for upstarts like you who barge into their club without an invitation."

"But you don't treat me like that," said Harry.

"That's because I'm not upper class," said Old Jack, laughing.

"Perhaps not, but my mum says you're first class," said Harry, "so that's what I want to be."

It didn't help that Old Jack couldn't tell Harry the real reason Mr. Hugo was always so offhand. He sometimes wished he hadn't been in the wrong place at the wrong time, and witnessed what had really happened the day the boy's father died.

"Have you fallen asleep again, old man?" said Harry. "Because I can't hang around chatting to you all day. I promised my mum I'd meet her at Clarks in the Broad because she wants to buy me a new pair of shoes. Not that I can see what's wrong with the pair I've got."

"Special lady, your mum," said Old Jack.

"That's why I'm buying her a watch," said Harry.

◄○►

The bell above the door rang as he entered the shop. Old Jack hoped that enough time had passed to ensure that Private Deakins wouldn't remember him.

"Good morning, sir. How can I help you?"

Old Jack couldn't fail to recognize Mr. Deakins immediately. He smiled and walked across to the display cabinet and studied the two watches on the top shelf. "I just need to know the price of this Ingersoll."

"The lady's or the gentleman's model, sir?" asked Mr. Deakins, coming out from behind the counter.

"The lady's," said Old Jack.

Deakins unlocked the cabinet with his one hand, deftly removed the watch from its stand, checked the label and said, "Sixteen shillings, sir."

"Good," said Old Jack, and placed a ten-bob note on the counter. Mr. Deakins looked even more puzzled. "When Harry Clifton asks you how much the watch is, Mr. Deakins, please tell him it's six shillings, because that's how much he will have saved by the time he stops working for you, and I know he's hoping to buy it as a present for his mother."

"You must be Old Jack," said Deakins. "He'll be so touched that you . . ."

"But you won't ever tell him," said Old Jack, looking Mr. Deakins in the eye. "I want him to believe that the price of the watch is six shillings."

"I understand," said Mr. Deakins, placing the watch back on the stand.

"And how much is the man's watch?"

"One pound."

"Would you allow me to put down another ten bob as a deposit, and then give you half a crown a week for the next month until I've paid off the full amount?"

"That is quite acceptable, sir. But wouldn't you like to try it on first?"

"No, thank you," said Old Jack. "It's not for me. I'm going to give it to Harry when he wins a scholarship to Bristol Grammar School."

"I had the same thought," said Mr. Deakins, "should my son Algy be fortunate enough to win one."

"Then you'd better order another one pretty quickly," said Old Jack, "because Harry tells me your son's a racing certainty."

Mr. Deakins laughed, and took a closer look at Old Jack. "Have we met before, sir?"

"I don't think so," said Old Jack, and left the shop without another word.

31

IF MUHAMMAD WON'T come to the mountain . . . Old Jack smiled to himself as he rose to greet Mr. Holcombe and offered him a seat.

"Would you care to join me in the buffet car for a cup of tea?" Old Jack asked. "Mrs. Clifton was kind enough to supply me with a quite excellent packet of Earl Gray."

"No, thank you sir," said Holcombe, "I've only just had breakfast."

"So, the boy just missed out on a scholarship," said Old Jack, assuming that was what the schoolmaster had come to see him about.

"Failed is how Harry looks upon it," said Holcombe, "despite coming seventeenth out of three hundred, and being offered a place in the school's A stream this September."

"But will he be able to accept the offer? It will place an extra financial burden on his mother."

"As long as there are no unexpected bombshells, she should be able to get Harry through the next five years."

"Even so, Harry won't be able to afford the little extras most of the other boys will take for granted."

"Possibly, but I have managed to cover some of his sundry expenses from the school's list, so he'll be able to consider at least two of the three extracurricular activities he's keen to sign up for."

"Let me guess," said Old Jack. "The choir, the theater club and . . . ?"

"Art appreciation," said Holcombe. "Miss Monday and Miss Tilly are taking responsibility for any trips the choir might make, I'm covering the theater club and . . ."

"So I get art appreciation," said Old Jack. "His new passion. I can still hold my own with Harry when it comes to Rembrandt and Vermeer, even this new chap, Matisse. Now he's trying to get me interested in a Spaniard called Picasso, but I can't see it myself."

"I've never heard of him," admitted Holcombe.

"And I doubt if you ever will," said Old Jack, "but don't tell Harry I said so." He picked up a small tin box, opened it, and took out three notes and almost all the coins he possessed.

"No, no," said Holcombe, "that isn't the reason I came to see you. In fact, I plan to visit Mr. Craddick later this afternoon, and I'm confident he'll—"

"I think you'll find that I take precedence over Mr. Craddick," said Old Jack, handing across the money.

"That's very generous of you."

"Money well spent," said Old Jack, "even if it is the widow's mite. At least my father would approve," he added as an afterthought.

"Your father?" repeated Holcombe.

"He's the resident canon at Wells Cathedral."

"I had no idea," said Holcombe. "So at least you're able to visit him from time to time."

"Sadly not. I fear I am a modern prodigal son," said Old Jack. Not wishing to go any further down that road, he said, "So tell me, young man, why did you want to see me?"

"I can't remember the last occasion anyone called me 'young man.'"

"Just be grateful that anyone still does," said Old Jack.

Holcombe laughed. "I've got a couple of tickets for the school play, *Julius Caesar*. As Harry is performing, I thought you might like to join me for the opening night."

"I knew he was auditioning," said Old Jack. "What part did he get?"

"He's playing Cinna," said Holcombe.

"Then we'll know him by his gait."

Holcombe bowed low. "Does that mean you'll join me?"

"I fear not," said Old Jack, raising a hand. "It's extremely kind of you to think of me, Holcombe, but I'm not yet ready for a live performance, even as just a member of the audience."

◄○►

Old Jack was disappointed to miss Harry's performance in the school play and had to be satisfied with being told the boy's version of how he had performed. The following year, when Holcombe suggested that perhaps Old Jack should attend because Harry's roles were getting bigger, he nearly gave in, but it wasn't until Harry played Puck, a year later, that he finally allowed the dream a reality.

Although he was still fearful of large crowds, Old Jack had decided that he would slip into the back of the school hall, where no one would see him or, even worse, recognize him.

It was while he was trimming his beard in the fifth-floor washroom of Barrington House that he noticed the screaming headline in a copy of the local rag that someone had left behind. *Tilly's tea shop burned to the ground. Arson suspected.* When he saw the photograph below it, he felt sick; Mrs. Clifton was standing on the pavement surrounded by her staff, surveying the burned-out remains of the shop. *Turn to page 11 for full story.* Old Jack obeyed the instruction, but there was no page 11.

He quickly left the washroom, hoping to find the missing page on Miss Potts's desk. He wasn't surprised to find that her desk was clear and her wastepaper basket had been emptied. He tentatively opened the door to the managing director's office, looked inside and spotted the missing page laid out on Mr. Hugo's desk. He sat down in the high-backed leather chair and began to read.

Jack's immediate reaction once he'd finished was to wonder if Harry would have to leave school.

The report noted that unless the insurance company paid the full amount on her premium, Mrs. Clifton would be facing bankruptcy. The reporter went on to say that a spokesman for the Bristol and West of England had made it clear that the company wouldn't be paying out a brass farthing until the police had eliminated all suspects from their inquiries. What else could possibly go wrong for the poor woman, Old Jack wondered.

The reporter had been careful not to refer to Maisie by name, but Old Jack wasn't in any doubt why her photograph was so prominently displayed on the front page. He continued to read the article. When he discovered that Detective Inspector Blakemore was in charge of the case, he felt a little more hopeful. It wouldn't take that particular gentleman long to work out that Mrs. Clifton built things up; she didn't burn them down.

As Old Jack placed the newspaper back on Mr. Hugo's desk, he noticed a letter for the first time. He would have ignored it, none of his business, if he hadn't seen the name "Mrs. Clifton" in the first paragraph.

He began to read the letter, and found it hard to believe it was Hugo Barrington who had put up the five hundred pounds that had made it possible for Mrs. Clifton to purchase Tilly's. Why would he want to help Maisie, he wondered. Was it possible he felt some remorse about the death of her husband? Or did he feel ashamed that he had sent an innocent man to prison for a crime he had not committed? Certainly he had given Tancock his old job back the moment he was released. Old Jack began to wonder if he should perhaps give Hugo the benefit of the doubt. He recalled Sir Walter's words: "He's not all bad, you know."

He read the letter once again. It was from Mr. Prendergast, the manager of the National Provincial Bank, who wrote that he had been pressing the insurance company to fulfill its contractual obligations and recompense Mrs. Clifton for the full value of the policy, which was £600. Mrs. Clifton, Prendergast pointed out, was the innocent party, and Detective Inspector Blakemore had recently informed the bank that she no longer played any part in his inquiries.

In the final paragraph of his letter, Prendergast suggested that he and Barrington should meet in the near future to resolve the matter, so that Mrs. Clifton could receive the full amount she was entitled to. Old Jack looked up when the little clock on the desk chimed seven times.

He switched off the light, ran into the corridor and down the stairs. He didn't want to be late for Harry's performance.

32

WHEN OLD JACK got home later that night, he picked up a copy of *The Times* Harry had left for him earlier in the week. He never bothered with the personal ads on the front page as he didn't need a new bowler hat, a pair of suspenders or a first edition of *Wuthering Heights*.

He turned the page to find a photo of King Edward VIII, enjoying a yachting holiday in the Mediterranean. Standing by his side was an American woman called Mrs. Simpson. The report was couched in ambiguous terms, but even the Thunderer was finding it hard to support the young King in his desire to marry a divorced woman. It made Old Jack sad, because he admired Edward, especially after his visit to the Welsh miners when he had so clearly been affected by their plight. But as his old nanny used to say, there'll be tears before bedtime.

Old Jack then spent some considerable time reading a report on the Tariff Reform Bill, which had just passed its second reading in the House, despite the firebrand Winston Churchill declaring that it was neither "fish nor fowl," and no one would benefit from it, including the government, when it came to an election. He couldn't wait to hear Sir Walter's unexpurgated views on that particular subject.

He turned a page to learn that the British Broadcasting Corporation had made its first television broadcast from Alexandra Palace. This was a concept he couldn't begin to comprehend. How could a picture be beamed into your home? He didn't even have a radio, and had absolutely no desire to own a television.

He moved on to the sports pages, to find a photograph of an elegantly dressed Fred Perry under the headline, *Three times Wimbledon champion tipped to win the American Open*. The tennis correspondent went on to suggest that some of the foreign competitors might be wearing shorts at Forest Hills, something else Jack couldn't come to terms with.

As he did whenever he read *The Times*, Old Jack saved the obituaries till last. He'd reached that age when men younger than himself were dying, and not just in wars.

When he turned the page, the color drained from his face, and he experienced an overwhelming sadness. He took his time reading the obituary of the Reverend Thomas Alexander Tarrant, Resident Canon of Wells Cathedral, described in the headline as a godly man. When Old Jack had finished reading his father's obituary, he felt ashamed.

—◦—

"Seven pounds four shillings?" repeated Old Jack. "But I thought you got a check for six hundred pounds from the Bristol and West of England Insurance Company, 'in full and final settlement,' if I recall the exact words."

"I did," said Maisie, "but by the time I'd paid back the original loan, the compound interest on that loan, as well as bank charges, I ended up with seven pounds and four shillings."

"I'm so naive," said Old Jack. "And to think that for a moment, just a moment, I actually thought Barrington was trying to be helpful."

"You're not half as naive as me," said Maisie. "Because if I had thought, even for one moment, that man was involved, I would never have taken a penny of his money, and because I did, I've lost everything. Even my job at the hotel."

"But why?" asked Old Jack. "Mr. Frampton always said you were irreplaceable."

"Well, it seems I'm not anymore. When I asked him why he'd sacked me, he refused to give a reason, other than to say he'd received a complaint about me from an 'unimpeachable source.' It can't be a coincidence that I was sacked the day after that 'unimpeachable source' dropped into the Royal Hotel for a chat with the manager."

"Did you see Barrington going into the hotel?" asked Old Jack.

"No, I didn't, but I saw him coming out. Don't forget, I was hiding in the back of his car, waiting for him."

"Of course," said Old Jack. "So what happened when you confronted him about Harry?"

"While we were in the car," said Maisie, "he virtually admitted to being responsible for Arthur's death."

"He finally came clean after all these years?" said Old Jack in disbelief.

"Not exactly," said Maisie. "More a slip of the tongue, but when I left the envelope with the invoice for next term's fees on the front seat of his car, he put it in his pocket and said he'd see what he could do to help."

"And you fell for it?"

"Hook, line and sinker," admitted Maisie, "because when he stopped the car he even got out to open the back door for me. But the moment I stepped out, he knocked me to the ground, tore up the bill and drove off."

"Is that how you got the black eye?"

Maisie nodded. "And he also warned me he'd have me committed to a mental asylum if I even thought about contacting his wife."

"That's nothing more than a bluff," said Old Jack, "because even he couldn't get away with that."

"You may be right," said Maisie, "but it's not a risk I'm willing to take."

"And if you did tell Mrs. Barrington that her husband was responsible for Arthur's death," said Old Jack, "all he'd have to do is let her know you're Stan Tancock's sister, and she'd dismiss it out of hand."

"Possibly," said Maisie. "But she wouldn't dismiss it out of hand if I told her her husband might be Harry's father . . ."

Old Jack was stunned into silence as he tried to take in the implications of Maisie's words. "I'm not only naive," he eventually managed, "but I'm also bone stupid. Hugo Barrington won't care if his wife does or doesn't believe he was involved in your husband's death. His greatest fear is Harry ever finding out that he might be his father . . ."

"But I would never tell Harry," said Maisie. "The last thing I'd want is for him to spend the rest of his life wondering who his father is."

"That is precisely what Barrington is banking on. And now he's broken you, he'll be hell-bent on destroying Harry."

"But why?" asked Maisie. "Harry's never done him any harm."

"Of course he hasn't, but if Harry were able to prove that he is Hugo Barrington's eldest son, he might just be in line to inherit not only the title, but everything that goes with it, and at the same time, Giles would end up with nothing."

It was Maisie's turn to be speechless.

"So, now we've discovered the real reason Barrington is so keen to have Harry thrown out of the grammar school, perhaps the time has come for me to pay a visit to Sir Walter, and tell him some unpalatable truths about his son."

"No, please don't do that," begged Maisie.

"Why not? It might be our one chance of keeping Harry at BGS."

"Possibly, but it would also guarantee that my brother Stan would get the sack, and God knows what else Barrington is capable of."

Old Jack didn't reply for some time. Then he said, "If you won't allow me to tell Sir Walter the truth, I'll have to start crawling around in the sewer that Hugo Barrington currently occupies."

33

"YOU WANT WHAT?" asked Miss Potts, not sure she'd heard him correctly.

"A private meeting with Mr. Hugo," said Old Jack.

"And am I permitted to inquire what the purpose of this meeting might be?" she said, making no attempt to hide the sarcasm in her voice.

"His son's future."

"Wait here for a moment. I'll see if Mr. Barrington is willing to see you."

Miss Potts knocked gently on the managing director's door and disappeared inside. She returned a moment later with a surprised look on her face.

"Mr. Barrington will see you now," she said, holding open the door.

Old Jack couldn't resist a smile as he strolled past her. Hugo Barrington looked up from behind his desk. He didn't offer the old man a seat, and made no attempt to shake hands with him.

"What possible interest can you have in Giles's future?" asked Barrington.

"None," admitted Old Jack. "It's your other son whose future I'm interested in."

"What the hell are you talking about?" said Barrington, a little too loudly.

"If you didn't know who I was talking about, you wouldn't have agreed to see me," replied Old Jack contemptuously.

The color drained from Barrington's face. Old Jack even

wondered if he was going to faint. "What do you want from me?" he finally said.

"All your life you've been a trader," said Old Jack. "I am in possession of something you'll want to trade."

"And what could that possibly be?"

"The day after Arthur Clifton mysteriously disappeared and Stan Tancock was arrested for a crime he didn't commit, I was asked by Detective Inspector Blakemore to make a statement of everything I'd witnessed that evening. Because you had Blakemore taken off the case, that statement remains in my possession. I have a feeling it would make very interesting reading if it were to fall into the wrong hands."

"I think you'll find that's blackmail," said Barrington, spitting out the words, "for which you can go to prison for a very long time."

"Some might consider it nothing more than a matter of civic duty for such a document to enter the public domain."

"And who do you imagine would be interested in the ravings of an old man? Certainly not the press, once my lawyers have explained the libel laws to them. And as the police closed the file some years ago, I can't see the chief constable going to the trouble and expense of reopening it on the word of an old man who might be considered at best eccentric and at worst mad. So I'm bound to ask, who else do you have in mind to share your preposterous allegations with?"

"Your father," said Old Jack, bluffing, but then Barrington didn't know about his promise to Maisie.

Barrington slumped back in his chair, only too aware of the influence Old Jack had with his father, even if he had never understood why. "How much do you expect me to pay for this document?"

"Three hundred pounds."

"That's daylight robbery!"

"It's no more and no less than the amount required to cover the fees and any little extras that will allow Harry Clifton to remain at Bristol Grammar School for the next two years."

"Why don't I just pay his fees at the beginning of each term, as I do for my own son?"

"Because you would stop paying one of your sons' fees the moment you got your hands on my statement."

"You'll have to take cash," said Barrington, taking a key from his pocket.

"No, thank you," said Old Jack. "I remember only too well what happened to Stan Tancock after you'd handed him your thirty pieces of silver. And I have no desire to spend the next three years in prison for a crime I didn't commit."

"Then I'll have to call the bank if I'm to write out a check for such a large amount."

"Be my guest," said Old Jack, gesturing toward the phone on Barrington's desk.

Barrington hesitated for a moment before picking up the handset. He waited for a voice to come on the line. "TEM 3731," he said.

Another wait, before another voice said, "Yes?"

"Is that you, Prendergast?"

"No, sir," said the voice.

"Good, you're just the man I need to speak to," Barrington replied. "I'll be sending a Mr. Tar around to see you in the next hour, with a check for three hundred pounds made payable to Bristol Municipal Charities. Would you see that it's processed immediately, and make sure you phone me straight back."

"If you want me to ring you back, just say 'Yes, that's right,' and I'll call in a couple of minutes," the voice said.

"Yes, that's right," said Barrington, and put the phone down.

He opened the drawer of his desk, took out a checkbook and wrote the words *Pay Bristol Municipal Charities* and, on a separate line, *Three hundred pounds*. He then signed the check and passed it to Old Jack, who studied it carefully and nodded.

"I'll just put it in an envelope," said Barrington. He pressed the buzzer under his desk. Old Jack glanced at Miss Potts as she entered the room.

"Yes, sir?"

"Mr. Tar is leaving to go to the bank," said Barrington, placing the check in the envelope. He sealed it and addressed it to

Mr. Prendergast, adding the word PRIVATE in bold letters, then handed it to Old Jack.

"Thank you," said Jack. "I'll deliver the document to you personally as soon as I get back."

Barrington nodded, just as the phone on his desk began to ring. He waited for Old Jack to leave the room before he picked it up.

Old Jack decided to take the tram into Bristol, feeling that the expense was justified on such a special occasion. When he walked into the bank twenty minutes later, he told the young man on the reception that he had a letter for Mr. Prendergast. The receptionist didn't seem particularly impressed, until Old Jack added, "It's from Mr. Hugo Barrington."

The young man immediately deserted his post, led Old Jack across the banking hall and down a long corridor to the manager's office. He knocked on the door, opened it and announced, "This gentleman has a letter from Mr. Barrington, sir."

Mr. Prendergast leaped up from behind his desk, shook hands with the old man and ushered him to a seat on the other side of the desk. Old Jack handed the envelope to Prendergast, with the words, "Mr. Barrington asked me to give this to you personally."

"Yes, of course," said Prendergast, who immediately recognized the familiar hand of one of his most valued customers. He slit open the envelope and extracted a check. He looked at it for a moment, before saying, "There must be some mistake."

"There's no mistake," said Old Jack. "Mr. Barrington would like the full amount to be paid to Bristol Municipal Charities at your earliest convenience, as he instructed you over the phone only half an hour ago."

"But I haven't spoken to Mr. Barrington this morning," said Prendergast, passing the check back to Old Jack.

Old Jack stared in disbelief at a blank check. It only took him a few moments to realize that Barrington must have switched the checks when Miss Potts entered the room. The true genius of his action was to address the envelope to Mr. Prendergast and mark it private, thus ensuring it wouldn't be opened until it had been handed to the manager. But the one mystery Jack couldn't fathom was: who had been on the other end of the phone?

Old Jack hurried out of the office without saying another word to Prendergast. He crossed the banking hall and ran out into the street. He only had to wait a few minutes for a tram to the docks. He couldn't have been away for much more than an hour by the time he walked back through the gates and into the dockyard.

A man he didn't recognize was striding toward him. He had a military air about him and Old Jack wondered if the limp had been caused by an injury he'd suffered in the Great War.

Old Jack hurried past him and on down the quayside. He was relieved to see that the carriage door was closed, and when he opened it he was even more pleased to find that everything was just as he'd left it. He sank to his knees and lifted the corner of the carpet, but the police statement was no longer there. Detective Inspector Blakemore would have described the theft as the work of a professional.

34

OLD JACK TOOK his place in the fifth row of the congregation, hoping no one would recognize him. The cathedral was so packed that people who had been unable to find a seat in the side chapels stood in the aisles and were crammed in at the back.

The Bishop of Bath and Wells brought tears to Old Jack's eyes when he talked about his father's unquestioning faith in God, and how, since the premature death of his wife, the canon had devoted himself to serving the community, "The proof of which," proclaimed the Bishop, raising his arms to acknowledge the vast congregation, "can be seen by the number of those present, who have come to honor him from so many walks of life, and to pay their respects.

"And although the man knew no vanity, he could not hide a certain pride in his only son, Jack, whose selfless courage, bravery and willingness to sacrifice his own life in South Africa during the Boer War saved so many of his comrades, and led to him being awarded the Victoria Cross." He paused, looked down into the fifth row and said, "And how delighted I am to see him in the congregation today."

Several people began looking around for a man they had never seen before. Jack bowed his head in shame.

At the end of the service, many members of the congregation came up to tell Captain Tarrant how much they had admired his father. The words "dedication," "selflessness," "generosity" and "love" fell from everyone's lips.

Jack felt proud of being his father's son, while at the same time ashamed that he had excluded him from his life, in the same way as he had the rest of his fellow men.

As he was leaving, he thought he recognized an elderly gentleman standing by the great gates, clearly waiting to speak to him. The man stepped forward and raised his hat. "Captain Tarrant?" he inquired with a voice that suggested authority.

Jack returned the compliment. "Yes, sir?"

"My name is Edwin Trent. I had the privilege of being your father's solicitor, and, I'd like to think, one of his oldest and closest friends."

Jack shook him warmly by the hand. "I remember you well, sir. You taught me a love of Trollope and an appreciation of the finer points of spin bowling."

"It's kind of you to remember," Trent chuckled. "I wonder if I might accompany you on your way back to the station?"

"Of course, sir."

"As you know," said Trent as they began walking toward the town, "your father was resident canon of this cathedral for the past nine years. You'll also know that he cared nothing for worldly goods, and shared even the little he had with those less fortunate than himself. If he were to be canonized, he would surely be the patron saint of vagabonds."

Old Jack smiled. He recalled going to school one morning without breakfast because three tramps were sleeping in the hallway and, to quote his mother, they had eaten them out of house and home.

"So when his will comes to be read," continued Trent, "it will show that just as he entered this world with nothing, he has also left it with nothing—other than a thousand friends, that is, which he would have considered a veritable fortune. Before he died, he entrusted me with one small task should you attend his funeral, namely that of handing you the last letter he ever wrote." He extracted an envelope from an inside pocket of his overcoat and handed it to Old Jack, raised his hat once more and said, "I have carried out his request, and am proud to have met his son once again."

"I am obliged, sir. I only wish that I hadn't made it necessary for him to have to write in the first place." Jack raised his hat and the two men parted.

Old Jack decided that he would not read his father's letter until he was on the train, and had begun the journey back to Bristol. As the engine shunted out of the station, billowing clouds of gray smoke, Jack settled back in a third-class compartment. As a child, he remembered asking his father why he always traveled third class, to which he had replied, "Because there isn't a fourth class." It was ironic that, for the past thirty years, Jack had been living in first class.

He took his time unsealing the envelope, and even after he had extracted the letter, he left it folded while he continued to think about his father. No son could have asked for a better mentor or friend. When he looked back on his life, all his actions, judgments and decisions were nothing more than pale imitations of his father's.

When he finally unfolded the letter, another flood of memories came rushing back the moment he saw the familiar bold, copperplate hand in jet-black ink. He began to read.

The Close
Wells Cathedral
Wells, Somerset

26th August, 1936

My beloved son,

If you were kind enough to attend my funeral, you must now be reading this letter. Allow me to begin by thanking you for being among the congregation.

Old Jack raised his head and looked out at the passing countryside. He felt guilty once again for treating his father in such an inconsiderate and thoughtless manner, and now it was too late to ask for his forgiveness. His eyes returned to the letter.

When you were awarded the Victoria Cross, I was the proudest father in England, and your citation still hangs above my desk to this very day. But then, as the years passed, my happiness turned to sorrow, and I asked our Lord what I had done that I should be so punished by losing not only your dear mother, but also you, my only child.

I accept that you must have had some noble purpose for turning your head and your heart against this world, but I wish you had shared your reason for so doing with me. But, should you read this letter, perhaps you might grant me one last wish.

Old Jack removed the handkerchief from his top pocket and wiped his eyes before he was able to continue reading.

God gave you the remarkable gift of leadership and the ability to inspire your fellow men, so I beg you not to go to your grave knowing that when the time comes for you to face your maker, you will, as in the parable Matthew 25, v14–30, have to confess that you buried the one talent He gave you.

Rather, use that gift for the benefit of your fellow men, so that when your time comes, as it surely must, and those same men attend your funeral, the Victoria Cross will not be the only thing they remember when they hear the name Jack Tarrant.

Your loving father

"Are you all right, my luv?" asked a lady who had moved from the other side of the carriage to sit next to Old Jack.

"Yes, thank you," he said, the tears streaming down his face. "It's just that I was released from prison today."

GILES BARRINGTON

1936–1938

35

I was thrilled when I saw Harry walk through the school gates on the first day of term. I'd spent the summer hols at our villa in Tuscany, so I wasn't in Bristol when Tilly's was burned to the ground and didn't find out about it until I returned to England the weekend before term began. I had wanted Harry to join us in Italy, but my father wouldn't hear of it.

I've never met anyone who didn't like Harry, with the exception of my father, who won't even allow his name to be mentioned in the house. I once asked Mama if she could explain why he felt so strongly, but she didn't seem to know any more than I did.

I didn't press the point with my old man, as I've never exactly covered myself in glory in his eyes. I nearly got myself expelled from my prep school for stealing—heaven knows how he managed to fix that—and after that I let him down by failing to get into Eton. I told Papa when I came out of the exam that I couldn't have tried harder, which was the truth. Well, half the truth. I would have got away with it if my coconspirator had only kept his mouth shut. At least it taught me a simple lesson: if you make a deal with a fool, don't be surprised when they act foolishly.

My coconspirator was the Earl of Bridport's son, Percy. He was facing an even greater dilemma than I was, because seven generations of Bridports had been educated at Eton, and it was looking as if young Percy was going to ruin that rather fine batting average.

Eton has been known to bend the rules when it comes to members of the aristocracy and will occasionally allow a stupid boy to darken its doors, which is why I selected Percy for my little subterfuge in the first place. It was after I overheard the Frob saying to another beak, "If Bridport was any brighter, he'd be a half-wit," that I knew I didn't need to look any further for my accomplice.

Percy was as desperate to be offered a place at Eton as I was to be rejected, so I saw this as no more than an opportunity for both of us to achieve our purpose.

I didn't discuss my plan with Harry or Deakins. Harry would undoubtedly have disapproved, he's such a morally upright fellow, and Deakins wouldn't have been able to understand why anyone would want to fail an exam.

On the day before the examination was due to take place my father drove me to Eton in his swish new Bugatti, which could do a hundred miles an hour, and once we hit the A4 he proved it. We spent the night at the Swann Arms, the same hotel in which he had stayed over twenty years before when he took the entrance exam. Over dinner, Papa didn't leave me in any doubt how keen he was that I should go to Eton and I nearly had a change of heart at the last moment, but I had given my word to Percy Bridport, and felt I couldn't let him down.

Percy and I had shaken hands on the deal back at St. Bede's, agreeing that when we entered the examination hall, we would give the recorder the other's name. I rather enjoyed being addressed as "my lord" by all and sundry, even if it was only for a few hours.

The examination papers were not as demanding as the ones I'd sat a fortnight earlier for Bristol Grammar, and I felt I'd done more than enough to ensure that Percy would be returning to Eton in September. However, they were difficult enough for me to feel confident that his lordship would not let me down.

Once we'd handed in our papers and reverted to our true personas, I went off to tea with my pa, in Windsor. When he asked me how it had gone, I told him I'd done the best I possibly could. He seemed satisfied by this, and even began to relax, which only made me feel more guilty. I didn't enjoy the journey back to Bristol, and felt even worse when I got home and my mother asked me the same question.

Ten days later, I received an *I'm sorry to have to inform you* letter from Eton. I had only managed 32 percent. Percy scored 56 percent and was offered a place for the Michaelmas term, which delighted his father and was met with incredulity by the Frob.

Everything would have worked out just fine, if Percy hadn't told a friend how he'd managed to get into Eton. The friend told another friend, who told another friend, who told Percy's father. The Earl of Bridport MC, being an honorable man, immediately informed the headmaster of Eton. This resulted in Percy being expelled before he'd even set foot in the place. If it hadn't been for a personal intervention by the Frob, I might have suffered the same fate at Bristol Grammar.

My father tried to convince the headmaster of Eton that it was simply a clerical error, and that, as I'd actually scored 56 percent in the exam, I should be reinstated in Bridport's place. This piece of logic was rejected by return of post, as Eton wasn't in need of a new cricket pavilion. I duly reported to Bristol Grammar School on the first day of term.

—◇—

During my first year, I restored my reputation somewhat by scoring three centuries for the Colts and ended the season being awarded my colors. Harry played Cinna in *Julius Ceasar,* and Deakins was Deakins, so no one was surprised when he won the First Form prize.

During my second year, I became more aware of the financial constraints Harry's mother must be experiencing when I noticed that he was wearing his shoes with the laces undone, and he admitted they were pinching because they were so tight.

So when Tilly's was burned to the ground only weeks before we were expected to enter the sixth form, I was not altogether surprised to learn that Harry thought he might not be able to stay on at the school. I thought about asking my father if he might be able to help, but Mama told me I would be wasting my time. That's why I was so delighted when I saw him walking through the school gates on the first day of term.

He told me that his mother had begun a new job at the Royal

Hotel, working nights, and it was proving to be far more lucrative than she had originally thought possible.

During the next summer hols I would, once again, have liked to invite Harry to join the family in Tuscany, but I knew my father would not consider the idea. But as the Arts Appreciation Society, of which Harry was now secretary, was planning a trip to Rome, we agreed to meet up there, even if it did mean I would have to visit the Villa Borghese.

—<o>—

Although we were living in a little bubble of our own down in the West Country, it would have been impossible not to be aware of what was taking place on the continent.

The rise of the Nazis in Germany, and the Fascists in Italy, didn't seem to be affecting the average Englishman, who was still enjoying a pint of cider and a cheese sandwich at his local on a Saturday, before watching, or in my case playing, cricket on the village green in the afternoon. For years this blissful state of affairs had been able to continue because another war with Germany didn't bear thinking about. Our fathers had fought in the war to end all wars, but now the unmentionable seemed to be on everyone's lips.

Harry told me in no uncertain terms that if war was declared, he wouldn't be going to university but would join up immediately, just as his father and uncle had done some twenty years before. My father had "missed out," as he put it, because unfortunately he was color-blind, and those in authority thought he'd serve the war effort better by remaining at his post, playing an important role in the docks. Though I've never been quite sure exactly what that important role was.

—<o>—

In our final year at BGS, both Harry and I decided to enter our names for Oxford; Deakins had already been offered an open scholarship to Balliol College. I wanted to go to the House, but was informed most politely by the entrance tutor that Christ Church rarely took grammar school boys, so I settled for Brasenose, which had once been described by Bertie Wooster as a college "where brains are neither here nor there."

As Brasenose was also the college with the most cricket blues, and I had scored three centuries in my final year as captain of BGS, one of them at Lord's for a Public Schools XI, I felt I must be in with a chance. In fact, my form master, Dr. Paget, told me that when I went for my interview they would probably throw a cricket ball at me as I entered the room. If I caught it, I would be offered a place. If I caught it one-handed, a scholarship. This turned out to be apocryphal. However, I'm bound to admit that during drinks with the college principal, he asked me more questions about Hutton than Horace.

There were other highs and lows during my last two years at school: Jesse Owens winning four gold medals at the Olympic Games in Berlin, right under Hitler's nose, was a definite high, while the abdication of Edward VIII because he wished to marry an American divorcee was an undoubted low.

The nation seemed to be divided on whether the King should have abdicated, as were Harry and I. I failed to understand how a man born to be King could be willing to sacrifice the throne to marry a divorced woman. Harry was far more sympathetic to the King's plight, saying that we couldn't begin to understand what the poor man was going through until we fell in love ourselves. I dismissed this as codswallop, until that trip to Rome that was to change both our lives.

36

IF GILES IMAGINED he'd worked hard during his final days at St. Bede's, in those last two years at Bristol Grammar School both he and Harry became acquainted with hours only Deakins was familiar with.

Dr. Paget, their sixth-form master, told them in no uncertain terms that if they hoped to be offered a place at Oxford or Cambridge, they would have to forget any other activities, as they would need to spend every waking moment preparing for the entrance exams.

Giles was hoping to captain the school's First XI in his final year, while Harry was keen to land the lead in the school play. Dr. Paget raised an eyebrow when he heard this, even though *Romeo and Juliet* was the set text for Oxford that year. "Just be sure you don't sign up for anything else," he said firmly.

Harry reluctantly resigned from the choir, which gave him two more free evenings a week to study. However, there was one activity no pupil could exempt himself from: every Tuesday and Thursday, at four o'clock, all the boys had to be standing to attention on the parade ground, fully kitted out and ready for inspection as members of the Combined Cadet Force.

"Can't allow the Hitler Youth to imagine that if Germany is foolish enough to declare war on us a second time, we won't be ready for them," bellowed the RSM.

Every time ex-Regimental Sergeant Major Roberts delivered these words, it sent a shiver through the ranks of schoolboys, who realized as each day passed that it was becoming more and more likely they would be serving on the front line as junior officers in some foreign field, rather than going up to university as undergraduates.

Harry took the RSM's words to heart and was quickly promoted to cadet officer. Giles took them less seriously, knowing that if he was called up, he could, like his father, take the easy way out and remind them of his color-blindness to avoid coming face to face with the enemy.

Deakins showed little interest in the whole process, declaring with a certainty that brooked no argument, "You don't need to know how to strip a bren gun when you're in the intelligence corps."

By the time the long summer nights began to draw to a close, they were all ready for a holiday before they would return for their final year, at the end of which they would have to face the examiners once again. Within a week of term ending, all three of them had left for their summer break: Giles to join his family at their villa in Tuscany, Harry to Rome with the school's Arts Appreciation Society, while Deakins entombed himself in Bristol Central library, avoiding contact with any other human beings, despite the fact that he'd already been offered a place at Oxford.

—<o>—

Over the years, Giles had come to accept that if he wanted to see Harry during the holidays, he had to make sure his father didn't find out what he was up to, otherwise the best-laid schemes of mice and . . . But in order to achieve this, he often had to get his sister Emma to join in the subterfuge, and she never failed to extract her pound of flesh before agreeing to become his accomplice.

"If you take the lead over dinner tonight, I'll follow up," said Giles once he'd outlined his latest scheme to her.

"Sounds like the natural order of things," said Emma scornfully.

After the first course had been served, Emma innocently asked her mother if she could possibly take her to the Villa Borghese the following day, as it had been recommended as a must by her art mistress. She was well aware that Mama had already made other plans.

"I'm so sorry, darling," she said, "but your father and I are going to lunch with the Hendersons in Arezzo tomorrow. You're most welcome to join us."

"There's nothing to stop Giles taking you into Rome," interjected his father from the other end of the table.

"Do I have to?" said Giles, who had just been about to make the same suggestion.

"Yes, you do," replied his father firmly.

"But what's the point, Pa? By the time we get there, we'll have to turn round and come back. It's hardly worth it."

"Not if you were to spend the night at the Plaza Hotel. I'll call them first thing in the morning, and book a couple of rooms."

"Are you sure they're grown up enough for that?" asked Mrs. Barrington, sounding a little anxious.

"Giles will be eighteen in a few weeks. It's time he grew up and took some responsibility." Giles bowed his head as if he had given in meekly.

The following morning, a taxi drove him and Emma to the local station just in time to catch the early morning train to Rome.

"Be sure to take care of your sister," were his father's last words before they left the villa.

"I will," promised Giles as the car drove off.

Several men rose to offer Emma their seat as she entered the carriage, while Giles was left standing for the entire journey. On arrival in Rome, they took a taxi to the Via del Corso, and once they'd booked into their hotel they continued on to the Villa Borghese. Giles was struck by how many young men not much older than himself were in uniform, while almost every pillar and lamppost they passed displayed a poster of Mussolini.

Once the taxi had dropped them off, they made their way up through the gardens, passing more men in uniform and even more posters of "Il Duce" before they finally reached the palatial Villa Borghese.

Harry had written to tell Giles they would be setting out on their official tour at ten o'clock. He checked his watch—a few minutes past eleven, with luck the tour would be nearly over. He bought two tickets, handed one to Emma, bounded up the steps to the galleria and went in search of the school party. Emma took her time admiring the Bernini statues that dominated the first four rooms, but then she wasn't in a hurry. Giles went from gallery to gallery until he spotted a group of young men dressed in dark claret jackets and black flannel trousers, who were crowded around a small portrait of an elderly man dressed in a cream silk cassock with a white mitre on his head.

"There they are," he said, but Emma was nowhere to be seen. Not giving his sister another thought, he headed over to the attentive group. The moment he saw her, he quite forgot the reason he had come to Rome.

"Caravaggio was commissioned to paint this portrait of Pope Paul V in 1605," she said, with a slight accent. "You will notice that it was not finished, and that is because the artist had to flee from Rome."

"Why, miss?" demanded a young boy in the front row, who was clearly determined to take Deakins's place at some time in the future.

"Because he became involved in a drunken brawl, during which he ended up killing a man."

"Did they arrest him?" asked the same boy.

"No," said the tour guide, "Caravaggio always managed to move on to the next city before the forces of justice could catch up with him, but in the end the Holy Father decided to grant him a pardon."

"Why?" demanded the same boy.

"Because he wanted Caravaggio to carry out several more commissions for him. Some of them are among the seventeen works that can still be seen in Rome today."

At that moment, Harry spotted Giles gazing in awe in the direction of the painting. He left the group and walked across to join him. "How long have you been standing there?" he asked.

"Long enough to fall in love," said Giles, his eyes still fixed on the tour guide.

Harry laughed when he realized it wasn't the painting Giles

was staring at, but the elegant, self-assured young woman who was addressing the boys. "I think she's a bit out of your age group," said Harry, "and I suspect even your price range."

"I'm willing to take that risk," said Giles as the guide led her little group into the next room. Giles followed obediently and positioned himself so he had a clear view of her, while the rest of the group studied a statue of *Paolina Borghese* by Canova, "arguably the greatest sculptor of all time," she said. Giles wasn't going to disagree with her.

"Well, that brings us to the end of our tour," she announced. "But if you have any more questions I will be here for a few more minutes, so don't hesitate to ask."

Giles didn't hesitate.

Harry watched in amusement as his friend strode up to the young Italian woman and began chatting to her as if they were old friends. Even the little boy from the front row didn't dare to interrupt him. Giles rejoined Harry a few minutes later, a large grin plastered across his face.

"She's agreed to have dinner with me tonight."

"I don't believe you," said Harry.

"But a problem has arisen," he added, ignoring his friend's Doubting Thomas look.

"More than one, I suspect."

". . . which can be overcome with your assistance."

"You need a chaperone to accompany you," suggested Harry, "just in case things get out of hand."

"No, you ass. I want you to take care of my sister while Caterina introduces me to Rome's nightlife."

"Not a hope," said Harry. "I didn't come all the way to Rome just to act as your babysitter."

"But you're my best friend," pleaded Giles. "If you won't help me, who else can I turn to?"

"Why don't you try Paolina Borghese? I doubt if she has any plans for tonight."

"All you have to do is take her out for dinner, and make sure she's in bed by ten."

"Forgive me for mentioning it, Giles, but I thought you'd come to Rome to have dinner with me?"

"I'll give you a thousand lire if you take her off my hands. And we can still have breakfast at my hotel in the morning."

"I'm not that easily bribed."

"And," said Giles, playing his trump card, "I'll also give you my recording of Caruso singing *La Bohème*."

Harry turned to find a young girl standing by his side.

"By the way," said Giles, "this is my sister, Emma."

"Hello," said Harry. Turning back to Giles, he said, "You've got yourself a deal."

—◇—

Harry joined Giles for breakfast at the Palace Hotel the following morning, when his friend greeted him with the same immodest smile he always wore just after he'd scored a century.

"So, how was Caterina?" Harry asked, not wanting to hear his reply.

"Beyond my wildest dreams."

Harry was about to question him more closely when a waiter appeared by his side. "*Cappuccino, per favore.*" Then he asked, "So how far did she let you go?"

"All the way," said Giles.

Harry's mouth fell open, but no words came out. "Did you . . ."

"Did I what?"

"Did you . . ." Harry tried again.

"Yes?"

"See her naked?"

"Yes, of course."

"The whole body?"

"Naturally," said Giles as a cup of coffee was placed in front of Harry.

"The bottom half as well as the top?"

"Everything," said Giles. "And I mean everything."

"Did you touch her breasts?"

"I licked her nipples actually," said Giles, taking a sip of coffee.

"You did what?"

"You heard me," said Giles.

"But did you, I mean, did you . . ."

"Yes, I did."

"How many times?"

"I lost count," said Giles. "She was insatiable. Seven, perhaps eight. She just wouldn't let me get to sleep. I'd still be there now if she hadn't had to be at the Vatican museum at ten this morning to lecture the next bunch of brats."

"But what if she gets pregnant?" said Harry.

"Don't be so naive, Harry. Try to remember she's an Italian." After another sip of coffee, he asked, "So, how did my sister behave herself?"

"The food was excellent, and you owe me your Caruso recording."

"That bad? Well, we can't all be winners."

Neither of them had noticed Emma enter the room until she was standing by their side. Harry leaped up and offered her his seat. "Sorry to leave you," he said, "but I have to be at the Vatican museum by ten."

"Give Caterina my love!" shouted Giles as Harry almost ran out of the breakfast room.

Giles waited until Harry was out of sight before he asked his sister, "So, how did last night go?"

"Could have been worse," she said, picking up a croissant. "A bit serious, isn't he?"

"You should meet Deakins."

Emma laughed. "Well, at least the food was good. But don't forget, I now own your gramophone."

37

GILES LATER DESCRIBED it as the most memorable night of his life—for all the wrong reasons.

The annual play is one of the major events in the Bristol Grammar School calendar, not least because the city boasts a fine theater tradition, and 1937 was to prove a vintage year.

The school, like so many others in the country, performed one of Shakespeare's set texts for the year. The choice had been between *Romeo and Juliet* and *A Midsummer Night's Dream*. Dr. Paget chose the tragedy rather than the comedy, not least because he had a Romeo and he didn't have a Bottom.

For the first time in the school's history, the young ladies of Red Maids' on the other side of the city were invited to audition for the girls' parts, but not before several discussions had taken place with Miss Webb, the headmistress, who had insisted on a set of ground rules that would have impressed a mother superior.

The play was to be performed on three consecutive evenings in the last week of term. As always, the Saturday night was sold out first, because former pupils and the parents of the cast wished to attend the closing night.

Giles was standing anxiously in the foyer checking his watch every few moments as he waited impatiently for his parents and younger sister to arrive. He hoped that Harry would give another fine performance, and his father would finally come round to accepting him.

The critic from the *Bristol Evening World* had described Harry's performance as "mature beyond his years," but he had saved the highest praise for Juliet, reporting that he had not seen the death scene performed more movingly even at Stratford.

Giles shook hands with Mr. Frobisher as he walked into the foyer. His old housemaster introduced his guest, a Mr. Holcombe, before they went through to the great hall to take their seats.

A murmur rippled around the audience when Captain Tarrant walked down the center aisle and took his place in the front row. His recent appointment as a governor of the school had been met with universal approval. As he leaned across to have a word with the chairman of the governors, he spotted Maisie Clifton sitting just a few rows behind. He gave her a warm smile, but didn't recognize the man she was sitting with. The next surprise came when he studied the cast list.

The headmaster and Mrs. Barton were among the last members of the audience to enter the great hall. They took their places in the front row alongside Sir Walter Barrington and Captain Tarrant.

Giles was becoming more nervous with each passing minute. He was beginning to wonder if his parents would turn up before the curtain rose.

"I'm so sorry, Giles," said his mother when they finally appeared. "It's my fault, I lost track of time," she added as she and Grace hurried into the hall. His father followed a yard behind and raised his eyebrows when he saw his son. Giles didn't hand him a program as he wanted it to be a surprise, although he had shared the news with his mother who, like him, hoped her husband would finally treat Harry as if he were a friend of the family, and not an outsider.

The curtain rose only moments after the Barringtons had taken their seats, and a hush of anticipation descended on the packed audience.

When Harry made his first entrance, Giles glanced in his father's direction. As there didn't appear to be any immediate reaction, he began to relax for the first time that evening. But this happy state of affairs only lasted until the ballroom scene, when Romeo, and Hugo, saw Juliet for the first time.

Some people in the seats near the Barringtons became irritated by a restless man who was spoiling their enjoyment of the play with his loud whispering and demands to see a program. They became even more annoyed after Romeo said, "Is she not Capulet's daughter?" at which point Hugo Barrington stood up and barged along the row, not caring whose feet he trod on. He then marched down the center aisle, pushed his way through the swing doors and disappeared into the night. It was some time before Romeo fully regained his composure.

Sir Walter tried to give the impression he hadn't noticed what was going on behind him, and although Captain Tarrant frowned, his eyes never left the stage. Had he turned round, he would have seen Mrs. Clifton was ignoring Barrington's unscripted exit as she concentrated on every word the two young lovers had to say.

During the interval, Giles went in search of his father but couldn't find him. He checked the car park, but there was no sign of the Bugatti. When he returned to the foyer, he saw his grandfather bending down and whispering in his mother's ear.

"Has Hugo gone completely mad?" asked Sir Walter.

"No, he's sane enough," said Elizabeth, making no attempt to hide her anger.

"Then what in heaven's name does he think he's up to?"

"I have no idea."

"Could it possibly have something to do with the Clifton boy?"

She would have replied if Jack Tarrant hadn't walked across to join them.

"Your daughter has a remarkable talent, Elizabeth," he said after kissing her hand, "as well as the advantage of inheriting your beauty."

"And you're an old flatterer, Jack," she said, before adding, "I don't think you've met my son, Giles."

"Good evening, sir," said Giles. "It's a great honor to meet you. May I congratulate you on your recent appointment."

"Thank you, young man," said Tarrant. "And how do you feel about your friend's performance?"

"Remarkable, but did you know—"

"Good evening, Mrs. Barrington."

"Good evening, headmaster."

"I must be joining a long queue of those who wish to add their . . ."

Giles watched as Captain Tarrant slipped away to join Harry's mother, and wondered how they knew each other.

"How lovely to see you, Captain Tarrant."

"And you, Mrs. Clifton, and how glamorous you're looking tonight. If Cary Grant had known that such beauty existed in Bristol, he would never have deserted us for Hollywood." He then lowered his voice. "Did you have any idea that Emma Barrington was playing Juliet?"

"No, Harry didn't mention it to me," said Maisie. "But then, why should he?"

"Let's hope that the affection they are displaying for one another on stage is nothing more than good acting, because if it's how they really feel about each other, we may have an even bigger problem on our hands." He looked around to make sure no one was eavesdropping on their conversation. "I presume you still haven't said anything to Harry?"

"Not a word," said Maisie. "And from Barrington's ill-mannered behavior it seems he was also taken by surprise."

"Good evening, Captain Tarrant," said Miss Monday, touching Jack's arm. Miss Tilly was by her side. "How good of you to come all the way down from London to see your protégé."

"My dear Miss Monday," said Tarrant, "Harry's every bit as much your protégé and he'll be so pleased that you traveled all the way up from Cornwall to see his performance." Miss Monday beamed, as a bell sounded to indicate the audience should return to their seats.

Once everyone had settled back in their places, the curtain rose for the second half, although one seat in the sixth row remained conspicuously empty. The death scene brought tears to the eyes of some who had never shed a tear in public, while Miss Monday hadn't wept that much since Harry's voice had broken.

The moment the final curtain fell, the audience rose as one. Harry and Emma were greeted by a storm of applause as they walked to the front of the stage, holding hands, and grown men, who rarely showed their feelings, cheered.

When they turned to bow to each other, Mrs. Barrington smiled, and blushed. "Good heavens, they weren't acting," she said, loud enough for Giles to hear. The same thought had also crossed the minds of Maisie Clifton and Jack Tarrant long before the actors took their final bow.

Mrs. Barrington, Giles and Grace went backstage to find Romeo and Juliet still holding hands as people queued up to lavish praise on them.

"You were great," said Giles, slapping his friend on the back.

"I was all right," said Harry, "but Emma was magnificent."

"So when did all this happen?" he whispered.

"It began in Rome," admitted Harry with an impish grin.

"And to think I sacrificed my Caruso recording, not to mention my gramophone, to bring you two together."

"As well as paying for our first dinner date."

"Where's Papa?" asked Emma, looking around.

Grace was about to tell her sister what had happened when Captain Tarrant appeared.

"Congratulations, my boy," he said. "You were quite splendid."

"Thank you sir," said Harry, "but I don't think you've met the real star of the show."

"No, but let me assure you, young lady, if I was forty years younger, I'd see off any of my rivals."

"You don't have any rivals for my affection," said Emma. "Harry never stops telling me how much you've done for him."

"That's a two-way street," said Jack as Harry spotted his mother and threw his arms around her.

"I'm so proud of you," said Maisie.

"Thank you, Mum. But let me introduce you to Emma Barrington," he said, placing an arm around Emma's waist.

"Now I know why your son is so good-looking," said Emma as she shook Harry's mother by the hand. "May I introduce my mother," she added.

It was a meeting Maisie had thought about for many years, but this was not a scenario that had ever crossed her mind. She was apprehensive as she shook hands with Elizabeth Barrington, but was greeted with such a friendly smile that it quickly became clear she was unaware of any possible connection between them.

"And this is Mr. Atkins," said Maisie, introducing the man who had been sitting beside her during the performance.

Harry had never come across Mr. Atkins before. Looking at his mother's fur coat, he wondered if Atkins was the reason he now had three pairs of shoes.

He was about to speak to Mr. Atkins, when he was interrupted by Dr. Paget, who was keen to introduce him to Professor Henry Wyld. Harry recognized the name at once.

"I hear that you're hoping to come up to Oxford to read English," said Wyld.

"Only if I can be taught by you, sir."

"I see that Romeo's charm has not been left behind on the stage."

"And this is Emma Barrington, sir."

Oxford's Merton Professor of English Language and Literature gave a slight bow. "You were quite magnificent, young lady."

"Thank you, sir," said Emma. "I am also hoping to be taught by you," she added. "I've applied to Somerville for next year."

Jack Tarrant glanced at Mrs. Clifton, and couldn't miss the unmasked horror in her eyes.

"Grandfather," said Giles as the chairman of the governors joined them. "I don't think you know my friend, Harry Clifton."

Sir Walter shook Harry warmly by the hand, before throwing his arms around his granddaughter. "You two made an old man proud," he said.

It was becoming painfully clear to Jack and Maisie that the two "star-crossed lovers" had no idea of the problems they had set in motion.

◄○►

Sir Walter ordered his chauffeur to drive Mrs. Barrington and the children back to the Manor House. Despite Emma's triumph, her mother made no attempt to hide her feelings as the car made its way toward Chew Valley. As they drove through the gates and up to the house, Giles noticed that some lights were still on in the drawing room.

Once the chauffeur had dropped them off, Elizabeth told Giles, Emma and Grace to go to bed, in a tone of voice none of them had heard for many years, while she headed for the drawing room. Giles and Emma reluctantly climbed the wide staircase but sat down on the top step the moment their mother was out of sight, while Grace obediently went to her room. Giles even wondered if his mother had left the door open on purpose.

When Elizabeth entered the room, her husband didn't bother to stand up. She noticed a half-empty bottle of whiskey and a tumbler on the table by his side.

"No doubt you have some explanation for your unforgivable behavior?"

"I don't have to explain anything I do to you."

"Emma somehow managed to rise above your appalling behavior tonight."

Barrington poured himself another tumbler of whiskey and took a gulp. "I have arranged for Emma to be removed from Red Maids immediately. Next term she will be enrolled at a school far enough away to ensure she never sees that boy again."

On the stairs, Emma burst into tears. Giles wrapped an arm around her.

"What can Harry Clifton possibly have done to make you behave in such a shameful way?"

"It's none of your business."

"Of course it's my business," said Elizabeth, trying to remain calm. "We are discussing our daughter and your son's closest friend. If Emma has fallen in love with Harry, and I suspect she has, I can't think of a nicer or more decent young man for her to lose her heart to."

"Harry Clifton is the son of a whore. That's why her husband left her. And I repeat, Emma will never be allowed to come in contact with the little bastard again."

"I'm going to bed before I lose my temper," said Elizabeth. "Don't even think of joining me in your present state."

"I wasn't thinking of joining you in any state," said Barrington, pouring himself another whiskey. "You haven't given me any pleasure in the bedroom for as long as I can remember."

Emma leaped up and ran to her room, locking the door behind her. Giles didn't move.

"You are obviously drunk," said Elizabeth. "We'll discuss this in the morning, when you're sober."

"There will be nothing to discuss in the morning," slurred Barrington as his wife left the room. A moment later his head fell back on the cushion and he began to snore.

◄○►

When Jenkins pulled back the shutters in the drawing room just before eight the following morning he showed no surprise when he found his master slumped in an armchair, sound asleep and still wearing his dinner jacket.

The morning sunlight caused Barrington to stir. He blinked, and peered at the butler before he checked his watch.

"There will be a car coming to pick up Miss Emma in about an hour's time, Jenkins, so be sure she's packed and ready."

"Miss Emma is not here, sir."

"What? Then where is she?" demanded Barrington as he tried to stand up, but wobbled unsteadily for a moment before falling back into the chair.

"I have no idea, sir. She and Mrs. Barrington left the house just after midnight."

38

"WHERE DO YOU think they've gone?" asked Harry, once Giles had described what happened after he had arrived back at the Manor House.

"I've no idea," said Giles. "I was asleep when they left the house. All I could get out of Jenkins was that a taxi had taken them to the station just after midnight."

"And you say your father was drunk when you returned home last night?"

"As a skunk, and he hadn't sobered up by the time I came down for breakfast this morning. He was shouting and screaming at anyone who crossed his path. He even tried to blame me for everything. That was when I decided to go and stay with my grandparents."

"Do you think your grandfather might know where they are?"

"I don't think so, although he didn't seem that surprised when I told him what had happened. Grandma said I could stay with them for as long as I wanted to."

"They can't be in Bristol," said Harry, "if the taxi took them to the station."

"They could be anywhere by now," said Giles.

Neither of them spoke again for some time, until Harry suggested, "Your villa in Tuscany perhaps?"

"Unlikely," said Giles. "That's the first place Papa would think of, so they wouldn't be safe there for long."

"So it has to be somewhere your father would think twice about before going after them." Both boys fell silent again, until

Harry said, "I can think of someone who might know where they are."

"And who's that?"

"Old Jack," said Harry, who still couldn't quite bring himself to call him Captain Tarrant. "I know he's become a friend of your mother's, and she certainly trusts him."

"Do you know where he might be at the moment?"

"Anyone who reads *The Times* knows that," said Harry scornfully.

Giles punched his friend on the arm. "So where is he, clever clogs?"

"He'll be at his office in London. Soho Square, if I remember correctly."

"I've always wanted an excuse to spend a day in London," said Giles. "It's just a pity I've left all my money back at the house."

"Not a problem," said Harry. "I'm flush. That Atkins fellow gave me a fiver, although he did say I was to spend it on books."

"Don't worry," said Giles, "I can think of an alternative plan."

"Like what?" asked Harry, looking hopeful.

"We can just sit around and wait for Emma to write to you."

It was Harry's turn to punch his friend. "OK," he said. "But we'd better get going before anyone finds out what we're up to."

◄◦►

"I'm not in the habit of traveling third class," said Giles as the train pulled out of Temple Meads.

"Well, you'd better get used to it while I'm paying," said Harry.

"So tell me, Harry, what's your friend Captain Tarrant up to? I know the government has appointed him Director of the Citizens Displacement Unit, which sounds pretty impressive, but I'm not sure what he actually does."

"What it says," said Harry. "He's responsible for finding accommodation for refugees, in particular those families who are escaping the tyranny of Nazi Germany. He says he's carrying on his father's work."

"Class act, your friend Captain Tarrant."

"You don't know the half of it," said Harry.

"Tickets, please."

The two boys spent most of the journey trying to work out where Emma and Mrs. Barrington could possibly be, but by the time the train pulled into Paddington Station, they still hadn't come to any firm conclusions.

They took the tube to Leicester Square, emerged into the sunlight and went in search of Soho Square. As they made their way through the West End, Giles became so distracted by the bright neon lights and shop windows full of goods he'd never seen before that Harry occasionally had to remind him why they'd actually come to London.

When they reached Soho Square, neither of them could have missed the steady flow of bedraggled men, women and children, heads bowed, shuffling in and out of a vast building on the far side of the square.

The two young men dressed in blazers, gray flannels and ties looked strangely incongruous as they entered the building and followed the arrows directing them to the third floor. Several of the refugees stood to one side to allow them to pass, assuming they must be there on official business.

Giles and Harry joined the long queue outside the director's office, and might have been there for the rest of the day if a secretary had not come out and spotted them. She walked straight up to Harry and asked if he had come to see Captain Tarrant.

"Yes," said Harry. "He's an old friend."

"I know," said the woman. "I recognized you immediately."

"How?" asked Harry.

"He has a photograph of you on his desk," she said. "Follow me. Captain Tarrant will be delighted to see you."

Old Jack's face lit up when the two boys—he should stop thinking of them as boys, they were now young men—walked into his office. "It's good to see you both," he said, jumping up from behind his desk to greet them. "So who are you running away from this time?" he added with a smile.

"My father," said Giles quietly.

Old Jack crossed the room, closed the door and sat the two young men down on an uncomfortable sofa. He drew up a chair and listened carefully as they told him everything that had happened since they'd seen him at the play the previous evening.

"I saw your father leave the theater, of course," said Old Jack, "but it would never have crossed my mind he could treat your mother and sister quite so appallingly."

"Do you have any idea where they might be, sir?" asked Giles.

"No. But if I had to guess, I'd say they were staying with your grandfather."

"No, sir, I spent the morning with Grandpa, and even he doesn't know where they are."

"I didn't say which grandfather," said Jack.

"Lord Harvey?" said Harry.

"That would be my bet," said Jack. "They'd feel safe with him, and confident that Barrington would think twice before going after them."

"But Grandpa has at least three homes that I'm aware of," said Giles. "So I wouldn't know where to begin looking."

"How stupid of me," said Harry. "I know exactly where he is."

"You do?" said Giles. "Where?"

"At his country estate in Scotland."

"You sound very certain," said Jack.

"Only because last week he dropped Emma a line to explain why he wouldn't be able to attend the school play. It seems he always spends December and January in Scotland. But I'm damned if I can remember the address."

"Mulgelrie Castle, near Mulgelrie, Highlands," said Giles.

"Most impressive," said Jack.

"Not really, sir. It's just years of Mama making me write thank-you letters to all my relations on Boxing Day. But as I've never been to Scotland, I haven't got a clue where it is."

Old Jack got up and removed a large atlas from the bookshelf behind his desk. He looked up Mulgelrie in the index, flicked over several pages and then laid it on the desk in front of him. Running a finger from London to Scotland, he said, "You'll have to take the overnight sleeper to Edinburgh, and then change to a local train for Mulgelrie."

"I don't think we've got enough money left for that," said Harry, checking his wallet.

"Then I'll have to issue you both with rail warrants, won't I?" said Jack. He opened his desk drawer, pulled out a large buff-colored pad and tore off two forms. He filled them in, signed and stamped them. "After all," he added, "you are clearly stateless refugees in search of a home."

"Thank you, sir," said Giles.

"One last word of advice," said Old Jack as he rose from behind his desk. "Hugo Barrington is not a man who likes to be crossed, and while I'm fairly confident he won't do anything to annoy Lord Harvey, that doesn't necessarily apply to you, Harry. So be on your guard until you're safely inside Mulgelrie Castle. Should you at any time come across a man with a limp," he added, "be wary of him. He works for Giles's father. He's clever and resourceful, but more important, he has no allegiance to anyone except his paymaster."

39

GILES AND HARRY were directed to another third-class carriage, but they were both so tired that despite the frequent opening and closing of carriage doors during the night, the clattering of the wheels over points and the regular blast of the train's whistle, they slept soundly.

Giles woke with a start as the train pulled into Newcastle a few minutes before six. He looked out of the window to be greeted by a dull gray day and the sight of lines of soldiers waiting to board the train. A sergeant saluted a second lieutenant who didn't look much older than Giles and asked, "Permission to board the train, sir?" The young man returned his salute and replied in a softer voice, "Carry on, sergeant," and the soldiers began to file onto the train.

The ever-present threat of war, and the question of whether he and Harry would be in uniform before they had the chance to go up to Oxford, was never far from Giles's mind. His uncle Nicholas, whom he'd never met, an officer just like the young man on the platform, had led a platoon of soldiers and been cut down at Ypres. Giles wondered what would be the names of the battlefields that would be commemorated with poppies every year if there was to be another Great War to end all wars.

His thoughts were interrupted when he noticed a passing reflection in the carriage window. He swung round, but the figure was no longer there. Had Captain Tarrant's warning caused him to overreact, or was it just a coincidence?

Giles looked across at Harry, who was still sound asleep, but then he probably hadn't slept for the past two nights. As the train shunted into Berwick-on-Tweed, Giles noticed the same man walking past their compartment. Just a glance, and he was gone; no longer a coincidence. Was he checking to see which station they got off at?

Harry finally woke, blinked and stretched his arms. "I'm starving," he said.

Giles leaned over and whispered, "I think there's someone on this train who's following us."

"What makes you say that?" asked Harry, suddenly wide awake.

"I've seen the same man pass our carriage once too often."

"Tickets, please!"

Giles and Harry handed their warrants to the ticket collector. "How long does this train stop at each station?" he asked once the man had clipped them.

"Now, that all depends on whether we're runnin' on time or not," he replied a little wearily, "but never less than four minutes is the company regulation."

"What is the next station?" asked Giles.

"Dunbar. We should be there in about thirty minutes. But you've both got warrants for Mulgelrie," he added before moving on to the next compartment.

"What was all that about?" asked Harry.

"I'm trying to find out if we're being followed," said Giles, "and the next part of my plan will involve you."

"What role will I be playing this time?" said Harry, sitting on the edge of his seat.

"Certainly not Romeo," said Giles. "When the train stops at Dunbar, I want you to get off while I watch if anyone follows you. Once you're on the platform, walk quickly toward the ticket barrier, then turn back, go into the waiting room and buy a cup of tea. Don't forget you've only got four minutes to be back on board before the train sets off again. And whatever you do, don't look back, or he'll know we're onto him."

"But if there is someone following us, surely he'll be more interested in you than me?"

"I don't think so," said Giles, "and certainly not if Captain

Tarrant is right, because I have a feeling your friend knows more than he's willing to admit."

"That doesn't exactly fill me with confidence," said Harry.

Half an hour later, the train shuddered to a halt in Dunbar. Harry opened the carriage door, stepped out onto the platform and headed for the exit.

Giles caught no more than a glimpse of the man as he hurried after Harry.

"Got you," Giles said, then leaned back and closed his eyes, confident that once the man realized Harry had only got off to buy a cup of tea, he would look in his direction just to make sure he hadn't also left the carriage.

Giles opened his eyes again when Harry returned to the compartment holding a bar of chocolate.

"Well," said Harry, "did you spot anyone?"

"Sure did," said Giles. "In fact, he's just getting back on the train."

"What does he look like?" asked Harry, trying not to sound anxious.

"I only caught a glimpse of him," said Giles, "but I'd say he's around forty, a little over six foot, smartly dressed, with very short hair. The one thing you can't miss is his limp."

"So now we know what we're up against, Sherlock, what next?"

"First, Watson, it's important to remember that we have several things going for us."

"I can't think of one," said Harry.

"Well, for a start, we know we're being followed, but he doesn't know we know. We also know where we're going, which he clearly doesn't. We're also fit, and less than half his age. And with that limp, he won't be able to move all that quickly."

"You're rather good at this," said Harry.

"I do have a built-in advantage," said Giles. "I am my father's son."

◄◦►

By the time the train pulled into Edinburgh Waverley, Giles had gone over his plan with Harry a dozen times. They stepped out of the carriage and walked slowly down the platform toward the barrier.

"Don't even think about looking back," said Giles as he produced his rail warrant, then headed toward a line of taxis.

"The Royal Hotel," said Giles to the cabbie. "And can you let me know if another taxi follows us?" he added before joining Harry in the back.

"Right you are," said the cabbie, as he eased off the rank and joined the traffic.

"How do you know there's a Royal Hotel in Edinburgh?" asked Harry.

"There's a Royal Hotel in every city," said Giles.

A few minutes later the cabbie said, "I cannae be sure, but the next cab off the rank isn't far behind us."

"Good," said Giles. "How much is the fare to the Royal?"

"Two shillings, sir."

"I'll give you four if you can lose him."

The driver immediately put his foot down on the accelerator, causing both of his passengers to be thrown back into their seats. Giles recovered quickly and looked through the back window to see the taxi behind them had also speeded up. They had gained sixty or seventy yards, but Giles realized that advantage wouldn't last for long.

"Cabbie, take the next turning on the left and then slow down for a moment. After we jump out, I want you to continue on to the Royal and don't stop until you reach the hotel." An outstretched arm appeared. Harry placed two florins into the palm.

"When I jump out," said Giles, "just follow me, and then do exactly as I do." Harry nodded.

The taxi swung round the corner and slowed down for a moment just as Giles opened the door. He leaped out on to the pavement, toppled over, quickly picked himself up, then dashed into the nearest shop, throwing himself on the floor. Harry followed only seconds later, slammed the door behind him and was lying by his friend's side just as the second cab shot around the corner.

"Can I help you, sir?" asked a sales assistant, hands on hips, looking down at the two young men lying prostrate on the ground.

"You already have," said Giles, rising to his feet and giving her a warm smile. He brushed himself down, said "Thank you," and left the shop without another word.

When Harry stood up, he came face to face with a slim-waisted mannequin wearing only a corset. He turned bright red, ran out of the shop and joined Giles on the pavement.

"I don't expect the man with the limp will be booking into the Royal for the night," said Giles, "so we'd better get moving."

"Agreed," said Harry as Giles flagged down another cab. "Waverley station," he said before climbing into the back.

"Where did you learn how to do all that?" asked Harry in admiration, as they headed back in the direction of the station.

"You know, Harry, you should read a little less Joseph Conrad and a little more John Buchan if you want to know how to travel in Scotland while being pursued by a fiendish foe."

The journey to Mulgelrie was considerably slower and far less exciting than the one to Edinburgh had been, and there was certainly no sign of any man with a limp. When the engine finally dragged its four carriages and two passengers into the little station, the sun had already disappeared behind the highest mountain. The station master was standing by the exit waiting to check their tickets when they got off the last train that day.

"Any hope of getting a taxi?" Giles asked as they handed over their warrants.

"No, sir," replied the station master. "Jock goes home for tea around six o'clock, and he'll nae be back for another hour."

Giles thought twice about explaining the logic of Jock's actions to the station master, before he asked, "Then perhaps you'd be kind enough to tell us how we can get to Mulgelrie Castle."

"You'll have to walk," said the station master helpfully.

"And which direction might it be?" asked Giles, trying not to sound exasperated.

"It's about three miles up yonder," the man said, pointing up the hill. "You cannae miss it."

"Up yonder" turned out to be the only accurate piece of

information the station master had offered, because after the two of them had been walking for over an hour, it was pitch black and there was still no sign of any castle.

Giles was beginning to wonder if they were going to have to spend their first night in the Highlands sleeping in a field with only a flock of sheep to keep them company, when Harry shouted, "There it is!"

Giles stared through the misty gloom and although he still couldn't quite make out the outline of a castle, his spirits were lifted by flickering lights coming from several windows. They trudged on until they reached a massive pair of wrought-iron gates which had not been locked. As they made their way up the long driveway Giles could hear barking, but he couldn't see any dogs. After about another mile they came to a bridge spanning a moat, and on the far side, a heavy oak door that didn't look as if it welcomed strangers.

"Leave the talking to me," said Giles as they staggered across the bridge and came to a halt outside the door.

Giles banged three times with the side of his fist, and within moments the door was pulled open to reveal a giant of a man dressed in a kilt with a dark lovat jacket, white shirt and white bow tie.

The head steward looked down on the weary, bedraggled objects that stood in front of him. "Good evening, Mr. Giles," he said, although Giles had never set eyes on the man before. "His lordship has been expecting you for some time, and wondered if you would care to join him for dinner?"

40

LORD HARVEY HANDED the telegram to Giles and chuckled. "Sent by our mutual friend, Captain Tarrant. He only turned out to be wrong about what time you'd arrive."

"We had to walk all the way from the station," protested Giles between mouthfuls.

"Yes, I did consider sending the car to meet you off the last train," said Lord Harvey, "but there's nothing like a bracing Highland walk to work up a good appetite."

Harry smiled. He'd hardly spoken since they'd come down for dinner, and as Emma had been placed at the far end of the table he had to satisfy himself with the occasional wistful gaze, wondering if they'd ever be left alone together.

The first course was a thick Highland broth, which Harry finished a little too quickly, but when Giles was served a second helping, he also allowed his bowl to be refilled. Harry would have asked for a third helping if everyone else hadn't continued making polite conversation while they waited for him and Giles to finish so that the main course could be served.

"There's no need for either of you to be anxious about anyone wondering where you are," said Lord Harvey, "because I've already sent telegrams to Sir Walter and to Mrs. Clifton, to assure them you are both safe and well. I didn't bother to get in touch with your father, Giles," he added without further comment. Giles glanced across the table to see his mother purse her lips.

Moments later the dining room doors swung open and several liveried servants entered and whisked away the soup bowls. Three more servants followed, carrying silver salvers on which rested what looked to Harry like six small chickens.

"I do hope you like grouse, Mr. Clifton," said Lord Harvey, the first person ever to call him Mr., as a bird was placed in front of him. "I shot these myself."

Harry couldn't think of an appropriate response. He watched as Giles picked up his knife and fork and began to slice tiny pieces off the bird, bringing back memories of their first meal together at St. Bede's. By the time the plates were cleared, Harry had only managed about three morsels and wondered how old he would have to be before he could say, "No, thank you, I'd prefer another bowl of soup."

Things improved a little when a large plate of different fruits, some of which Harry had never seen before, was placed in the center of the table. He would have liked to ask his host their names and the countries they originated from, but memories of his first banana came to mind, when he had definitely slipped. He satisfied himself with following Giles's lead, watching carefully to see which had to be peeled, which had to be cut and which you could simply take a bite out of.

When he'd finished, a servant appeared and placed a bowl of water by the side of his plate. He was just about to pick it up and drink it, when he saw Lady Harvey place her fingers in hers and moments later a servant passed her a linen napkin so she could dry her hands. Harry dipped his fingers in the water and, like magic, a napkin immediately appeared.

After dinner, the ladies retired to the drawing room. Harry wanted to join them so he could at last catch up with Emma and tell her everything that had happened since she'd poisoned herself. But no sooner had she left the room than Lord Harvey sat back down, a sign for the under-butler to offer his lordship a cigar while another servant poured him a large glass of Cognac.

Once he'd taken a sip, he nodded and glasses were placed in front of Giles and Harry. The butler closed the humidor before filling their glasses with brandy.

"Well," said Lord Harvey after two or three luxuriant puffs. "Am I to understand that you are both hoping to go up to Oxford?"

"Harry's a safe bet," said Giles. "But I'll need to score a couple of centuries during the summer, and preferably one at Lord's if the examiners are going to overlook my more obvious deficiencies."

"Giles is being modest, sir," said Harry. "He has just as good a chance of being offered a place as I do. After all, he's not only the captain of cricket, he's also school captain."

"Well, if you are successful, I can assure you that you'll experience three of the happiest years of your life. That's assuming Herr Hitler isn't foolish enough to insist on a replay of the last war in the vain hope that he'll be able to reverse the result."

The three of them raised their glasses and Harry took his first sip of brandy. He didn't like the taste and was wondering if it would be thought discourteous if he didn't finish it, when Lord Harvey came to his rescue.

"Perhaps it's time for us to join the ladies," he said, draining his glass. He put his cigar in an ashtray, rose from his place and marched out of the dining room, not waiting for a second opinion. The two young men followed him across the hall and into the drawing room.

Lord Harvey took the seat next to Elizabeth, while Giles winked at Harry and went across to join his grandmother. Harry sat next to Emma on the sofa.

"How gallant of you to come all this way, Harry," she said, touching his hand.

"I'm so sorry about what happened after the play. I only hope I wasn't responsible for causing the problem in the first place."

"How could you possibly be responsible, Harry? You've never

done anything that could have caused my father... Mama that way."

"But it's no secret that your father doesn't think w... together, even on stage."

"Let's talk about it tomorrow morning," Emma... "We can go for a long walk in the hills and be on our o... only the Highland cattle to overhear us."

"I'll look forward to that," said Harry. He would have... hold her hand, but there were too many eyes continually... ing in their direction.

"You two young men must be very tired after such an ex... ing journey," said Lady Harvey. "Why don't you both go o... bed, and we'll see you at breakfast in the morning."

Harry didn't want to go to bed; he wanted to stay with Em... and try to find out if she'd discovered why her father was so o... posed to them being together. But Giles rose immediately, kisse... his grandmother and mother on the cheek and said goodnigh... leaving Harry with no choice but to join him. He leaned across... and kissed Emma on the cheek, thanked his host for a wonderful... evening and followed Giles out of the room.

As they walked down the hall, Harry paused to admire a paint- ing of a bowl of fruit by an artist called Peploe when Emma came dashing out of the drawing room, threw her arms around his neck and kissed him gently on the lips.

Giles continued up the stairs as if he hadn't noticed, while Harry kept his eyes on the drawing-room door. Emma broke away when she heard it opening behind her.

"'Good night, good night, parting is such sweet sorrow,'" she whispered.

"'That I shall say good night till it be morrow,'" Harry replied.

◄○►

"Where are you two off to?" asked Elizabeth Barrington as she came out of the breakfast room.

"We're going to climb Crag Cowen," said Emma. "Don't wait up, because you may never see us again."

Her mother laughed. "Then make sure you wrap up well,

cause even the sheep catch cold in the Highlands." She waited til Harry had closed the door behind them before she added, Giles, your grandfather wishes to see us in his study at ten o'clock." t sounded to Giles more like a command than a request.

"Yes, Mother," he said, before looking through the window and watching Harry and Emma walking down the path toward Crag Cowen. They'd only gone a few yards before Emma took Harry's hand. Giles smiled as they turned the corner and disappeared behind a row of pines.

When the clock in the hall began to strike, Giles had to walk quickly along the corridor to make sure he reached his grandfather's study before the tenth chime. His grandparents and his mother stopped talking the moment he entered the room. They had clearly been waiting for him.

"Have a seat, dear boy," said his grandfather.

"Thank you, sir," Giles replied, and sat down on a chair between his mother and his grandmother.

"I suppose this would best be described as a council of war," said Lord Harvey, looking up from his high-backed leather chair as if he were addressing a board meeting. "I'll try to bring everyone up to date before we decide what the best course of action should be." Giles was flattered that his grandfather now considered him to be a full member of the family board.

"I telephoned Walter last night. He was just as appalled by Hugo's conduct at the play as I was when Elizabeth told me about it, although I had to fill him in on what happened when she returned to the Manor House." Giles's mother bowed her head, but didn't interrupt. "I went on to tell him that I'd had a long talk with my daughter, and that we felt there were only two possible courses of action."

Giles sat back in his chair, but didn't relax.

"I left Walter in no doubt that if Elizabeth were even to consider returning to the Manor House, it would be necessary for Hugo to make several concessions. First, he must apologize unequivocally for his appalling behavior."

Giles's grandmother nodded in agreement.

"Second, he will never again, and I repeated, never again,

suggest that Emma should be taken out of her school, and he will in future fully support her efforts to gain a place at Oxford. God knows it's hard enough for a young man to make the grade nowadays, but it's damn nigh impossible for a woman.

"My third and most important demand, and on this I was quite adamant, is that he explain to us all why he continues to treat Harry Clifton so appallingly. I suspect it might have something to do with Harry's uncle stealing from Hugo. The sins of the father are one thing, but an uncle . . . I refuse to accept, as he has so often claimed to Elizabeth, that he considers Clifton unworthy to mix with his children simply because his father was a docker and his mother is a waitress. Perhaps Hugo has forgotten that my grandfather was a jobbing clerk in a firm of wine merchants, while his own grandfather left school at the age of twelve and started out as a docker like young Clifton's father, and just in case anyone has forgotten, I'm the first Lord Harvey in this family, and you don't get much more nouveau than that."

Giles wanted to cheer.

"Now, none of us can have failed to notice," continued Lord Harvey, "how Emma and Harry feel about each other, which is hardly surprising as they are two exceptional young people. If, in the fullness of time, their relationship blossoms, no one would be more delighted than Victoria and I. On that subject, Walter was in full agreement with me."

Giles smiled. He liked the idea of Harry becoming a member of the family, even though he didn't believe his father would ever accept it.

"I told Walter," continued his grandfather, "that if Hugo felt unable to abide by these terms, Elizabeth would be left with no choice but to institute divorce proceedings immediately. I would also have to resign from the board of Barrington's, and make public my reasons for doing so."

Giles was saddened by this, as he knew there had never been a divorce in either family.

"Walter kindly agreed to get back to me in the next few days, after he's had a chance to talk things over with his son, but he did tell me that Hugo has already promised to stop drinking, and that he appears to be genuinely contrite. Let me finish by reminding you that this is a family matter and should not in any circumstances be discussed with outsiders. We must hope that this proves to be nothing more than an unfortunate incident that will soon be forgotten."

◄○►

The following morning, Giles's father telephoned and asked to speak to him. He apologized profusely, saying how sorry he was to have blamed Giles for something that was entirely his own fault. He begged Giles to do everything in his power to convince his mother and Emma to return to Gloucestershire so they could all spend Christmas together at the Manor House. He also hoped that, as his father-in-law had suggested, the incident would be quickly forgotten. He made no mention of Harry Clifton.

41

ONCE THEY'D DISEMBARKED from the train at Temple Meads, Giles and his mother waited in the car while Emma said goodbye to Harry.

"They've just spent the last nine days together," said Giles. "Have they forgotten that they'll be seeing each other again tomorrow?"

"And probably the next day," said Giles's mother. "But try not to forget, unlikely though it might seem, that it could even happen to you one day."

Emma eventually joined them, but when they drove off she continued to look out of the back window and didn't stop waving until Harry was out of sight.

Giles was keen to get home and finally discover what it was that Harry could have done to make his father treat him so cruelly over the years. Surely it couldn't be worse than stealing from the tuck shop or deliberately failing your exams. He'd considered a dozen possibilities but none of them made any sense. Now, at last, he hoped he was going to find out the truth. He glanced across at his mother. Although she rarely displayed her emotions, she was clearly becoming more and more agitated as they approached Chew Valley.

Giles's father was standing on the top step waiting to greet them when the car drew up outside the house; no sign of Jenkins. He apologized immediately to Elizabeth and then the children, before telling them how much he'd missed them.

"Tea is set up in the drawing room," he said. "Please join me there as soon as you're ready."

Giles was the first back downstairs and he sat uneasily in a chair opposite his father. While they waited for his mother and Emma to join them, his father confined himself to asking Giles how he'd enjoyed Scotland, and to explain that Nanny had taken Grace into Bristol to buy her school uniform. At no time did he mention Harry. When Giles's mother and sister entered the room a few minutes later, his father immediately stood up. Once they were seated, he poured them all a cup of tea. He clearly didn't want any servants to overhear what he was about to reveal.

Once everyone had settled, Giles's father sat on the edge of his seat and began to speak softly.

"Let me begin by saying to all three of you how unacceptable my behavior was on the night of what everyone has described as Emma's great triumph. That your father was not there for the curtain call was bad enough, Emma," he said, looking directly at his daughter, "but the way I treated your mother when you returned home that night was quite unforgivable, and I realize it may take some time before such a deep wound can be healed."

Hugo Barrington placed his head in his hands and Giles noticed that he was trembling. He eventually steadied himself.

"You have all, for different reasons, asked to know why I have treated Harry Clifton so badly over the years. It is true that I cannot bear to be in his presence, but the fault is entirely of my own making. When you learn the reason, you might begin to understand, and possibly even sympathize."

Giles glanced at his mother, who was sitting stiffly in her chair. There was no way of telling how she felt.

"Many years ago," continued Barrington, "when I first became managing director of the company, I convinced the board that we should branch out into shipbuilding, despite my father's reservations. I signed a contract with a Canadian company to build a merchant ship called the *Maple Leaf*. That not only turned out to be a financial disaster for the company, but a personal catastrophe for me, from which I have never fully recovered and doubt if I ever will. Allow me to explain.

"One afternoon a docker burst into my office insisting that his work mate was trapped inside the hull of the *Maple Leaf* and if I didn't give the order to break it open, his life would be lost. Naturally I went down to the dock immediately and the ganger assured me there was absolutely no truth in the story. However, I insisted the men down tools so that we could listen for any sound coming from inside the hull. I waited for some considerable time, but as there was no sound, I gave the order for them to return to work, as we were already several weeks behind schedule.

"I assumed the docker in question would sign on for his usual shift the following day. But not only did he not turn up, he was never seen again. The possibility of his death has been on my conscience ever since." He paused, raised his head and said, "That man's name was Arthur Clifton, and Harry is his only son."

Emma began to sob.

"I want you to imagine, if you possibly can, what I go through whenever I see that young man, and how he would feel were he ever to find out that I might have been responsible for his father's death. That Harry Clifton has become Giles's closest friend, and fallen in love with my daughter, is the stuff of a Greek tragedy."

Once again, he buried his head in his hands and didn't speak for some time. When he finally looked up, he said, "If you wish to ask me any questions, I will do my best to answer them."

Giles waited for his mother to speak first. "Were you responsible for sending an innocent man to jail for a crime he did not commit?" Elizabeth asked quietly.

"No, my dear," said Barrington. "I hope you know me well enough to realize I am not capable of such a thing. Stan Tancock was a common thief, who broke into my office and robbed me. Because he was Arthur Clifton's brother-in-law, and for no other reason, I gave him back his job the day he was released from prison." Elizabeth smiled for the first time.

"Father, I wonder if I might be allowed to ask a question," said Giles.

"Yes, of course."

"Did you have Harry and me followed when we traveled up to Scotland?"

"Yes, I did, Giles. I was desperate to find out where your mother and Emma were so I could apologize to them for my disgraceful behavior. Please try to forgive me."

Everyone turned their attention to Emma, who hadn't yet spoken. When she did, her words took them all by surprise. "You'll have to tell Harry everything you've told us," she whispered, "and if he is willing to forgive you, you must then welcome him into our family."

"I would be delighted to welcome him into the family, my darling, although it would be understandable if he never wanted to speak to me again. But I cannot tell him the truth about what happened to his father."

"Why not?" demanded Emma.

"Because Harry's mother has made it clear that she does not want him ever to find out how his father died, as he has been brought up to believe he was a brave man who was killed in the war. Up until this moment, I have kept my promise never to reveal to anyone what took place on that dreadful day."

Elizabeth Barrington rose, walked across to her husband and kissed him gently. Barrington broke down and sobbed. A moment later Giles joined his parents and placed an arm around his father's shoulders.

Emma didn't move.

42

"HAS YOUR MOTHER always been that good-looking?" said Giles. "Or am I just getting older?"

"I've no idea," said Harry. "All I can say is that *your* mother always looks so elegant."

"Much as I love the dear creature, she looks positively prehistoric compared to yours," said Giles as Elizabeth Barrington, parasol in one hand and handbag in the other, bore down upon them.

Giles, like every other boy, had been dreading what outfit his mother might turn up in. As for the selection of hats, it was worse than Ascot, with every mother and daughter trying to outdo each other.

Harry looked more carefully at his mother, who was chatting to Dr. Paget. He had to admit that she was attracting more attention than most of the other mothers, which he found a little embarrassing. But he was pleased that she no longer appeared to be burdened by financial worries, and assumed the man standing on her right had something to do with that.

However grateful he was to Mr. Atkins, he didn't care for the idea of him becoming his stepfather. Mr. Barrington may in the past have been over-zealous about his daughter, but Harry could not deny that he felt just as protective when it came to his mother.

She had recently told him that Mr. Frampton was so pleased with her work at the hotel that he had promoted her to night supervisor and given her another pay raise. And certainly Harry no longer had to wait for his trousers to be too short before they were replaced. But even he had been surprised when she hadn't commented about the cost of his traveling to Rome with the Arts Appreciation Society.

"How nice to see you, Harry, on your day of triumph," said Mrs. Barrington. "Two prizes, if I remember correctly. I'm only sorry that Emma can't be with us to share in your glory, but as Miss Webb pointed out, her gels cannot be expected to take the morning off for someone else's speech day, even if her brother is the school captain."

Mr. Barrington came across to join them, and Giles watched his father carefully as he shook hands with Harry. There was still a distinct lack of warmth on his father's part, although no one could deny that he was making every effort to conceal it.

"So, when are you expecting to hear from Oxford, Harry?" asked Barrington.

"Some time next week, sir."

"I'm confident they'll offer you a place, although I suspect it will be a close-run thing for Giles."

"Don't forget he's also had his moment of glory," said Harry.

"I don't recall that," said Mrs. Barrington.

"I think Harry's referring to the century I scored at Lord's, Mama."

"Admirable though that might be, for the life of me I can't see how it will help you get into Oxford," said his father.

"Normally I would agree with you, Papa," said Giles, "were it not for the fact that the Professor of History was sitting next to the President of the MCC at the time."

The laughter that followed was drowned out by the sound of bells. The boys began to move rapidly in the direction of the great hall, with their parents following dutifully a few paces behind them.

Giles and Harry took their places among the prefects and prize-winners in the front three rows.

"Do you recall our first day at St. Bede's?" said Harry, "when we all sat in the front row, quite terrified of Dr. Oakshott?"

"I was never terrified of the Shot," said Giles.

"No, of course you weren't," said Harry.

"But I do remember when we came down for breakfast on the first morning that you licked your porridge bowl."

"And I remember you swore you'd never mention it again," whispered Harry.

"And I promise I never will again," replied Giles not whispering. "What was the name of that frightful bully who slippered you on our first night?"

"Fisher," said Harry. "And it was the second night."

"Wonder what he's up to now?"

"He's probably running a Nazi youth camp."

"Then that's a good enough reason to go to war," said Giles as everyone in the hall rose to welcome the chairman of the governors and his board.

The crocodile of smartly dressed men made their way slowly down the aisle and up on to the stage. The last person to take his seat was Mr. Barton, the headmaster, but not before he'd ushered the guest of honor into the center chair in the front row.

Once everyone had settled, the headmaster rose to welcome the parents and guests, before delivering the school's annual report. He began by describing 1938 as a vintage year, and for the next twenty minutes he elaborated on this claim, giving details of the school's academic and sporting achievements. He ended by inviting the Right Honorable Winston Churchill MP, Chancellor of Bristol University and Member of Parliament for Epping, to address the school and present the prizes.

Mr. Churchill rose slowly from his place and stared down at the audience for some time before he began.

"Some guests of honor begin their speeches by telling their audience that they never won any prizes when they were at school, in fact they were always bottom of the class. I cannot make such a claim: although I certainly never won a prize, at least I was never bottom of the class—I was second to bottom." The boys roared and cheered, while the masters smiled. Only Deakins remained unmoved.

The moment the laughter had subsided, Churchill scowled. "Our nation today faces another of those great moments in history, when the British people may once again be asked to decide the fate of the free world. Many of you present in this great hall . . ." He lowered his voice and concentrated his attention on the rows of boys seated in front of him, not once looking in the direction of their parents.

"Those of us who lived through the Great War will never forget the tragic loss of life our nation suffered, and the effect it has had on an entire generation. Of the twenty boys in my class at Harrow who went on to serve in the front line, only three of them lived long enough to cast a vote. I only hope that whoever delivers this speech in twenty years' time will not need to refer to that barbaric and unnecessary waste of life as the *First* World War. With that single hope, I wish you all long, happy and successful lives."

Giles was among the first to rise and give the guest of honor a standing ovation as he returned to his seat. He felt that if Britain were left with no choice but to go to war, this was the one man who should take over from Neville Chamberlain and become Prime Minister. When everyone had resumed their places some minutes later, the headmaster invited Mr. Churchill to present the prizes.

Giles and Harry cheered when Mr. Barton not only announced that Deakins was scholar of the year but added, "This morning I received a telegram from the Master of Balliol College, Oxford, to say that Deakins has been awarded the senior classics scholarship. I might add," continued Mr. Barton, "that he is the first boy to achieve this distinction in the school's four-hundred-year history."

Giles and Harry were on their feet immediately, as a gangly, six-foot-two-inch boy with pebble glasses, wearing a suit that hung on him as if it had never left its coathanger, made his way slowly up onto the stage. Mr. Deakins wanted to leap up and take a photograph of his son being presented with his prize by Mr. Churchill, but didn't do so, for fear it might be frowned upon.

Harry received a warm reception when he was awarded the English prize, as well as the school reading prize. The headmaster added, "None of us will ever forget his performance as

Romeo. Let us all hope that Harry will be among those who receive a telegram next week offering them a place at Oxford."

When Mr. Churchill presented Harry with his prize, he whispered, "I never went to university. I only wish I had. Let's hope you receive that telegram, Clifton. Good luck."

"Thank you, sir," said Harry.

But the biggest cheer of the day was reserved for Giles Barrington when he went up to receive the headmaster's prize for captain of the school and captain of cricket. To the guest of honor's surprise, the chairman of the governors leaped up from his place and shook hands with Giles before he reached Mr. Churchill.

"My grandson, sir," Sir Walter explained with considerable pride.

Churchill smiled, gripped Giles by the hand and, looking up at him, said, "Be sure you serve your country with the same distinction with which you have clearly served your school."

That was the moment when Giles knew exactly what he would do if Britain went to war.

Once the ceremony was over, the boys, parents and masters rose as one to sing "Carmen Bristoliense."

> *Sit clarior, sit dignior, quotquot labuntur menses:*
> *Sit primus nobis hic decor, Sumus Bristolienses.*

Once the last chorus had rung out, the headmaster led the guest of honor and his staff off the stage, out of the great hall and into the afternoon sunshine. Moments later, everyone else poured out onto the lawn to join them for tea. Three boys in particular were surrounded by well-wishers, as well as by a bevy of sisters who thought Giles was "just cute."

"This is the proudest day of my life," said Harry's mother as she embraced him.

"I know how you feel, Mrs. Clifton," said Old Jack, shaking Harry by the hand. "I only wish Miss Monday had lived long enough to see you today, because I don't doubt it would have also been the happiest day of her life."

Mr. Holcombe stood to one side and waited patiently to add his congratulations. Harry introduced him to Captain Tarrant, unaware that they were old friends.

When the band had stopped playing, and the captains and the kings had departed, Giles, Harry and Deakins sat alone on the grass and reminisced about things past, no longer schoolboys.

43

A TELEGRAM WAS delivered to Harry's study by a junior boy on Thursday afternoon. Giles and Deakins waited patiently for him to open it, but instead he handed the little brown envelope to Giles.

"Passing the buck again," said Giles as he ripped it open. He couldn't hide his surprise when he read the contents.

"You failed," said Giles, sounding shocked. Harry collapsed back into his chair. "To win a scholarship. However," Giles added, reading the telegram aloud, "*We are delighted to offer you an exhibition to Brasenose College, Oxford. Many congratulations. Details to follow in the next few days. W.T.S. Stallybrass, Principal.* Not bad, but you're clearly not in Deakins's class."

"And which class are you in?" said Harry, immediately regretting his words.

"One scholar, one exhibitionist—"

"Exhibitioner," corrected Deakins.

"And one commoner," said Giles, ignoring his friend. "Has a nice ring about it."

Eleven other telegrams were delivered to successful applicants from Bristol Grammar School that day, but none was addressed to Giles Barrington.

"You should let your mother know," said Giles as they walked into the hall for supper. "She probably hasn't slept all week worrying about it."

Harry looked at his watch. "It's too late, she'll already have left for work. I won't be able to tell her until tomorrow morning."

"Why don't we go and surprise her at the hotel?" said Giles.

"I can't do that. She'd think it unprofessional to interrupt her while she's at work, and I don't feel I can make an exception, even for this," he said, waving the telegram triumphantly.

"But don't you think she has a right to know?" said Giles. "After all, she's sacrificed everything to make it possible for you. Frankly, if they offered me a place at Oxford, I'd interrupt Mama even if she was addressing the Mothers' Union. Don't you agree, Deakins?"

Deakins removed his glasses and began to polish them with a handkerchief, always a sign that he was deep in thought. "I'd ask Paget's opinion, and if he raises no objection—"

"Good idea," said Giles. "Let's go and see the Page."

"Are you coming, Deakins?" asked Harry, but then noticed that Deakins's glasses had been returned to the end of his nose, a sign that he had been transported to another world.

"Many congratulations," said Dr. Paget once he'd read the telegram. "And well deserved, if I may say so."

"Thank you, sir," said Harry. "I wondered if it would be possible for me to go to the Royal Hotel so I can tell my mother the news?"

"I can't see any reason why not, Clifton."

"Can I trot along with him?" asked Giles innocently.

Paget hesitated. "Yes, you can, Barrington. But don't even think about having a drink or smoking while you're in the hotel."

"Not even one glass of champagne, sir?"

"No, Barrington, not even a glass of cider," said Paget firmly.

As the two young men strolled out of the school gates, they passed a lamplighter who was standing on his bicycle, stretching up to light a street lamp. They chatted about the summer hols, when Harry would be joining Giles's family in Tuscany for the first time, and agreed they would have to be back in time to see the Australians when they played against Gloucestershire at the county ground. They discussed the possibility, or, according to Harry, the probability, of war being declared now that everyone had been issued with a gas mask. But neither of them touched on another subject that was on both of their minds: would Giles be joining Harry and Deakins at Oxford in September?

As they approached the hotel, Harry had second thoughts about interrupting his mother while she was at work, but Giles had already barged through the revolving doors and was standing in the foyer waiting for him.

"It will only take a couple of minutes," said Giles when Harry joined him. "Just tell her the good news and we can go straight back to school." Harry nodded.

Giles asked the doorman where the Palm Court was, and he directed them to a raised area at the far end of the foyer. After climbing the half dozen steps, Giles walked up to the desk and, keeping his voice low, asked the receptionist, "Can we have a quick word with Mrs. Clifton?"

"Mrs. Clifton?" asked the girl. "Has she made a reservation?" She ran her finger down a list of bookings.

"No, she works here," said Giles.

"Oh, I'm new here," said the girl, "but I'll just ask one of the waitresses. They're bound to know."

"Thank you."

Harry remained on the bottom step, his eyes searching the room for his mother.

"Hattie," the receptionist asked a passing waitress, "does a Mrs. Clifton work here?"

"Not any longer she doesn't," came back the immediate reply. "She left a couple of years ago. Haven't heard a dicky-bird from her since."

"There must be some mistake," said Harry, bounding up the steps to join his friend.

"Do you have any idea where we might find her?" asked Giles, keeping his voice low.

"No," said Hattie. "But you could have a word with Doug, the night porter. He's been here forever."

"Thank you," said Giles and, turning to Harry, added, "There's bound to be a simple explanation, but if you'd prefer to leave it . . ."

"No, let's find out if Doug knows where she is."

Giles walked slowly across to the porter's desk, giving Harry enough time to change his mind, but he didn't say a word. "Are you Doug?" he asked a man dressed in a faded blue frockcoat with buttons that no longer shone.

"I am, sir," he replied. "How can I help you?"

"We're looking for Mrs. Clifton."

"Maisie don't work here any longer, sir. She must have left at least a couple of years back."

"Do you know where she is working now?"

"I've no idea, sir."

Giles took out his purse, extracted half a crown and placed it on the counter. The porter eyed it for some time before he spoke again. "It's just possible you'll find her at Eddie's Nightclub."

"Eddie Atkins?" inquired Harry.

"I believe that's correct, sir."

"Well, that explains it," said Harry. "And where is Eddie's Nightclub?"

"Welsh Back, sir," replied the porter as he pocketed the half a crown.

Harry left the hotel without another word and jumped into the back of a waiting cab. Giles got in beside him. "Don't you think we should get back to school?" said Giles, looking at his watch. "You can always tell your mother in the morning."

Harry shook his head. "It was you who said you'd interrupt your mother even if she was addressing the Mothers' Union," Harry reminded him. "Eddie's Nightclub, Welsh Back, please, cabbie," he said firmly.

Harry didn't speak during the short journey. When the cab turned into a dark alley and came to a halt outside Eddie's, he got out and walked toward the entrance.

Harry banged firmly on the door. A shutter slid open and a pair of eyes stared at the two young men. "The entrance fee is five shillings each," said a voice behind the eyes. Giles pushed a ten-shilling note through the hole. The door swung open immediately.

The two of them made their way down a dimly lit staircase to the basement. Giles saw her first and quickly turned to leave, but it was too late. Harry was staring, transfixed, at a row of girls seated on stools at the bar, some chatting to men, others on their own. One of them, wearing a white see-through blouse, a short black leather skirt and black stockings, approached them and said, "Can I help you, gents?"

Harry ignored her. His eyes had settled on a woman at the far end of the bar who was listening intently to an older man who had his hand on her thigh. The girl looked to see who he was staring at. "I must say, you know class when you see it," she said. "Mind you, Maisie can be choosy, and I have to warn you, she doesn't come cheap."

Harry turned and bolted back up the steps, pulled open the door and ran out onto the street, with Giles chasing after him. Once Harry was on the pavement, he fell to his knees and was violently sick. Giles knelt and put his arm around his friend, trying to comfort him.

A man who had been standing in the shadows on the other side of the road limped away.

EMMA BARRINGTON

1932–1939

44

I'll never forget the first time I saw him.

He came to tea at the Manor House to celebrate my brother's twelfth birthday. He was so quiet and reserved that I wondered how he could possibly be Giles's best friend. The other one, Deakins, was really strange. He never stopped eating and hardly said a word all afternoon.

And then Harry spoke, a soft, gentle voice that made you want to listen. The birthday party had apparently been going swimmingly until my father burst into the room, and then he hardly spoke again. I'd never known my father to be so off-hand with anyone, and I couldn't understand why he should behave in that way toward a complete stranger. But even more inexplicable was Papa's reaction when he asked Harry when his birthday was. How could such an innocuous question bring on such an extreme reaction? A moment later my father got up and left the room, without even saying goodbye to Giles and his guests. I could see that Mama was embarrassed by his behavior, although she poured another cup of tea and pretended not to notice.

A few minutes later, my brother and his two friends left to go back to school. He turned and smiled at me before leaving, but just like my mother, I pretended not to notice. But when the front door closed I stood by the drawing-room window and watched as the car disappeared down the driveway and out of sight. I thought I saw him looking out of the back window, but I couldn't be sure.

After they had left, Mama went straight to my father's study and I could hear raised voices, which had recently become more and more common. When she came back out, she smiled at me as if nothing unusual had happened.

"What's the name of Giles's best friend?" I asked.

"Harry Clifton," she replied.

—◁◦▷—

The next time I saw Harry Clifton was at the Advent carol service at St. Mary Redcliffe. He sang "O Little Town of Bethlehem," and my best friend, Jessica Braithwaite, accused me of swooning as if he was the new Bing Crosby. I didn't bother to deny it. I saw him chatting to Giles after the service and I would have liked to congratulate him, but Papa seemed to be in a hurry to get home. As we left, I saw his nanny giving him a huge hug.

I was also at St. Mary Redcliffe the evening his voice broke, but at the time I didn't understand why so many heads were turning and some members of the congregation began to whisper among themselves. All I know is that I never heard him sing again.

When Giles was driven to the grammar school on his first day, I begged my mother to let me go along, but only because I wanted to meet Harry. But my father wouldn't hear of it, and despite my bursting into controlled tears, they still left me standing on the top step with my younger sister Grace. I knew Papa was cross about Giles not being offered a place at Eton, something I still don't understand, because a lot of boys more stupid than my brother passed the exam. Mama didn't seem to mind which school Giles went to, whereas I was delighted he was going to Bristol Grammar, because it meant I'd have a better chance of seeing Harry again.

In fact I must have seen him at least a dozen times during the next three years, but he was never able to recall any of those occasions, until we met up in Rome.

The family were all staying at our villa in Tuscany that summer when Giles took me to one side and said he needed to ask my advice. He only ever did that when he wanted something. But this time it turned out to be something I wanted just as much as he did.

"So what are you expecting me to do this time?" I asked.

"I need an excuse to go into Rome tomorrow," he said, "because I'm meant to be meeting up with Harry."

"Harry who?" I said, feigning indifference.

"Harry Clifton, stupid. He's on a school trip to Rome and I promised to get away and spend the day with him." He didn't need to spell out that Papa wouldn't have approved. "All you have to do," he continued, "is ask Mama if she could take you to Rome for the day."

"But she'll need to know why I want to go into Rome."

"Tell her you've always wanted to visit the Villa Borghese."

"Why the Villa Borghese?"

"Because that's where Harry will be at ten o'clock tomorrow morning."

"But what happens if Mama agrees to take me? Then you'll be stymied."

"She won't. They're having lunch with the Hendersons in Arezzo tomorrow, so I'll volunteer to be your chaperone."

"And what do I get in exchange?" I demanded, as I didn't want Giles to know how keen I was to see Harry.

"My gramophone," he said.

"For keeps, or just to borrow?"

Giles didn't speak for some time. "Forever," he said reluctantly.

"Hand it over now," I said, "or you can forget it." To my surprise he did.

I was even more amazed when, the next day, my mother fell for his little ploy. Giles didn't even have to offer to act as my chaperone; Papa insisted that he accompany me. My deceitful brother made a show of protesting, but finally gave in.

I rose early the following morning and spent some considerable time thinking about what I should wear. It would have to be fairly conservative if my mother wasn't to become suspicious, but on the other hand I wanted to make sure Harry noticed me.

While we were on the train to Rome, I disappeared into the lavatory and put on a pair of mother's silk stockings and just a touch of lipstick, not enough for Giles to notice.

Once we'd checked into our hotel, Giles wanted to leave immediately for the Villa Borghese. So did I.

As we walked through the gardens and up toward the villa, a soldier turned to look at me. It was the first time that had happened, and I could feel my cheeks reddening.

No sooner had we entered the gallery than Giles went off in search of Harry. I hung back, pretending to take a great deal of interest in the paintings and statues. I needed to make an entrance.

When I eventually caught up with them, I found Harry chatting to my brother, although Giles wasn't even pretending to listen to him, as he was clearly besotted by the tour guide. If he'd asked me, I could have told him he didn't have a chance. But older brothers rarely listen to their sisters when it comes to women; I would have advised him to comment on her shoes, which made me quite envious. Men think the Italians are only famous for designing cars. One exception to this rule is Captain Tarrant, who knows exactly how to treat a lady. My brother could learn a lot from him. Giles simply regarded me as his gauche little sister, not that he would have known what the word gauche meant.

I picked my moment, then strolled across and waited for Giles to introduce us. Imagine my surprise when Harry invited me to join him for dinner that night. My only thought was that I hadn't packed a suitable evening dress. Over dinner, I discovered that my brother had paid Harry a thousand lire to take me off his hands, but he had refused until Giles also agreed to part with his Caruso recording. I told Harry he'd got the records and I'd got the gramophone. He didn't catch on.

As we crossed the road on the way back to the hotel, he held my hand for the first time, and when we reached the other side, I didn't let go. I could tell it was the first time Harry had held a girl's hand, because he was so nervous he was sweating.

I tried to make it easy for him to kiss me when we got back to my hotel, but he just shook hands and said good night as if we were old chums. I hinted that perhaps we might bump into each other again once we were back in Bristol. This time he responded more positively, and even suggested the most romantic location for our next date: the city's central library. He explained that it was somewhere Giles would never come across us. I happily agreed.

It was just after ten when Harry left and I went up to my room.

A few minutes later I heard Giles unlocking his bedroom door. I had to smile. His evening with Caterina can't have been worth a Caruso recording and a gramophone.

When the family returned to Chew Valley a couple of weeks later, there were three letters waiting for me on the hall table, each with the same handwriting on the envelope. If my father noticed, he said nothing.

During the next month, Harry and I spent many happy hours together in the city library without anyone becoming suspicious, not least because he'd discovered a room where no one was likely to find us, even Deakins.

Once term began and we weren't able to see each other as often, I quickly became aware just how much I missed Harry. We wrote every other day, and tried to grab a few hours together at the weekends. And that's how it might have continued, had it not been for the unwitting intervention of Dr. Paget.

Over coffee at Carwardine's one Saturday morning, Harry, who had become quite bold, told me that his English master had persuaded Miss Webb to allow her girls to take part in the Bristol Grammar School play that year. By the time the auditions were held three weeks later, I knew the part of Juliet by heart. Poor innocent Dr. Paget couldn't believe his luck.

Rehearsals meant not only that the two of us could be together for three afternoons a week, but that we were allowed to play the parts of young lovers. By the time the curtain went up on the first night, we were no longer acting.

The first two performances went so well that I couldn't wait for my parents to attend the closing night, although I didn't tell my father I was playing Juliet as I wanted it to be a surprise. It wasn't long after my first entrance that I became distracted by someone noisily leaving the auditorium. But Dr. Paget had told us on several occasions never to look into the audience, it broke the spell, so I had no idea who had left so publicly. I prayed it wasn't my father, but when he didn't come backstage after the performance I realized my prayer had not been answered. What made it worse was my certainty that his little outburst was aimed at Harry, although I still didn't know why.

When we returned home that night, Giles and I sat on the stairs and listened to my parents having another row. But it was different this time, because I'd never heard my father be so unkind to Mama. When I could bear it no longer, I went to my room and locked myself in.

I was lying on my bed, thinking about Harry, when I heard a gentle knock on the door. When I opened it, my mother made no attempt to hide the fact that she'd been crying, and told me to pack a small suitcase because we would be leaving shortly. A taxi drove us to the station and we arrived just in time to catch the milk train to London. During the journey, I wrote to Harry to let him know what had happened and where he could get in touch with me. I posted the letter in a box on King's Cross station before we boarded another train for Edinburgh.

Imagine my surprise when the following evening Harry and my brother turned up at Mulgelrie Castle, just in time for dinner. We spent an unexpected and glorious nine days in Scotland together. I didn't ever want to return to Chew Valley, even though my father had rung and apologized unreservedly for the way he'd behaved on the night of the play.

But I knew that eventually we would have to go home. I promised Harry on one of our long morning walks that I would try to find out the reason for my father's continued hostility toward him.

When we arrived back at the Manor House, Papa could not have been more conciliatory. He tried to explain why he had treated Harry so badly over the years, and my mother and Giles seemed to accept his explanation. But I wasn't convinced he had told us the whole story.

What made things even more difficult for me was that he forbade me to tell Harry the truth about how his father had died, as his mother was adamant that it should remain a family secret. I had a feeling that Mrs. Clifton knew the real reason my father didn't approve of Harry and me being together, although I would have liked to tell them both that nothing and no one could keep us apart. However, it all came to a head in a way I could never have predicted.

I was just as impatient as Harry to find out if he'd been offered a place at Oxford, and we arranged to meet outside the library on the morning after he received the telegram letting him know the result.

I was a few minutes late that Friday morning, and when I saw him sitting on the top step, head in hands, I knew he must have failed.

45

HARRY LEAPED UP and threw his arms around Emma the moment he saw her. He continued to cling to her, something he'd never done in public before, which confirmed her belief that it could only be bad news.

Without a word passing between them, he took her by the hand, led her into the building, down a circular wooden staircase and along a narrow brick corridor until he came to a door marked "Antiquities." He peered inside to make sure that no one else had discovered their hiding place.

The two of them sat opposite each other at a small table where they had spent so many hours studying during the past year. Harry was trembling, and not because of the chill in the windowless room that was lined on all sides by shelves of leatherbound books covered in dust, some of which looked as if they hadn't been opened for years. In time they would become antiquities in their own right.

It was some time before Harry spoke.

"Do you think there is anything I could say or do that would stop you loving me?"

"No, my darling," said Emma, "absolutely nothing."

"I've found out why your father has been so determined to keep us apart."

"I already know," said Emma, bowing her head slightly, "and I promise you it makes no difference."

"How can you possibly know?" said Harry.

"My father told us the day we returned from Scotland, but he swore us to secrecy."

"He told you my mother was a prostitute?"

Emma was stunned. It was some time before she recovered enough to speak. "No, he did not," she said vehemently. "How could you say anything so cruel?"

"Because it's the truth," said Harry. "My mother hasn't been working at the Royal Hotel for the past two years, as I thought, but at a nightclub called Eddie's."

"That doesn't make her a prostitute," said Emma.

"The man sitting at the bar with a glass of whiskey in one hand and the other on her thigh wasn't hoping for stimulating conversation."

Emma leaned across the table and touched Harry gently on the cheek. "I'm so sorry, my darling," she said, "but it makes no difference to how I feel about you, and it never will."

Harry managed a weak smile, but Emma remained silent, knowing it could only be a few moments before he asked her the inevitable question.

"If that wasn't the secret your father asked you to keep," he said, suddenly serious again, "what did he tell you?"

It was Emma's turn to hold her head in her hands, aware that he'd left her with no choice but to tell him the truth. Like her mother, she was no good at dissembling.

"What did he tell you?" Harry repeated, more emphatically.

Emma held on to the edge of the table as she tried to steady herself. Finally she summoned up the strength to look at Harry. Although he was only a few feet away, he could not have been more distant. "I need to ask you the same question you asked me," said Emma. "Is there anything I could say or do that would stop you loving me?"

Harry leaned across and took her hand. "Of course not," he said.

"Your father wasn't killed in the war," she said softly. "And my father was probably responsible for his death." She gripped his hand firmly before revealing everything her father had told them the day they returned from Scotland.

When she'd finished, Harry looked dazed and was unable to speak. He tried to stand up but his legs gave way beneath him, like a boxer who'd taken one punch too many, and he fell back into his chair.

"I've known for some time that my father couldn't have died in the war," Harry said quietly, "but what I still don't understand is why my mother didn't simply tell me the truth."

"And now you do know the truth," said Emma, trying to hold back the tears, "I would understand if you wanted to break off our relationship after what my father has put your family through."

"It's not your fault," said Harry, "but I'll never forgive him." He paused before adding, "And I won't be able to face him once he finds out the truth about my mother."

"He need never find out," said Emma, taking him by the hand again. "It will always be a secret between us."

"That's not possible any longer," said Harry.

"Why not?"

"Because Giles saw the man who followed us to Edinburgh standing in a doorway opposite Eddie's Nightclub."

"Then it's my father who's prostituted himself," said Emma, "because not only did he lie to us yet again, but he's already gone back on his word."

"How?"

"He promised Giles that man would never follow him again."

"That man wasn't interested in Giles," said Harry. "I think he was following my mother."

"But why?"

"Because if he was able to prove how my mother earned her living, he must have hoped it would convince you to give me up."

"How little he knows his own daughter," said Emma, "because I'm now even more determined that nothing will keep us apart. And he certainly can't stop me admiring your mother even more than I did before."

"How can you say that?" said Harry.

"She works as a waitress to support her family, ends up owning Tilly's, and when it's burned to the ground she's accused of arson, but holds her head high, knowing she is innocent. She finds herself another job at the Royal Hotel, and when she's sacked, she still refuses to give up. She receives a check for six hundred pounds, and for a moment believes all her problems are solved, only to discover she's in fact penniless just at the time when she needs money to make sure you can stay at school. In desperation, she then turns to . . ."

"But I wouldn't have wanted her to . . ."

"She would have known that, Harry, but she still felt it was a sacrifice worth making."

Another long silence followed. "Oh my God," said Harry. "How can I ever have thought badly of her." He looked up at Emma. "I need you to do something for me."

"Anything."

"Can you go and see my mother? Use any excuse, but try to find out if she saw me in that dreadful place last night."

"How will I know, if she isn't willing to admit it?"

"You'll know," said Harry quietly.

"But if your mother did see you, she's bound to ask me what you were doing there."

"I was looking for her."

"But why?"

"To tell her that I've been offered a place at Oxford."

◄○►

Emma slipped into a pew at the back of Holy Nativity and waited for the service to end. She could see Mrs. Clifton sitting in the third row, next to an old lady. Harry had seemed a little less tense when they'd met again earlier that morning. He'd been very clear what he needed to find out, and she promised not to stray beyond her remit. They had rehearsed every possible scenario several times, until she was word perfect.

After the elderly priest had given the final blessing, Emma stepped out into the center of the aisle and waited, so Mrs. Clifton couldn't possibly miss her. When Maisie saw Emma, she couldn't hide a look of surprise, but it was quickly replaced by a welcoming smile. She walked quickly toward her and introduced the old lady who was with her. "Mum, this is Emma Barrington, she's a friend of Harry's."

The old lady gave Emma a toothy grin. "There's a great deal of difference between being his friend and being his girlfriend. Which are you?" she demanded.

Mrs. Clifton laughed, but it was clear to Emma that she was just as interested to hear her reply.

"I'm his girlfriend," said Emma proudly.

The old lady delivered another toothy grin, but Maisie didn't smile.

"Well, that's all right then, isn't it?" Harry's grandmother said, before adding, "I can't stand around here all day chatting, I've got dinner to make." She began to walk away, but then turned back and asked, "Would you like to join us for dinner, young lady?"

This was a question that Harry had anticipated, and for which he'd even scripted a reply. "That's very kind of you," said Emma, "but my parents will be expecting me."

"Quite right too," said the old lady. "You should always respect your parents' wishes. I'll see you later, Maisie."

"May I walk with you, Mrs. Clifton?" asked Emma as they stepped out of the church.

"Yes, of course, my dear."

"Harry asked me to come and see you, because he knew you'd want to know that he's been offered a place at Oxford."

"Oh, that's wonderful news," said Maisie, throwing her arms around Emma. She suddenly released her, and asked, "But why didn't he come and tell me himself?"

Another scripted reply. "He's stuck in detention," said Emma, hoping she didn't sound over-rehearsed, "writing out passages from Shelley. I'm afraid my brother's to blame. You see, after he heard the good news, he smuggled a bottle of champagne into school, and they were caught celebrating in his study last night."

"Is that so wicked?" asked Maisie, grinning.

"Dr. Paget seemed to think so. Harry's dreadfully sorry."

Maisie laughed so uproariously that Emma had no doubt she'd no idea her son had visited the club last night. She would have liked to ask one more question that still puzzled her, but Harry couldn't have been more emphatic: "If my mother doesn't want me to know how my father died, so be it."

"I'm sorry you can't stay to lunch," said Maisie, "because there was something I wanted to tell you. Perhaps another time."

46

HARRY SPENT THE following week waiting for another bomb-shell to drop. When it did, he cheered out loud.

Giles received a telegram on the last day of term telling him he'd been offered a place at Brasenose College, Oxford, to read History.

"By the skin of his teeth," was the expression Dr. Paget used when he informed the headmaster.

Two months later, one scholar, one exhibitioner and one commoner arrived in the ancient university city, by different modes of transport, to begin their three-year undergraduate courses.

Harry signed up for the dramatic society and the officer training corps, Giles for the union and the cricket club, while Deakins settled himself down in the bowels of the Bodleian library, and, like a mole, was rarely seen above ground. But then, he had already decided that Oxford was where he was going to spend the rest of his life.

Harry couldn't be so sure how he would be spending the rest of his life, while the Prime Minister continued to fly back and forth to Germany, finally returning to Heston airport with a smile on his face, waving a piece of paper and telling people what they wanted to hear. Harry wasn't in any doubt that Britain was on the brink of war. When Emma asked him why he was so convinced, he replied, "Haven't you noticed that Herr Hitler never bothers to visit us? We are always the importunate suitor, and in the end we will be spurned." Emma ignored his opinion, but then, like Mr. Chamberlain, she didn't want to believe he might be right.

Emma wrote to Harry twice a week, sometimes three times, despite the fact that she was working flat out preparing for her own entrance exams to Oxford.

—◦—

When Harry returned to Bristol for the Christmas vacation, the two of them spent as much time together as possible, although Harry made sure he kept out of the way of Mr. Barrington.

Emma turned down the chance to spend her holiday with the rest of the family in Tuscany, not hiding the fact from her father that she'd rather be with Harry.

As her entrance exam drew nearer, the number of hours Emma spent in the Antiquities room would have impressed even Deakins, but then Harry was coming to the conclusion that she was about to impress the examiners just as much as his reclusive friend had done the year before. Whenever he suggested this to Emma, she would remind him that there were twenty male students at Oxford for every female.

"You could always go to Cambridge," Giles foolishly suggested.

"Where they're even more prehistoric," Emma responded. "They still don't award degrees to women."

Emma's greatest fear was not that she wouldn't be offered a place at Oxford, but that by the time she took it up, war would have been declared, and Harry would have signed up and departed for some foreign field that was not forever England. All her life she had been continually reminded of the Great War by the number of women who still wore black every day, in memory of their husbands, lovers, brothers and sons who had never returned from the Front, in what nobody was any longer calling the war to end all wars.

She had pleaded with Harry not to volunteer if war was declared, but at least to wait until he was called up. But after Hitler had marched into Czechoslovakia and annexed the Sudetenland, Harry never wavered in his belief that war with Germany was inevitable, and that the moment it was declared, he would be in uniform the following day.

When Harry invited Emma to join him for the Commem Ball

at the end of his first year, she resolved not to discuss the possibility of war. She also made another decision.

—◦—

Emma traveled up to Oxford on the morning of the ball and checked into the Randolph Hotel. She spent the rest of the day being shown around Somerville, the Ashmolean and the Bodleian by Harry, who was confident she would be joining him as an undergraduate in a few months' time.

Emma returned to the hotel, giving herself plenty of time to prepare for the ball. Harry had arranged to pick her up at eight.

He strolled through the front door of the hotel a few minutes before the appointed hour. He was dressed in a fashionable midnight blue dinner jacket which his mother had given him for his nineteenth birthday. He called Emma's room from the front desk to tell her he was downstairs and would wait for her in the foyer.

"I'll be straight down," she promised.

As the minutes passed, Harry began to pace around the foyer, wondering what Emma meant by "straight down." But Giles had often told him that she'd learned how to tell the time from her mother.

And then he saw her, standing at the top of the staircase. He didn't move as she walked slowly down, her strapless turquoise silk dress emphasizing her graceful figure. Every other young man in the foyer looked as if he'd be happy to change places with Harry.

"Wow," he said as she reached the bottom step. "Who needs Vivien Leigh? By the way, I love the shoes." Emma felt the first part of her plan was falling into place.

They walked out of the hotel and strolled arm in arm toward Radcliffe Square. As they entered the gates of Harry's college, the sun began to dip behind the Bodleian. No one entering Brasenose that evening would have thought that Britain was only a few weeks away from a war in which over half the young men who danced the night away would never graduate.

But nothing could have been further from the thoughts of the gay young couples dancing to the music of Cole Porter and Jerome

314

Kern. While several hundred undergraduates and their guests consumed crates of champagne and ate their way through a mountain of smoked salmon, Harry rarely let Emma out of his sight, fearful that some ungallant soul might attempt to steal her away.

Giles drank a little too much champagne, ate far too many oysters and didn't dance with the same girl twice the entire evening.

At two o'clock in the morning, the Billy Cotton Dance Band struck up the last waltz. Harry and Emma clung to each other as they swayed to the rhythm of the orchestra.

When the conductor finally raised his baton for the National Anthem, Emma couldn't help noticing that all the young men around her, whatever state of inebriation they were in, stood rigidly to attention as they sang "God Save the King."

Harry and Emma walked slowly back to the Randolph chatting about nothing of any consequence, just not wanting the evening to end.

"Well, at least you'll be back in a fortnight's time to sit your entrance exam," said Harry as they climbed the steps to the hotel, "so it won't be too long before I see you again."

"True," said Emma, "but there'll be no time for any distractions until I've completed the last paper. Once that's out of the way, we can spend the rest of the weekend together."

Harry was about to kiss her goodnight, when she whispered, "Would you like to come up to my room? I've got a present for you. I wouldn't want you to think I'd forgotten your birthday."

Harry looked surprised, as did the hall porter when the young couple walked up the staircase together hand in hand. When they reached Emma's room, she fumbled nervously with the key before finally pushing open the door.

"I'll just be a moment," she said as she disappeared into the bathroom.

Harry sat down in the only chair in the room and tried to think of what he'd most like for his birthday. When the bathroom door opened, Emma was framed in the half light. The elegant strapless gown had been replaced by a hotel towel.

Harry could hear his heart beating as she walked slowly toward him.

"I think you're a little overdressed, my darling," Emma said, as she slipped off his jacket and let it fall to the floor. Next she undid his bow tie before unbuttoning his shirt, and both joined the jacket. Two shoes and two socks followed, before she slowly pulled down his trousers. She was about to remove the one remaining obstacle in her path, when he gathered her up in his arms and carried her across the bedroom.

As he dumped her unceremoniously onto the bed, the towel fell to the floor. Emma had often imagined this moment since they'd returned from Rome, and assumed that her first attempts at making love would be awkward and clumsy. But Harry was gentle and considerate, although he was clearly every bit as nervous as she was. After they'd made love, she lay in his arms, not wanting to fall asleep.

"Did you like your birthday present?" she asked.

"Yes I did," said Harry. "But I hope it's not going to be another year before I can unwrap the next one. That reminds me, I've got a present for you too."

"But it's not my birthday."

"It's not a birthday present."

He jumped out of bed, picked his trousers up off the floor and rummaged around in the pockets until he came across a small leather box. He returned to the bedside, fell to one knee and said, "Emma, my darling, will you marry me?"

"You look quite ridiculous down there," said Emma, frowning. "Get back into bed before you freeze to death."

"Not until you've answered my question."

"Don't be silly, Harry. I decided that we were going to be married the day you came to the Manor House for Giles's twelfth birthday."

Harry burst out laughing as he placed the ring on the third finger of her left hand.

"I'm sorry it's such a small diamond," he said.

"It's as big as the Ritz," she said as he climbed back into bed. "And as you seem to have everything so well organized," she teased, "what date have you chosen for our wedding?"

"Saturday, July the twenty-ninth, at three o'clock."

"Why then?"

"It's the last day of term, and in any case, we can't book the university church after I've gone down."

Emma sat up, grabbed the pencil and pad from the bedside table and started to write.

"What are you doing?" asked Harry.

"I'm working on the guest list. If we've only got seven weeks . . ."

"That can wait," said Harry, taking her back in his arms. "I feel another birthday coming on."

<o>

"She's too young to be thinking about marriage," said Emma's father, as if she wasn't in the room.

"She's the same age I was when you proposed to me," Elizabeth reminded him.

"But you weren't about to sit the most important exam of your life, just weeks before the wedding."

"That's exactly why I've taken over all the arrangements," said Elizabeth. "That way Emma won't have any distractions until her exams are over."

"Surely it would be better to put the wedding off for a few months. After all, what's the hurry?"

"What a good idea, Daddy," said Emma, speaking for the first time. "Perhaps we could also ask Herr Hitler if he'd be kind enough to put off the war for a few months, because your daughter wants to get married."

"And what does Mrs. Clifton think about all of this?" her father asked, ignoring his daughter's comment.

"Why should she be anything other than delighted by the news?" Elizabeth asked him. He didn't respond.

<o>

An announcement of the forthcoming marriage between Emma Grace Barrington and Harold Arthur Clifton was published in *The Times* ten days later. The first banns were read from the pulpit of St. Mary's by the Reverend Styler on the following Sunday and over three hundred invitations were sent out during the next week. No one was surprised when Harry asked Giles to be his best man, with Captain Tarrant and Deakins as the principal ushers.

But Harry was shocked when he received a letter from Old Jack, declining his kind invitation because he couldn't leave his post in the current circumstances. Harry wrote back, begging him to reconsider and at least attend the wedding, even if he felt unable to take on the task of being an usher. Old Jack's reply left Harry even more confused: "I feel my presence might turn out to be an embarrassment."

"What is he talking about?" said Harry. "Surely he knows that we'd all be honored if he came."

"He's almost as bad as my father," said Emma. "He's refusing to give me away, and says he's not even sure he'll come."

"But you told me he'd promised to be more supportive in the future."

"Yes, but that all changed the moment he heard we were engaged."

"I can't pretend that my mother sounded all that enthusiastic when I told her the news either," Harry admitted.

⋖◇⋗

Emma didn't see Harry again until she returned to Oxford to sit her exams, and even then not until she'd completed the final paper. When she came out of the examination hall, her fiancé was waiting on the top step, a bottle of champagne in one hand and two glasses in the other.

"So, how do you think you got on?" he asked as he filled her glass.

"I don't know," sighed Emma, as dozens of other girls poured out of the examination hall. "I didn't realize what I was up against until I saw that lot."

"Well, at least you've got something to distract you while you wait for the results."

"Just three weeks to go," Emma reminded him. "That's more than enough time for you to change your mind."

"If you don't win a scholarship, I may have to reconsider my position. After all, I can't be seen associating with a commoner."

"And if I do win a scholarship, I may have to reconsider my position and look for another scholar."

"Deakins is still available," said Harry as he topped up her glass.

"It will be too late by then," said Emma.

"Why?"

"Because the results are due to be announced on the morning of our wedding."

Emma and Harry spent most of the weekend locked away in her little hotel room, endlessly going over the wedding arrangements when they weren't making love. By Sunday night, Emma had come to one conclusion.

"Mama has been quite magnificent," she said, "which is more than I can say for my father."

"Do you think he'll even turn up?"

"Oh yes. Mama's talked him into coming, but he's still refusing to give me away. What's the latest on Old Jack?"

"He hasn't even replied to my last letter," said Harry.

47

"HAVE YOU PUT on a little weight, darling?" asked Emma's mother as she tried to fasten the last clasp on the back of her daughter's wedding dress.

"I don't think so," replied Emma, looking at herself critically in the full-length mirror.

"Stunning," was Elizabeth's verdict as she stood back to admire the bride's outfit.

They had traveled to London several times to have the dress fitted by Madame Renée, the proprietor of a small, fashionable boutique in Mayfair, thought to be patronized by Queen Mary and Queen Elizabeth. Madame Renée had personally supervised each fitting, and the Victorian embroidered lace around the neck and hem, something old, blended quite naturally with the silk bodice and empire bell skirt that was proving so fashionable that year, something new. The little cream tear-drop hat, Madame Renée had assured them, was what women of fashion would be wearing next year. The only comment Emma's father made on the subject came when he saw the bill.

Elizabeth Barrington glanced at her watch. Nineteen minutes to three. "No need to rush," she told Emma when there was a knock on the door. She was sure she'd hung the Do Not Disturb sign on the doorknob and told the chauffeur not to expect them before three. At the rehearsal the previous day, the journey from the hotel to the church had taken seven minutes. Elizabeth intended Emma to be fashionably late. "Keep them waiting for a few minutes, but don't give them any cause for concern." A second knock.

"I'll get it," Elizabeth said, and went to the door. A young porter in a smart red uniform handed her a telegram, the eleventh that day. She was about to close the door when he said, "I was told to inform you, madam, that this one is important."

Elizabeth's first thought was to wonder who could possibly have canceled at the last moment. She only hoped it wouldn't mean reorganizing the top table at the reception. She tore open the telegram and read the contents.

"Who's it from?" asked Emma, adjusting the angle of her hat by another inch and wondering if it was perhaps a little too risqué.

Elizabeth handed her the telegram. Once Emma had read it, she burst into tears.

"Many congratulations, darling," said her mother, taking a handkerchief out of her handbag and beginning to dry her daughter's tears. "I'd hug you, but I don't want to crease your dress."

Once Elizabeth was satisfied that Emma was ready, she spent a moment checking her own outfit in the mirror. Madame Renée had pronounced, "You mustn't outdo your daughter on her big day, but at the same time, you can't afford to go unnoticed." Elizabeth particularly liked the Norman Hartnell hat, even if it was not what the young were calling "chic."

"Time to leave," she declared after one more look at her watch. Emma smiled as she glanced at the going-away outfit she would change into once the reception was over, when she and Harry would travel up to Scotland for their honeymoon. Lord Harvey had offered them Mulgelrie Castle for a fortnight, with the promise that no other member of the family would be allowed within ten miles of the estate during that time and, perhaps more important, Harry could ask for three portions of Highland broth every night, without a suggestion of grouse to follow.

Emma followed her mother out of the suite and along the corridor. By the time she reached the top of the staircase, she felt sure her legs were about to give way. As she descended the stairs, other guests stood aside so that nothing would impede her progress.

A porter held open the front door of the hotel for her, while Sir Walter's chauffeur stood by the back door of the Rolls so the bride could join her grandfather. As Emma sat down beside him, carefully arranging her dress, Sir Walter placed his monocle in his right eye and declared, "You look quite beautiful, young lady. Harry is indeed a most fortunate man."

"Thank you, Grandpa," she said, kissing him on the cheek. She glanced out of the rear window to see her mother climbing into a second Rolls-Royce, and a moment later the two cars moved off to join the afternoon traffic as they began their sedate journey to the university church of St. Mary's.

"Is Daddy at the church?" asked Emma, trying not to sound anxious.

"Among the first to arrive," said her grandfather. "I do believe he's already regretting allowing me the privilege of giving you away."

"And Harry?"

"Never seen him so nervous. But Giles seems to have everything under control, which must be a first. I know he's spent the last month preparing his best man's speech."

"We're both lucky to have the same best friend," said Emma. "You know, Grandpa, I once read that every bride has second thoughts on the morning of her wedding."

"That's natural enough, my dear."

"But I've never had a second thought about Harry," said Emma, as they came to a halt outside the university church. "I know we'll spend the rest of our lives together."

She waited for her grandfather to step out of the car before she gathered up her dress and joined him on the pavement.

Her mother rushed forward to check Emma's outfit one last time before she would allow her to enter the church. Elizabeth handed her a small bouquet of pale pink roses as the two brides-maids, Emma's younger sister Grace and her school friend Jessica, gathered up the end of the train.

"You next, Grace," said her mother, bending down to unruffle her bridesmaid's dress.

"I hope not," said Grace, loud enough for her mother to hear.

Elizabeth stepped back and nodded. Two sidesmen pulled open the heavy doors, the sign for the organist to strike up Mendelssohn's "Wedding March," and the congregation to rise and welcome the bride.

As Emma stepped into the church, she was taken by surprise to see how many people had traveled to Oxford to share in her happiness. She walked slowly down the aisle on her grandfather's arm, the guests turning to smile at her as she made her way toward the altar.

She noticed Mr. Frobisher sitting next to Mr. Holcombe on the right-hand side of the aisle. Miss Tilly, who was wearing quite a daring hat, must have come all the way from Cornwall, while Dr. Paget gave her the warmest of smiles. But nothing compared with the smile that appeared on her own face when she spotted Captain Tarrant, head bowed, wearing a morning suit that didn't quite fit. Harry would be so pleased he had decided to come after all. In the front row sat Mrs. Clifton, who had clearly spent some time selecting her outfit because she looked so fashionable. A smile crossed Emma's lips, but she was surprised and disappointed that her future mother-in-law didn't turn to look at her as she passed.

And then she saw Harry, standing on the altar steps next to her brother as they waited for the bride. Emma continued up the aisle on the arm of one grandfather, while the other stood bolt upright in the front row, next to her father, who she thought looked a little melancholy. Perhaps he really was regretting his decision not to give her away.

Sir Walter stood to one side as Emma climbed the four steps to join her future husband. She leaned over and whispered, "I nearly had a change of heart." Harry tried not to grin as he waited for the punch line. "After all, scholars of this university cannot be seen to marry beneath themselves."

"I'm so proud of you, my darling," he said. "Many congratulations."

Giles bowed low in genuine respect, and Chinese whispers broke out among the congregation as the news spread from row to row.

The music stopped, and the college chaplain raised his hands and said, *"Dearly beloved, we are gathered together here in the sight of God, and in the face of this congregation, to join together this Man and this Woman, in holy matrimony. . . ."*

Emma suddenly felt nervous. She had learned all the responses by heart but now she couldn't recall one of them.

"First it was ordained for the procreation of children . . ."

Emma tried to concentrate on the chaplain's words, but she couldn't wait to escape and be alone with Harry. Perhaps they should have gone up to Scotland the night before and eloped at Gretna Green; so much more convenient for Mulgelrie Castle, she'd pointed out to Harry.

"Into which holy estate these two persons present come now to be joined. Therefore if any man can show any just cause why they may not lawfully be joined together, let him now speak, or else hereafter forever hold his peace . . ."

The chaplain paused, to allow a diplomatic period of time to pass before he pronounced the words, *I require and charge you both,* when a clear voice declared, "I object!"

Emma and Harry both swung round to see who could possibly have uttered two such damning words.

The chaplain looked up in disbelief, wondering for a moment if he had misheard, but all over the church, heads were turning as the congregation tried to discover who had made the unexpected intervention. The chaplain had never experienced such a turn of events before, and tried desperately to recall what he was expected to do in the circumstances.

Emma buried her head in Harry's shoulder, while he searched among the chattering congregation, trying to find out who it was who had caused such consternation. He assumed it must be Emma's father, but when he looked down at the front row he saw Hugo Barrington, white as a sheet, was also trying to see who had brought the ceremony to a premature halt.

The Reverend Styler had to raise his voice to be heard above the growing clamor. "Would the gentleman who has objected to this marriage taking place please make himself known."

A tall, upright figure stepped out into the aisle. Every eye remained fixed on Captain Jack Tarrant as he made his way up to the altar before coming to a halt in front of the chaplain. Emma clung to Harry, fearful he was about to be pried away from her.

"Am I to understand, sir," said the chaplain, "that you feel this marriage should not be allowed to proceed?"

"That is correct, sir," said Old Jack quietly.

"Then I must ask you, the bride and groom and the members of their immediate family to join me in the vestry." Raising his voice, he added, "The congregation should remain in their places until I have considered the objection, and made my decision known."

Those who had been bidden were led by the chaplain into the vestry, followed by Harry and Emma. Not one of them spoke, although the congregation continued to whisper noisily among themselves.

Once the two families had crammed themselves into the tiny vestry, the Reverend Styler closed the door.

"Captain Tarrant," he began, "I must tell you that I alone am vested by law with the authority to decide whether this marriage should continue. Naturally I shall not come to any decision until I have heard your objections."

The only person in that overcrowded room who appeared calm was Old Jack. "Thank you, chaplain," he began. "Firstly, I must apologize to you all, and in particular to Emma and Harry, for my intervention. I have spent the past few weeks wrestling with my conscience before coming to this unhappy decision. I could have taken the easy way out and simply found some excuse for not attending this ceremony today. I have remained silent until now in the hope that in time any objection would prove irrelevant. But sadly that has not proved to be the case, for Harry and Emma's love for each other has in fact grown over the years, and not diminished, which is why it has become impossible for me to remain silent any longer."

Everyone was so gripped by Old Jack's words that only Elizabeth Barrington noticed her husband slip quietly out of the back door of the vestry.

"Thank you, Captain Tarrant," said the Reverend Styler. "While I accept your intervention in good faith, I need to know what specific charges you bring against these two young people."

"I bring no charge against Harry or Emma, both of whom I love and admire, and believe to be as much in the dark as the rest of you. No, my charge is against Hugo Barrington, who has known for many years that there is a possibility that he is the father of both of these unfortunate children."

A gasp went around the room as everyone tried to grasp the enormity of this statement. The chaplain said nothing until he was able to regain their attention. "Is there anyone present who can verify or refute Captain Tarrant's claim?"

"This can't possibly be true," said Emma, still clinging to Harry. "There must be some mistake. Surely my father can't . . ."

That was the moment everyone became aware that the father of the bride was no longer among them. The chaplain turned his attention to Mrs. Clifton, who was quietly sobbing.

"I can't deny Captain Tarrant's fears," she said haltingly. It was some time before she continued. "I confess I did have a relationship with Mr. Barrington on one occasion." She paused again. "Only once, but, unfortunately, it was just a few weeks before I married my husband—" she raised her head slowly— "so I have no way of knowing who Harry's father is."

"I should point out to you all," said Old Jack, "that Hugo Barrington threatened Mrs. Clifton on more than one occasion, should she ever reveal his dreadful secret."

"Mrs. Clifton, may I be allowed to ask you a question?" said Sir Walter gently.

Maisie nodded, although her head remained bowed.

"Did your late husband suffer from color-blindness?"

"Not that I'm aware of," she said, barely loudly enough to be heard.

Sir Walter turned to Harry. "But I believe you do, my boy?"

"Yes I do, sir," said Harry without hesitation. "Why is that of any importance?"

"Because I am also color-blind," said Sir Walter. "As are my son and grandson. It is a hereditary trait that has troubled our family for several generations."

Harry took Emma in his arms. "I swear to you, my darling, I didn't know anything about this."

"Of course you didn't," said Elizabeth Barrington, speaking for the first time. "The only man who knew was my husband, and he didn't have the courage to come forward and admit it. If he had, none of this need ever have happened. Father," she said, turning to Lord Harvey, "can I ask you to explain to our guests why the ceremony will not be continuing."

Lord Harvey nodded. "Leave it to me, old gal," he said, touching her gently on the arm. "But what are you going to do?"

"I'm going take my daughter as far away from this place as possible."

"I don't want to go as far away as possible," Emma said, "unless it's with Harry."

"I fear your father has left us with no choice," said Elizabeth, taking her gently by the arm. But Emma continued to cling on to Harry until he whispered, "I'm afraid your mother's right, my darling. But one thing your father will never be able to do is stop me loving you, and if it takes the rest of my life, I'll prove he's not my father."

"Perhaps you'd prefer to leave by the rear entrance, Mrs. Barrington," suggested the chaplain. Emma reluctantly released Harry and allowed her mother to take her away.

The chaplain led them out of the vestry and down a narrow corridor to a door that he was surprised to find unlocked. "May God go with you, my children," he said before letting them out.

Elizabeth accompanied her daughter around the outside of the church to the waiting Rolls-Royces. She ignored those members of the congregation who had strayed outside for some fresh air or to smoke a cigarette and now made no attempt to conceal their curiosity when they spotted the two women climbing unceremoniously into the back of the limousine.

Elizabeth had opened the door of the first Rolls and bundled her daughter into the backseat before the chauffeur spotted them.

He had stationed himself by the great door, as he hadn't expected the bride and groom to appear for at least another half an hour, when a peal of bells would announce the marriage of Mr. and Mrs. Harry Clifton to the world. The moment the chauffeur heard the door slam, he stubbed out his cigarette, ran across to the car and jumped behind the wheel.

"Take us back to the hotel," Elizabeth said.

Neither of them spoke again until they had reached the safety of their room. Emma lay sobbing on the bed while Elizabeth stroked her hair, the way she had when she was a child.

"What am I going to do?" cried Emma. "I can't suddenly stop loving Harry."

"I'm sure you never will," said her mother, "but fate has decreed that you cannot be together until it can be proved who Harry's father is." She continued to stroke her daughter's hair, and thought she might even have fallen asleep, until Emma quietly added, "What will I tell my child when they ask who their father is?"

HARRY CLIFTON

1939–1940

48

The thing I remember most after Emma and her mother had left the church was how calm everyone appeared to be. No hysterics, no one fainted, there weren't even any raised voices. A visitor might have been forgiven for not realizing how many people's lives had just been irreparably damaged, even ruined. How very British, stiff upper lip and all that; no one willing to admit that their personal life had been shattered in the space of a single hour. Well, I have to admit, mine had.

I had stood in numbed silence as the different actors played out their roles. Old Jack had done no more or less than what he considered his duty, though the pallor of his skin and the deeply etched lines on his face suggested otherwise. He could have taken the easy way out and simply declined our invitation to the wedding, but Victoria Cross winners don't walk away.

Elizabeth Barrington was cast from that metal which, when put to the test, proved she was the equal of any man: a veritable Portia, who sadly hadn't married a Brutus.

As I looked around the vestry waiting for the chaplain to return, I felt saddest for Sir Walter, who had walked his granddaughter down the aisle, and had not gained a grandson, but rather lost a son, who, as Old Jack had warned me so many years ago, "was not cut from the same cloth" as his father.

My dear mother was fearful to respond when I tried to take her in my arms and reassure her of my love. She clearly believed she alone was to blame for everything that had taken place that day.

And Giles, he became a man when his father crept out of the

vestry to hide under some slimy stone, leaving the responsibility for his actions to others. In time, many of those present would become aware that what had taken place that day was every bit as devastating for Giles as for Emma.

Finally, Lord Harvey. He was an example to us all of how to behave in a crisis. Once the chaplain had returned and explained the legal implications of consanguinity to us, we agreed among ourselves that Lord Harvey should address the waiting congregation on behalf of both families.

"I would like Harry to stand on my right," he said, "as I wish everyone present to be left in no doubt, as my daughter Elizabeth made abundantly clear, that no blame rests on his shoulders.

"Mrs. Clifton," he said, turning to my mother, "I hope you will be kind enough to stand on my left. Your courage in adversity has been an example to us all, and to one of us in particular.

"I hope that Captain Tarrant will stand by Harry's side: only a fool blames the messenger. Giles should take his place beside him. Sir Walter, perhaps you would stand next to Mrs. Clifton, while the rest of the family take their places behind us. Let me make it clear to you all," he continued, "that I only have one purpose in this tragic business, namely to ensure that everyone gathered in this church today will be in no doubt of our resolve in this matter, so that no one will ever say we were a divided house."

Without another word, he led his small flock out of the vestry.

When the chattering congregation saw us filing back into the church, Lord Harvey didn't need to call for silence. Each one of us took our allocated place on the altar steps as if we were about to pose for a family photograph that would later find its way into a wedding album.

"Friends, if I may be so bold," began Lord Harvey, "I have been asked to let you know on behalf of our two families that sadly the marriage between my granddaughter, Emma Barrington, and Mr. Harry Clifton will not be taking place today, or for that matter on any other day." Those last four words had a finality about them that was chilling when you were the only person present who still clung to a vestige of hope that this might one day be resolved. "I must apologize to you all," he continued, "if you have been inconvenienced in any way, for that was surely not our purpose. May I conclude by thanking you for your presence here today, and wish you all a safe journey home."

I wasn't sure what would happen next, but one or two members of the congregation rose from their places and began to make their way slowly out of the church; within moments the trickle turned into a steady stream, until finally those of us standing on the altar steps were the only ones remaining.

Lord Harvey thanked the chaplain, and warmly shook hands with me before accompanying his wife down the aisle and out of the church.

My mother turned to me and tried to speak, but was overcome by her emotions. Old Jack came to our rescue, taking her gently by the arm and leading her away, while Sir Walter took Grace and Jessica under his wing. Not a day mothers or bridesmaids would want to recall for the rest of their lives.

Giles and I were the last to leave. He had entered the church as my best man, and now he left it wondering if he was my half-brother. Some people stand by you in your darkest hour, while others walk away; only a select few march toward you and become even closer friends.

Once we had bidden farewell to the Reverend Styler, who seemed unable to find the words to express how sorry he felt, Giles and I trudged wearily across the cobbled stones of the quad and back to our college. Not a word passed between us as we climbed the wooden staircase to my rooms and sank into old leather chairs and young maudlin silence.

We sat alone as day turned slowly into night. Sparse conversation that had no sequence, no meaning, no logic. When the first long shadows appeared, those heralds of darkness that so often loosen the tongue, Giles asked me a question I hadn't thought about for years.

"Do you remember the first time you and Deakins visited the Manor House?"

"How could I forget? It was your twelfth birthday, and your father refused to shake hands with me."

"Have you ever wondered why?"

"I think we found out the reason today," I said, trying not to sound too insensitive.

"No, we didn't," said Giles quietly. "What we found out today was the possibility that Emma might be your half-sister. I now realize the reason my father kept his affair with your mother secret for so many years was because he was far more worried you might find out you were his son."

"I don't understand the difference," I said, staring at him.

"Then it's important for you to recall the only question my father asked on that occasion."

"He asked when my birthday was."

"That's right, and when he discovered you were a few weeks older than me, he left the room without another word. And later, when we had to leave to go back to school, he didn't come out of his study to say good-bye, even though it was my birthday. It wasn't until today that I realized the significance of his actions."

"How can that minor incident still be of any significance after all these years?" I asked.

"Because that was the moment my father realized you might be his firstborn, and that when he dies it could be you, not me, who inherits the family title, the business, and all his worldly goods."

"But surely your father can leave his possessions to whomever he pleases, and that certainly wouldn't be me."

"I wish it was that simple," said Giles, "but as my grandpa so regularly reminds me, his father, Sir Joshua Barrington, was knighted by Queen Victoria in 1877 for services to the shipping industry. In his will, he stated that all his titles, deeds and possessions were to be left to the firstborn surviving son, in perpetuity."

"But I have no interest in claiming what clearly is not mine," I said, trying to reassure him.

"I'm sure you don't," said Giles, "but you may have no choice in the matter, because in the fullness of time, the law will require you to take your place as head of the Barrington family."

◄◦►

Giles left me just after midnight to drive to Gloucestershire. He promised to find out if Emma was willing to see me, as we'd parted without even saying good-bye, and said he would return to Oxford the moment he had any news.

I didn't sleep that night. So many thoughts were racing through my mind, and for a moment, just a moment, I even contemplated suicide. But I didn't need Old Jack to remind me that that was the coward's way out.

I didn't leave my rooms for the next three days. I didn't respond to gentle knocks on the door. I didn't answer the telephone when it rang. I didn't open the letters that were pushed under the door. It may have been inconsiderate of me not to respond to those who had only kindness in their hearts, but sometimes an abundance of sympathy can be more overwhelming than solitude.

Giles returned to Oxford on the fourth day. He didn't need to speak for me to realize his news wasn't going to give me succor. It turned out to be far worse than I had even anticipated. Emma and her mother had left for Mulgelrie Castle, where we had meant to be spending our honeymoon, with no relations to be allowed within ten miles. Mrs. Barrington had instructed her solicitors to begin divorce proceedings, but they were unable to serve any papers on her husband as no one had seen him since he'd crept unnoticed out of the vestry. Lord Harvey and Old Jack had both resigned from the board of Barrington's, but out of respect for Sir Walter neither had made their reasons for doing so public—not that that would stop the rumormongers having a field day. My mother had left Eddie's Nightclub and taken a job as a waitress in the dining room of the Grand Hotel.

"What about Emma?" I said. "Did you ask her . . ."

"I didn't have a chance to speak to her," said Giles. "They'd left for Scotland before I arrived. But she'd left a letter for you on the hall table." I could feel my heart beating faster as he handed me an envelope bearing her familiar handwriting. "If you feel like a little supper later, I'll be in my rooms."

"Thank you," I said, inadequately.

I sat in my chair by the window overlooking Cobb's quad, not wanting to open a letter that I knew wouldn't offer me a glimmer of hope. I finally tore open the envelope and extracted three pages written in Emma's neat hand. Even then, it was some time before I could read her words.

The Manor House
Chew Valley
Gloucestershire

July 29th, 1939

My Darling Harry,

It's the middle of the night, and I am sitting in my bedroom writing to the only man I will ever love.

Deep hatred for my father, whom I can never forgive, has been replaced by a sudden calm, so I must write these words before bitter recrimination returns to remind me of just how much that treacherous man has denied us both.

I only wish we'd been allowed to part as lovers, and not as strangers in a crowded room, the fates having decided we should never say the words "until death do us part," although I am certain I will go to my grave only having loved one man.

I will never be satisfied with just the memory of your love, for while there is the slightest hope that Arthur Clifton was your father, be assured, my darling, that I will remain constant.

Mama is convinced that given enough time, the memory of you, like the evening sun, will fade, and then finally disappear, before heralding a new dawn. Does she not recall telling me on the day of my wedding that our love for each other was so pure, so simple and so rare, that it would unquestionably withstand the test of time, which Mama confessed she could only envy, as she had never experienced such happiness.

But until I can be your wife, my darling, I am resolved that we must remain apart, unless, and until such time, it can be shown that we can be legally bound. No other man can hope to take your place and, if necessary, I will remain single, rather than settle for some counterfeit.

I wonder if the day will dawn when I do not reach out, ex-

pecting to find you by my side, and if it will ever be possible to fall asleep without whispering your name.

I would happily sacrifice the rest of my life to spend another year like the one we have just shared together, and no law made by God or man can change that. I still pray that the day will come when we can be joined together in the sight of that same God and those same men, but until then, my darling, I will always be your loving wife in all but name,

Emma

49

WHEN HARRY FINALLY summoned up the strength to open the countless letters that littered the floor, he came across one from Old Jack's secretary in London.

Soho Square
London

Wednesday, August 2nd, 1939

Dear Mr. Clifton,

You may not receive this letter until you've returned from your honeymoon in Scotland, but I wondered if Captain Tarrant stayed on in Oxford after the wedding. He didn't return to the office on Monday morning, and he hasn't been seen since, so I wondered if you had any idea where I might contact him.

I look forward to hearing from you.
Yours sincerely,

Phyllis Watson

Old Jack had clearly forgotten to let Miss Watson know he was going down to Bristol to spend a few days with Sir Walter, to make it clear that, although he had caused the wedding to be abandoned and had resigned from the board of Barrington's, he remained a close friend of the chairman's. As there wasn't a second letter from

Miss Watson among his pile of unopened mail, Harry assumed that Old Jack must have returned to Soho Square and was back behind his desk.

Harry spent the morning answering every one of the letters he'd left unopened; so many kind people offering sympathy—it wasn't their fault they reminded him of his unhappiness. Suddenly Harry decided he had to be as far away from Oxford as possible. He picked up the phone and told the operator he wanted to make a long-distance call to London. Half an hour later, she called back to tell him the number was continually engaged. Next, he tried Sir Walter at Barrington Hall, but the number just rang and rang. Frustrated by his failure to contact either of them, Harry decided to follow one of Old Jack's maxims: *Get off your backside and do something positive.*

He grabbed the suitcase he had packed for his honeymoon in Scotland, walked across to the lodge and told the porter he was going up to London and wouldn't be returning until the first day of term. "Should Giles Barrington ask where I am," he added, "please tell him I've gone to work for Old Jack."

"Old Jack," repeated the porter, writing the name down on a slip of paper.

On the train journey to Paddington, Harry read in *The Times* about the latest communiqués that were bouncing back and forth between the Foreign Office in London and the Reich Ministry in Berlin. He was beginning to think that Mr. Chamberlain was the only person who still believed in the possibility of peace in our time. *The Times* was predicting that Britain would be at war within days and that the Prime Minister couldn't hope to survive in office if the Germans defied his ultimatum and marched into Poland.

The Thunderer went on to suggest that in that eventuality, a coalition government would have to be formed, led by the Foreign Secretary, Lord Halifax (a safe pair of hands), and not Winston Churchill (unpredictable and irascible). Despite the paper's obvious distaste for Churchill, Harry didn't believe that Britain needed a "safe pair of hands" at this particular moment in history, but someone who was not frightened to bully a bully.

When Harry stepped off the train at Paddington, he was met by a wave of different colored uniforms coming at him from every direction. He'd already decided which service he would join the moment war was declared. A morbid thought crossed his mind as he boarded a bus for Piccadilly Circus: if he was killed while serving his country, it would solve all the Barrington family's problems—except one.

When the bus reached Piccadilly, Harry jumped off and began to weave his way through the clowns that made up the West End circus, through theater land and on past exclusive restaurants and overpriced nightclubs, which appeared determined to ignore any suggestion of war. The queue of displaced immigrants trooping in and out of the building in Soho Square appeared even longer and more bedraggled than on Harry's first visit. Once again, as he climbed the stairs to the third floor, several of the refugees stood aside, assuming he must be a member of staff. He hoped he would be within the hour.

When he reached the third floor, he headed straight for Miss Watson's office. He found her filling in forms, issuing rail warrants, arranging accommodation and handing out small amounts of cash to desperate people. Her face lit up when she saw Harry. "Do tell me Captain Tarrant's with you," were her first words.

"No, he isn't," said Harry. "I assumed he'd returned to London, which is why I'm here. I was wondering if you might be able to use an extra pair of hands."

"That's very kind of you, Harry," she said, "but the most useful thing you could do for me right now is to find Captain Tarrant. This place is bursting at the seams without him."

"The last I heard he was staying with Sir Walter Barrington at his home in Gloucester," said Harry, "but that was at least a fortnight ago."

"We haven't set eyes on him since the day he went to Oxford for your wedding," said Miss Watson as she tried to comfort two more immigrants who couldn't speak a word of English.

"Has anyone phoned his flat to see if he's there?" asked Harry.

"He doesn't have a phone," said Miss Watson, "and I've hardly been to my own home for the past two weeks," she added, nodding in the direction of a queue that stretched as far as the eye could see.

"Why don't I start there, and report back to you?"

"Would you?" said Miss Watson as two little girls began sobbing. "Don't cry, everything's going to be all right," she reassured the children as she knelt and placed an arm round them.

"Where does he live?" asked Harry.

"Number twenty-three, Prince Edward Mansions, Lambeth Walk. Take the number eleven bus to Lambeth, then you'll have to ask for directions. And thank you, Harry."

Harry turned and headed toward the stairs. Something wasn't right, he thought. Old Jack would never have deserted his post without giving Miss Watson a reason.

"I forgot to ask," Miss Watson shouted after him, "how was your honeymoon?"

Harry felt he was far enough away not to have heard her.

Back at Piccadilly Circus he boarded a double-decker bus overcrowded with soldiers. It drove down Whitehall, which was full of officers, and on through Parliament Square, where a vast crowd of onlookers was waiting for any snippets of information that might come out of the House of Commons. The bus continued its journey across Lambeth Bridge, and Harry got off when it reached Albert Embankment.

A paperboy who was shouting *Britain Awaits Hitler's Response* told Harry to take the second on the left, then the third on the right, and added for good measure, "I thought everyone knew where Lambeth Walk was."

Harry began to run like a man being pursued and he didn't stop until he came to a block of flats that was so dilapidated he could only wonder which Prince Edward it had been named after. He pushed open a door that wouldn't survive much longer on those hinges and walked quickly up a flight of stairs, stepping nimbly between piles of rubbish that hadn't been cleared for days.

When he reached the second floor, he stopped outside No. 23 and knocked firmly on the door, but there was no reply. He knocked again, louder, but still no one responded. He ran back down the stairs in search of someone who worked in the building, and when he reached the basement he found an old man slumped in an even older chair, smoking a roll-up and flicking through the pages of the *Daily Mirror*.

"Have you seen Captain Tarrant recently?" Harry asked sharply.

"Not for the past couple of weeks, sir," said the man, leaping to his feet and almost standing to attention when he heard Harry's accent.

"Do you have a master key that will open his flat?" asked Harry.

"I do, sir, but I'm not allowed to use it except in emergencies."

"I can assure you this is an emergency," said Harry, who turned and bounded back up the stairs, not waiting for his reply.

The man followed, if not quite as quickly. Once he'd caught up, he opened the door. Harry moved quickly from room to room, but there was no sign of Old Jack. The last door he came to was closed. He knocked quietly, fearing the worst. When there was no reply, he cautiously went in, to find a neatly made bed and no sign of anyone. He must still be with Sir Walter, was Harry's first thought.

He thanked the porter, walked back down the stairs and out onto the street as he tried to gather his thoughts. He hailed a passing taxi, not wanting to waste any more time on buses in a city that did not know him.

"Paddington Station. I'm in a hurry."

"Everyone seems to be in a hurry today," said the cabbie as he moved off.

Twenty minutes later Harry was standing on platform 6, but it was another fifty minutes before the train would depart for Temple Meads. He used the time to grab a sandwich—"Only got cheese, sir"—and a cup of tea and to phone Miss Watson to let her know that Old Jack hadn't been back to his flat. If it was possible, she sounded even more harassed than when he had left her. "I'm on my way to Bristol," he told her. "I'll ring you as soon as I catch up with him."

As the train made its way out of the capital, through the smog-filled back streets of the city and into the clean air of the countryside, Harry decided he had no choice but to go straight to Sir

Walter's office at the dockyard, even if it meant running into Hugo Barrington. Finding Old Jack surely outweighed any other consideration.

Once the train shunted into Temple Meads, Harry knew the two buses he needed to catch without having to ask the paperboy who was standing on the corner bellowing *"Britain Awaits Hitler's Response"* at the top of his voice. Same headline, but this time a Bristolian accent. Thirty minutes later, Harry was at the dockyard gates.

"Can I help you?" asked a guard who didn't recognize him.

"I have an appointment with Sir Walter," said Harry, hoping this would not be questioned.

"Of course, sir. Do you know the way to his office?"

"Yes, thank you," said Harry. He started walking slowly toward a building he'd never entered before. He began to think about what he would do if he came face to face with Hugo Barrington before he reached Sir Walter's office.

He was pleased to see the chairman's Rolls-Royce parked in its usual place, and even more relieved that there was no sign of Hugo Barrington's Bugatti. He was just about to enter Barrington House when he glanced at the railway carriage in the distance. Was it just possible? He changed direction and walked toward the Pullman *wagon-lit,* as Old Jack was wont to describe it after a second glass of whiskey.

When Harry reached the carriage he knocked gently on the glass pane as if it were a grand home. A butler did not appear, so he opened the door and climbed in. He walked along the corridor to first class, and there he was, sitting in his usual seat.

It was the first time Harry had ever seen Old Jack wearing his Victoria Cross.

Harry took the seat opposite his friend and recalled the first time he'd sat there. He must have been about five and his feet hadn't reached the ground. Then he thought of the time he'd run away from St. Bede's, and the shrewd old gentleman had persuaded him to be back in time for breakfast. He recalled when Old Jack had come to hear him sing a solo in the church, the time his voice had broken. Old Jack had dismissed this as a minor setback.

Then there was the day he learned he'd failed to win a scholarship to Bristol Grammar School, a major setback. Despite his failure, Old Jack had presented him with the Ingersoll watch he was still wearing today. It must have cost him every penny he possessed. In Harry's last year at school, Old Jack had traveled down from London to see him playing Romeo, and Harry had introduced him to Emma for the first time. And he would never forget his final speech day, when Jack had sat on stage as a governor of his old school and watched Harry being awarded the English prize.

And now, Harry would never be able to thank him for so many acts of friendship over the years that couldn't be repaid. He stared at a man he'd loved and had assumed would never die. As they sat there together in first class, the sun went down on his young life.

50

HARRY WATCHED AS the stretcher was placed in the ambulance. A heart attack, the doctor had said, before the ambulance drove away.

Harry didn't need to go and tell Sir Walter that Old Jack was dead, because when he woke the following morning, the chairman of Barrington's was sitting by his side.

"He told me he no longer had any reason to live," were Sir Walter's first words. "We have both lost a close and dear friend."

Harry's response took Sir Walter by surprise. "What will you do with this carriage, now that Old Jack is no longer around?"

"No one will be allowed anywhere near it, as long as I'm chairman," said Sir Walter. "It harbors too many personal memories for me."

"Me too," said Harry. "I spent more time here when I was a boy than I did in my own home."

"Or in the classroom for that matter," said Sir Walter with a wry smile. "I used to watch you from my office window. I thought what an impressive child you must be if Old Jack was willing to spend so much time with you."

Harry smiled when he remembered how Old Jack had come up with a reason why he should go back to school and learn to read and write.

"What will you do now, Harry? Return to Oxford and continue with your studies?"

"No, sir. I fear that we'll be at war by . . ."

"By the end of the month would be my guess," said Sir Walter.

"Then I'll leave Oxford immediately and join the navy. I've already told my college supervisor, Mr. Bainbridge, that that's what I plan to do. He assured me I can return and continue with my studies as soon as the war is over."

"Typical of Oxford," said Sir Walter, "they always take the long view. So will you go to Dartmouth and train as a naval officer?"

"No, sir, I've been around ships all my life. In any case, Old Jack started out as a private soldier and managed to work his way up through the ranks, so why shouldn't I?"

"Why not indeed?" said Sir Walter. "In fact, that was one of the reasons he was always considered to be a class above the rest of us who served with him."

"I had no idea you'd served together."

"Oh yes, I served with Captain Tarrant in South Africa," said Sir Walter. "I was one of the twenty-four men whose lives he saved on the day he was awarded the Victoria Cross."

"That explains so much that I've never really understood," said Harry. He then surprised Sir Walter a second time. "Do I know any of the others, sir?"

"The Frob," said Sir Walter. "But in those days he was Lieutenant Frobisher. Corporal Holcombe, Mr. Holcombe's father. And young Private Deakins."

"Deakins's father?" said Harry.

"Yes. Sprogg, as we used to call him. A fine young soldier. He never said much, but he turned out to be very brave. Lost an arm on that dreadful day."

The two men fell silent, each lost in his own thoughts of Old Jack, before Sir Walter asked, "So if you're not going to Dartmouth, my boy, may I ask how you plan to win the war single-handed?"

"I'll serve on any ship that will take me, sir, as long as they're willing to go in search of His Britannic Majesty's enemies."

"Then it's possible I may be able to help."

"That's kind of you, sir, but I want to join a war ship, not a passenger liner or a cargo vessel."

Sir Walter smiled again. "And so you will, dear boy. Don't forget, I'm kept informed about every ship that comes in and out of these docks and I know most of their captains. Come to think of it, I knew most of their fathers when they were captains. Why don't we go up to my office and see what ships are due in and out of the port in the next few days, and, more important, find out if any of them might be willing to take you on?"

"That's very decent of you, sir, but would it be all right if I visited my mother first? I might not have the chance to see her again for some time."

"Only right and proper, my boy," said Sir Walter. "And once you've been to see your mother, why don't you drop into my office later this afternoon? That should give me enough time to check on the latest shipping lists."

"Thank you, sir. I'll return as soon as I've told my mother what I plan to do."

"When you come back, just tell the man on the gate you've got an appointment with the chairman, then you shouldn't have any trouble getting past security."

"Thank you, sir," said Harry, masking a smile.

"And do pass on my kindest regards to your dear mother. A remarkable woman."

Harry was reminded why Sir Walter was Old Jack's closest friend.

<o>

Harry walked into the Grand Hotel, a magnificent Victorian building in the center of the city, and asked the doorman the way to the dining room. He walked across the lobby and was surprised to find a small queue at the maître d's desk, waiting to be allocated tables. He joined the back of the queue, recalling how his mother had always disapproved of him dropping in to see her at Tilly's or the Royal Hotel during working hours.

While Harry waited, he looked around the dining room, which was full of chattering people, none of whom looked as if they were anticipating a food shortage, or thinking of enlisting in the armed forces should the country go to war. Food was being whisked in and out of the swing doors on heavily laden silver trays, while a man in a chef's outfit was wheeling a trolley from table to table, slicing off slivers of beef, while another followed in his wake carrying a gravy boat.

Harry could see no sign of his mother. He was even beginning to wonder if Giles had only told him what he wanted to hear, when suddenly she burst through the swing doors, three plates balanced on her arms. She placed them in front of her customers so deftly they hardly noticed she was there, then returned to the kitchen. She was back a moment later, carrying three vegetable dishes. By the time Harry had reached the front of the queue he'd been re-minded of who had given him his boundless energy, uncritical enthusiasm and a spirit that didn't contemplate defeat. How would he ever be able to repay this remarkable woman for all the sacri-fices she had made—

"I'm sorry to have kept you waiting, sir," said the maître d', in-terrupting his thoughts, "but I don't have a table available at the moment. If you'd care to come back in about twenty minutes?"

Harry didn't tell him he didn't actually want a table, and not just because his mother was one of the waitresses, but because he wouldn't have been able to afford anything on the menu other than perhaps the gravy.

"I'll come back later," he said, trying to sound disappointed. About ten years later, he thought, by which time he suspected his mother would probably be the maître d'. He left the hotel with a smile on his face and took a bus back to the docks.

◄◦►

He was ushered straight through to Sir Walter's office by his sec-retary and found the chairman leaning on his desk, peering down at the port schedules, timetables and ocean charts that covered every inch of its surface.

"Have a seat, dear boy," said Sir Walter, before fixing his monocle in his right eye and looking sternly at Harry. "I've had a little time to think about our conversation this morning," he continued, sounding very serious, "and before we go any further, I need to be convinced that you're making the right decision."

"I'm absolutely certain," said Harry without hesitation.

"That may be, but I'm equally certain that Jack would have

advised you to return to Oxford and wait until you were called up."

"He may well have done so, sir, but he wouldn't have taken his own advice."

"How well you knew him," said Sir Walter. "Indeed, that's exactly what I expected you to say. Let me tell you what I've come up with so far," he continued, returning his attention to the papers that covered his desk. "The good news is that the Royal Navy battleship HMS *Resolution* is due to dock at Bristol in about a month's time, when it will refuel before awaiting further orders."

"A month?" said Harry, making no attempt to hide his frustration.

"Patience, boy," said Sir Walter. "The reason I chose the *Resolution* is because the captain is an old friend, and I'm confident I can get you on board as a deckhand, as long as the other part of my plan works out."

"But would the captain of the *Resolution* consider taking on someone with no seafaring experience?"

"Probably not, but if everything else falls into place, by the time you board the *Resolution* you will be an old sea dog."

Recalling one of Old Jack's favorite homilies, *I find I don't learn a lot while I'm talking*, Harry decided to stop interrupting and start listening.

"Now," Sir Walter continued, "I've identified three ships that are due to leave Bristol in the next twenty-four hours and are expected to return within three to four weeks, which will give you more than enough time to sign up as a deckhand on the *Resolution*."

Harry wanted to interrupt, but didn't.

"Let's begin with my first choice. The *Devonian* is bound for Cuba, with a manifest of cotton dresses, potatoes and Raleigh Lenton bicycles, and is due to return to Bristol in four weeks' time with a cargo of tobacco, sugar and bananas.

"The second ship on my shortlist is the SS *Kansas Star*, a passenger vessel that will be sailing to New York on the first tide tomorrow. It has been requisitioned by the United States government to transport American nationals back home before Britain finds itself at war with Germany.

"The third is an empty oil tanker, the SS *Princess Beatrice,* which is on its way back to Amsterdam to refuel and will return to Bristol with a full load before the end of the month. All three skippers are painfully aware that they need to be safely back in port as quickly as possible, because if war is declared, the two merchant vessels will be considered fair game by the Germans, while only the *Kansas Star* will be safe from the German U-boats skulking around the Atlantic just waiting for the order to sink anything flying a red or blue ensign."

"What crew are these ships in need of?" asked Harry. "I'm not exactly overqualified."

Sir Walter searched around his desk again, before extracting another sheet of paper. "The *Princess Beatrice* is short of a deck-hand, the *Kansas Star* is looking for someone to work in the kitch-ens, which usually means as a washer-upper or a waiter, while the *Devonian* needs a fourth officer."

"So that one can be removed from the shortlist."

"Funnily enough," said Sir Walter, "that's the position I con-sider you best qualified for. The *Devonian* has a crew of thirty-seven, and rarely goes to sea with a trainee officer, so no one would expect you to be anything other than a novice."

"But why would the captain consider me?"

"Because I told him you were my grandson."

51

HARRY WALKED ALONG the dock toward the *Devonian*. The small suitcase he was carrying made him feel like a schoolboy on his first day of term. What would the headmaster be like? Would he sleep in a bed next to a Giles or a Deakins? Would he come across an Old Jack? Would there be a Fisher on board?

Although Sir Walter had offered to accompany him and introduce him to the captain, Harry had felt that would not be the best way to endear himself to his new shipmates.

He stopped for a moment and looked closely at the ancient vessel on which he would be spending the next month. Sir Walter had told him that the *Devonian* had been built in 1913, when the oceans were still dominated by sail and a motorized cargo vessel would have been thought the latest thing. But now, twenty-six years later, it wouldn't be too long before she was decommissioned and taken to that area of the docks where old ships are broken up and their parts sold for scrap.

Sir Walter had also hinted that as Captain Havens only had one more year to serve before he retired, the owners might decide to scrap him at the same time as his ship.

The *Devonian*'s Articles of Agreement showed a crew of thirty-seven, but as on so many cargo ships, that number wasn't quite accurate: a cook and a washer-up picked up in Hong Kong didn't appear on the payroll, nor did the occasional deckhand or two who was fleeing the law and had no desire to return to his homeland.

Harry made his way slowly up the gangway. Once he'd stepped

on deck, he didn't move until he'd received permission to board. After all his years of hanging around the docks, he was well aware of ship's protocol. He looked up at the bridge and assumed the man he saw giving orders must be Captain Havens. Sir Walter had told him the senior officer on a cargo vessel was in fact a master mariner but should always be addressed on board as captain. Captain Havens was a shade under six foot, and looked nearer fifty than sixty. He was stockily built, with a weathered, tanned face and a dark neatly trimmed beard that, as he was going bald, made him look like George V.

When he spotted Harry waiting at the top of the gangway, the captain gave a crisp order to the officer standing next to him on the bridge, before making his way down onto the deck.

"I'm Captain Havens," he said briskly. "You must be Harry Clifton." He shook Harry warmly by the hand. "Welcome aboard the *Devonian*. You come highly recommended."

"I should point out, sir," began Harry, "that this is my first—"

"I'm aware of that," said Havens, lowering his voice, "but I'd keep it to yourself if you don't want your time on board to be a living hell. And whatever you do, don't mention you were at Oxford, because most of this lot," he said, indicating the seamen working on the deck, "will think it's just the name of another ship. Follow me. I'll show you the fourth officer's quarters."

Harry followed in the captain's wake, aware that a dozen suspicious eyes were watching his every move.

"There are two other officers on my ship," said the captain once Harry had caught up with him. "Jim Patterson, the senior engineer, spends most of his life down below in the boiler room, so you'll only see him at mealtimes, and sometimes not even then. He's served with me for the past fourteen years, and frankly I doubt if this old lady would still make it halfway across the Channel, let alone the Atlantic, if he wasn't down there to coax her along. My third officer, Tom Bradshaw, is on the bridge. He's only been with me for three years, so he's not yet earned his ticket. He keeps himself to himself, but whoever trained him knew what they were doing, because he's a damn fine officer."

Havens began to disappear down a narrow stairwell that led

to the deck below. "That's my cabin," he said as he continued down the corridor, "and that's Mr. Patterson's." He came to a halt in front of what appeared to be a broom cupboard. "This is your cabin." He pushed the door open but it only moved a few inches before it banged against a narrow wooden bed. "I won't come in as there isn't room for both of us. You'll find some clothes on the bed. Once you've changed, join me on the bridge. We'll be set-ting sail within the hour. Leaving the harbor will probably be the most interesting part of the voyage until we dock in Cuba."

Harry squeezed through the half-open door and had to close it behind him to allow enough room to change his clothes. He checked the gear that had been left, neatly folded, on his bunk: two thick blue sweaters, two white shirts, two pairs of blue trou-sers, three pairs of blue woolen socks and a pair of canvas shoes with thick rubber soles. It really was like being back at school. Every item had one thing in common: they all looked as if they'd been worn by several other people before Harry. He quickly changed into his seaman's gear, then unpacked his suitcase.

As there was only one drawer, Harry placed the little suitcase, full of his civilian clothes, under the bed—the only thing in the cabin that fitted perfectly. He opened the door, squeezed back into the corridor and went in search of the stairwell. Once he'd located it, he emerged back on deck. Several more pairs of suspi-cious eyes followed his progress.

"Mr. Clifton," said the captain as Harry stepped onto the bridge for the first time, "this is Tom Bradshaw, the third officer, who will be taking the ship out of the harbor as soon as we've been given clearance by the port authority. By the way, Mr. Brad-shaw," said Havens, "one of our tasks on this voyage will be to teach this young pup everything we know, so that when we re-turn to Bristol in a month's time the crew of HMS *Resolution* will mistake him for an old sea dog."

If Mr. Bradshaw commented, his words were drowned by two long blasts on a siren, a sound Harry had heard many times over the years, indicating that the two tugboats were in place and wait-ing to escort the *Devonian* out of the harbor. The captain pressed some tobacco into his well-worn briar pipe, while Mr. Bradshaw acknowledged the signal with two blasts of the ship's horn, to confirm that the *Devonian* was ready to depart.

"Prepare to cast off, Mr. Bradshaw," said Captain Havens, striking a match.

Mr. Bradshaw removed the cover from a brass voicepipe Harry hadn't noticed until that moment. "All engines slow ahead, Mr. Patterson. The tugboats are in place and ready to escort us out of harbor," he added, revealing a slight American accent.

"All engines slow ahead, Mr. Bradshaw," came back a voice from the boiler room.

Harry looked down over the side of the bridge and watched as the crew carried out their allotted tasks. Four men, two at the bow and two at the stern, were unwinding thick ropes from the capstans on the dock. Another two were hauling up the gangway. "Keep your eye on the pilot," said the captain between puffs on his pipe. "It's his responsibility to guide us out of the harbor and safely into the Channel. Once he's done that, Mr. Bradshaw will take over. If you turn out to be any good, Mr. Clifton, you may be allowed to take his place in about a year's time, but not until I've retired and Mr. Bradshaw has taken over command." As Bradshaw didn't give even the flicker of a smile, Harry remained silent and continued to watch everything going on around him. "No one is allowed to take my girl out at night," continued Captain Havens, "unless I'm sure he won't take any liberties with her." Again, Bradshaw didn't smile, but then he may have heard the comment before.

Harry found himself fascinated by how smoothly the whole operation was carried out. The *Devonian* eased away from the quayside and, with the help of the two tugboats, nosed her way slowly out of the docks, along the River Avon and under the suspension bridge.

"Do you know who built that bridge, Mr. Clifton?" the captain asked, taking his pipe out of his mouth.

"Isambard Kingdom Brunel, sir," said Harry.

"And why did he never live to see it opened?"

"Because the local council ran out of money, and he died before the bridge was completed."

The captain scowled. "Next you'll be telling me it's named after you," he said, putting his pipe back in his mouth. He didn't speak again until the tugboats had reached Barry Island, when they gave two more long blasts, released their lines and headed back to port.

The *Devonian* may have been an old lady, but it soon became clear to Harry that Captain Havens and his crew knew exactly how to handle her.

"Take over, Mr. Bradshaw," said the captain, as another pair of eyes appeared on the bridge, their owner carrying two mugs of hot tea. "There will be three officers on the bridge during this crossing, Lu, so be sure that Mr. Clifton also gets a mug of tea." The Chinese man nodded and disappeared below deck.

Once the harbor lights had disappeared over the horizon, the waves became larger and larger, causing the ship to roll from side to side. Havens and Bradshaw stood, feet apart, appearing to be glued to the deck, while Harry found himself regularly having to cling to something to make sure he didn't fall over. When Lu reappeared with a third mug of tea, Harry chose not to mention to the captain that it was cold, and that his mother usually added a lump of sugar.

Just as Harry was beginning to feel a little more confident, almost enjoying the experience, the captain said, "Not much more you can do tonight, Mr. Clifton. Why don't you go below and try to catch some shut-eye. Be back on the bridge by seven twenty to take over the breakfast watch." Harry was about to protest, when a smile appeared on Mr. Bradshaw's face for the first time.

"Goodnight, sir," said Harry before making his way down the steps and onto the deck. He wobbled slowly toward the narrow stairwell, feeling with every step he took that he was being watched by even more eyes. One voice said, loud enough for him to hear, "He must be a passenger."

"No, he's an officer," said a second voice.

"What's the difference?" Several men laughed.

Once he was back in his cabin, he undressed and climbed onto the thin wooden bunk. He tried to find a comfortable position without falling out or rolling into the wall as the ship swayed from side to side as well as lurching up and down. He didn't even have a wash basin to be sick in, or a porthole to be sick out of.

As he lay awake, his thoughts turned to Emma. He wondered if she was still in Scotland or had returned to the Manor House, or perhaps she'd already taken up residence at Oxford. Would Giles be wondering where he was, or had Sir Walter told him he'd gone to sea and would be joining the *Resolution* the moment he landed back in Bristol? And would his mother be wondering where he could be? Perhaps he should have broken her golden rule and interrupted her at work. Finally, he thought about Old Jack, and suddenly felt guilty when he realized he wouldn't be back in time for his funeral.

What Harry couldn't know was that his own funeral would take place before Old Jack's.

52

HARRY WAS WOKEN by the sound of four bells. He leaped up, hitting his head on the ceiling, threw on his clothes, squeezed into the corridor, shot up the stairwell, ran across the deck and bounded up the steps on to the bridge.

"Sorry I'm late, sir, I must have overslept."

"You don't have to call me sir when we're on our own," said Bradshaw, "the name's Tom. And as a matter of fact, you're over an hour early. The skipper obviously forgot to tell you it's seven bells for the breakfast watch, and four for the six o'clock watch. But as you're here, why don't you take over the wheel while I take a leak." The shock for Harry was to realize that Bradshaw wasn't joking. "Just be sure the arrow on the compass is always pointing sou'-sou'-west, then you can't go far wrong," he added, his American accent sounding more pronounced.

Harry took the wheel with both hands and stared intently at the little black arrow as he tried to keep the ship plowing through the waves in a straight line. When he looked back at the wake, he saw that the neat straight line Bradshaw had achieved with such apparent ease had been replaced by the sort of curves more associated with Mae West. Although Bradshaw was only away for a few minutes, Harry had rarely been more pleased to see anyone when he returned.

Bradshaw took over and the uninterrupted straight line quickly reappeared, although he only had one hand on the wheel.

"Remember, you're handling a lady," said Bradshaw. "You don't cling to her, but gently caress her. If you can manage that, she'll stay on the straight and narrow. Now try again, while I plot our seven bells position on the daily chart."

When one bell rang twenty-five minutes later and the captain appeared on the bridge to relieve Bradshaw, Harry's line in the ocean may not have been entirely straight, but at least it no longer appeared as if the ship was being steered by a drunken sailor.

—◁◦▷—

At breakfast, Harry was introduced to a man who could only have been the first engineer.

Jim Patterson's ghostly complexion made him look as if he'd spent most of his life below decks, and his paunch suggested he spent the rest of the time eating. Unlike Bradshaw, he never stopped talking, and it quickly became clear to Harry that he and the skipper were old friends.

The Chinese cook appeared, carrying three plates that could have been cleaner. Harry avoided the greasy bacon and fried tomatoes in favor of a piece of burned toast and an apple.

"Why don't you spend the rest of the morning finding your way around the ship, Mr. Clifton," suggested the captain after the plates had been cleared away. "You could even join Mr. Patterson in the engine room and see how many minutes you survive down there." Patterson burst out laughing, grabbed the last two pieces of toast and said, "If you think these are burned, wait until you've spent a few minutes with me."

—◁◦▷—

Like a cat that has been left alone in a new house, Harry began stalking around the outside of the deck as he tried to become familiar with his new kingdom.

He knew the ship was 475 feet long with a 56-foot beam and its top speed was fifteen knots, but he'd had no idea there would be so many nooks and crannies that undoubtedly served some purpose which, given time, he would learn. Harry also noticed there wasn't any part of the deck the captain couldn't keep a watchful eye on from the bridge, so there was no chance of escape for an idle seaman.

Harry took the stairwell down to the middle deck. The aft section consisted of the officers' quarters, amidships was the galley, and forward was a large open area of slung hammocks. How anyone could possibly sleep in one of those was beyond him. Then he noticed half a dozen sailors, who must have come off the dog watch, swaying gently from side to side with the rhythm of the ship and sleeping contentedly.

A narrow steel stairwell led down to the lower deck, where the wooden crates that held the 144 Raleigh bicycles, a thousand cotton dresses and two tons of potatoes were all safely secured, and wouldn't be opened until after the ship docked in Cuba.

Finally, he descended a narrow ladder that led to the boiler room, and Mr. Patterson's domain. He heaved open the heavy metal hatch and, like Shadrach, Meshach and Abednego, marched boldly into the fiery furnace. He stood and watched as half a dozen squat, muscle-bound men, their vests soiled with black dust, sweat pouring down their backs, shoveled coal into two gaping mouths that needed to be fed more than four meals a day.

As Captain Havens had predicted, it was only a few minutes before Harry had to stagger back into the corridor, sweating and gasping for breath. It was some time before he recovered enough to make his way back up onto the deck, where he fell on his knees and gulped in the fresh air. He could only wonder how those men could survive in such conditions and be expected to carry out three two-hour shifts a day, seven days a week.

Once Harry had recovered, he made his way back up to the bridge, armed with a hundred questions, from which star in the Plow points to the North Star, to how many nautical miles the ship could average per day, to how many tons of coal were required for . . . The captain happily answered them all, without once appearing exasperated by the young fourth officer's unquenchable thirst for knowledge. In fact, Captain Havens remarked to Mr. Bradshaw during Harry's break that what impressed him most about the lad was that he never asked the same question twice.

◄o►

During the next few days, Harry learned how to check the compass against the dotted line on the chart, how to gauge wind direction by watching seagulls, and how to take the ship through the trough of a wave and still maintain a constant course. By the end of the first week, he was allowed to take over the wheel whenever an officer took a meal break. By night, the captain taught him the names of the stars, which, he pointed out, were every bit as reliable as a compass, but he confessed his knowledge was limited to the northern hemisphere as the *Devonian* had never crossed the equator in all her twenty-six years on the high seas.

After ten days at sea, the captain was almost hoping for a storm, not only to stop the endless questions but also to see if there was anything that could throw this young man off his stride. Jim Patterson had already warned him that Mr. Clifton had survived for an hour in the boiler room that morning and was determined to complete a full shift before they docked in Cuba.

"At least you're spared his endless questions down there," remarked the captain.

"This week," responded the chief engineer.

Captain Havens wondered if a time would come when he learned something from his fourth officer. It happened on the twelfth day of the voyage, just after Harry had completed his first two-hour shift in the boiler room.

"Did you know that Mr. Patterson collects stamps, sir?" Harry asked.

"Yes, I did," replied the captain confidently.

"And that his collection now numbers over four thousand, including an unperforated Penny Black and a South African triangular Cape of Good Hope?"

"Yes, I did," repeated the captain.

"And that the collection is now worth more than his home in Mablethorpe?"

"It's only a cottage, damn it," said the captain, trying to hold his own, and before Harry could ask his next question, he added, "I'd be more interested if you could find out as much about Tom Bradshaw as you seem to have wormed out of my chief engineer.

Because frankly, Harry, I know more about you after twelve days than I do about my third officer after three years, and until now, I'd never thought of Americans as being a reserved race."

The more Harry thought about the captain's observation, the more he realized just how little he too knew about Tom, despite having spent many hours with him on the bridge. He had no idea if the man had any brothers or sisters, what his father did for a living, where his parents lived, or whether he even had a girl-friend. And only his accent gave away the fact that he was an American, because Harry didn't know which town, or even state, he hailed from.

Seven bells rang. "Would you take over the wheel, Mr. Clifton," said the captain, "while I join Mr. Patterson and Mr. Bradshaw for dinner? Don't hesitate to let me know if you spot anything," he added as he left the bridge, "especially if it's bigger than we are."

"Aye aye, sir," said Harry, delighted to be left in charge, even if it was only for forty minutes, although those forty minutes were being extended each day.

─◦─

It was when Harry asked him how many more days it would be before they reached Cuba that Captain Havens realized the preco-cious youth was already bored. He was beginning to feel some sympathy for the captain of HMS *Resolution,* who had no idea what he was letting himself in for.

Harry had recently been taking over the wheel after dinner so that the other officers could enjoy a few hands of gin rummy before returning to the bridge. And whenever the Chinaman took up Harry's mug of tea now, it was always piping hot, with the requested one lump of sugar.

Mr. Patterson was heard to remark to the captain one evening that should Mr. Clifton decide to take over the ship before they got back to Bristol, he wasn't sure whom he'd side with.

"Are you thinking of inciting a mutiny, Jim?" asked Havens as he poured his chief engineer another tot of rum.

"No, but I must warn you, skipper, that the young turk has already reorganized the shifts in the boiler room. So I know whose side my lads would be on."

"Then the least we can do," said Havens, pouring himself a glass of rum, "is order the flag officer to send a message to the *Resolution*, warning them what they'll be up against."

"But we don't have a flag officer," said Patterson.

"Then we'll have to clap the lad in irons," said the captain.

"Good idea, skipper. It's just a shame we don't have any irons."

"More's the pity. Remind me to pick some up as soon as we get back to Bristol."

"But you seem to have forgotten Clifton's leaving us to join the *Resolution* the moment we dock," Patterson said.

The captain swallowed a mouthful of rum before repeating, "More's the pity."

53

HARRY REPORTED TO the bridge a few minutes before seven bells to relieve Mr. Bradshaw, so he could go below and join the captain for dinner.

The length of time Tom left him in charge of the bridge was becoming longer and longer with each watch, but Harry never complained, because he enjoyed the illusion that for an hour a day the ship was under his command.

He checked the arrow on the compass and steered the course that had been set by the captain. He had even been entrusted with entering their position on the chart and writing up the daily log before he came off duty.

As Harry stood alone on the bridge, a full moon, a calm sea, and a thousand miles of ocean ahead of him, his thoughts drifted back to England. He wondered what Emma was doing at that moment.

Emma was sitting in her room at Somerville College, Oxford, tuning her radio to the Home Service so she could hear Mr. Neville Chamberlain address the nation.

"This is the BBC in London. You will now hear a statement from the Prime Minister."

"I am speaking to you from the Cabinet room, Ten Downing Street. This morning the British Ambassador in Berlin handed the German government a final note, stating that unless we heard from them by eleven o'clock, that they were prepared at once to withdraw their troops from Poland, a state of war would exist between us. I have to tell you now, that no such undertaking has

been received, and that consequently, this country is at war with Germany."

But as the *Devonian's* radio was unable to pick up the BBC, everyone on board went about their business as if it were a normal day.

Harry was still thinking about Emma when the first one shot past the bow. He wasn't sure what he should do. He was loath to disturb the captain during dinner for fear of being reprimanded for wasting his time. Harry was wide awake when he saw the second one, and this time he had no doubt what it was. Harry watched as the long, slender, shiny object slithered below the surface toward the bow of the ship. He instinctively swung the wheel to starboard but the ship veered to port. It wasn't quite what he'd intended, but the mistake gave him enough time to raise the alarm because the object shot past the bow, missing the ship by several yards.

This time he didn't hesitate and jammed the palm of his hand on the klaxon, which immediately emitted a loud blast. Moments later Mr. Bradshaw appeared on deck and began racing toward the bridge, closely followed by the captain, pulling on his jacket.

One by one, the rest of the crew came rushing out of the bowels of the ship and headed straight for their stations, assuming it must be an unscheduled fire drill.

"What's the problem, Mr. Clifton?" asked Captain Havens calmly as he stepped onto the bridge.

"I think I saw a torpedo, sir, but as I've never seen one before, I can't be sure."

"Could it have been a dolphin enjoying our leftovers?" suggested the captain.

"No, sir, it wasn't a dolphin."

"I've never seen a torpedo either," Havens admitted as he took over the wheel. "Which direction was it coming from?"

"Nor'-nor'-east."

"Mr. Bradshaw," said the captain, "all crew to emergency stations and prepare to lower the lifeboats on my command."

"Aye aye, sir," said Bradshaw, who slid down the railings onto the deck and immediately began to organize the crew.

"Mr. Clifton, keep your eyes peeled and tell me the moment you spot anything."

Harry grabbed the binoculars and began a slow sweep of the ocean. At the same time, the captain bellowed down the voice-pipe, "All engines reverse, Mr. Patterson, all engines reverse, and stand by for further orders."

"Aye aye, sir," said a startled chief engineer, who hadn't heard that order since 1918.

"Another one," said Harry. "Nor'-nor'-east, coming directly toward us."

"I see it," said the captain. He swung the wheel to the left and the torpedo missed them by only a few feet. He knew he was unlikely to pull off that trick again.

"You were right, Mr. Clifton. That wasn't a dolphin," said Havens matter-of-factly. Under his breath he added, "We must be at war. The enemy has torpedoes, and all I've got is a hundred and forty-four Raleigh bicycles, a few sacks of potatoes and some cotton dresses." Harry kept his eyes peeled.

The captain remained so calm that Harry felt almost no sense of danger. "Number four coming directly at us, sir," he said. "Nor'-nor'-east again."

Havens gamely tried to maneuver the old lady one more time, but she didn't respond quickly enough to his unwelcome advances and the torpedo ripped into the ship's bow. A few minutes later Mr. Patterson reported that a fire had broken out below the waterline and that his men were finding it impossible to douse the flames with the ship's primitive foam hoses. The captain didn't need to be told that he was facing a hopeless task.

"Mr. Bradshaw, prepare to abandon ship. All crew to stand by the lifeboats and await further orders."

"Aye aye, sir," shouted Bradshaw from the deck.

Havens bellowed down the voicepipe. "Mr. Patterson, get yourself and your men out of there immediately, and I mean immediately, and report to the lifeboats."

"We're on our way, skipper."

"Another one, sir," said Harry. "Nor'-nor'-west, heading toward the starboard side, amidships."

The captain swung the wheel once again, but he knew this time he would not be able to ride the punch. Seconds later, the torpedo ripped into the ship, which began to list to one side.

"Abandon ship!" shouted Havens, reaching for the tannoy. "Abandon ship!" he repeated several times, before he turned to Harry, who was still scanning the sea through his binoculars.

"Make your way to the nearest lifeboat, Mr. Clifton, and sharpish. There's no point in anyone remaining on the bridge."

"Aye aye, sir," said Harry.

"Captain," came a voice from the engine room, "number four hold is jammed. I'm trapped belowdecks along with five of my men."

"We're on our way, Mr. Patterson. We'll have you out of there in no time. Change of plan, Mr. Clifton. Follow me." The captain shot down the stairs, his feet barely touching the steps, with Harry just inches behind him.

"Mr. Bradshaw," shouted the captain as he dodged in and out of the oil-fed, lapping flames, which had reached the upper deck, "get the men into the lifeboats sharpish and abandon ship."

"Aye aye, sir," said Bradshaw, who was clinging onto the ship's railings.

"I need an oar. And make sure you have one lifeboat on standby ready to take Mr. Patterson and his men from the boiler room."

Bradshaw grabbed an oar from one of the lifeboats and, with the help of another seaman, managed to pass it to the captain. Harry and the skipper took one end each and stumbled along the deck toward number four hold. Harry was puzzled what use an oar could possibly be against torpedoes, but this wasn't the time to be asking questions.

The captain charged on, past the Chinaman, who was on his knees, head bowed, praying to his God.

"Get yourself into the lifeboat, now, you stupid bugger!" shouted Havens. Mr. Lu rose unsteadily to his feet, but didn't move. As Harry staggered past, he shoved the man in the direction of the third officer, causing Mr. Lu to topple forward and almost fall into Mr. Bradshaw's arms.

When the captain reached the hatch above number four hold, he wedged the thin end of the oar into an arched hook, jumped up and threw all his weight onto the blade. Harry quickly joined him and together they managed to lever up the massive iron plate until there was a gap of about a foot.

"You pull the men out, Mr. Clifton, while I try to keep the hatch open," said Havens, as two hands appeared through the gap.

Harry let go of the oar, fell to his knees and crawled toward the open hatch. As he grabbed the man's shoulders, a wave of water swept over him and into the hold. He yanked the seaman out and shouted at him to report straight to the lifeboats. The second man was more agile and managed to pull himself out without out Harry's assistance, while the third was in such a blind panic that he shot through the hole and banged his head on the hatch lid before staggering off after his shipmates. The next two followed in quick succession and scrambled on their hands and knees in the direction of the last remaining lifeboat. Harry waited for the chief engineer to appear, but there was no sign of him. The ship lurched further over and Harry had to cling to the deck to stop himself falling head-first into the hold.

He peered down into the darkness and spotted an outstretched hand. He put his head through the hole and leaned down as far as he could without falling in, but couldn't quite reach the second officer's fingers. Mr. Patterson tried several times to jump up, but with each attempt his efforts were hampered as more water poured in on top of him. Captain Havens could see what the problem was but couldn't come to their assistance, because if he let go of the oar the hatch lid would come crashing down on Harry.

Patterson, who was now up to his knees in water, shouted, "For God's sake you two, get yourselves into the lifeboats before it's too late!"

"Not a chance," said the captain. "Mr. Clifton, get yourself down there and push the bastard up, then you can follow."

Harry didn't hesitate. He lowered himself backward, feet first, into the hold, gripping the ledge with his fingertips. Finally he let go and dropped into the darkness. The sloshing, oily, freezing water broke his fall and once he'd regained his balance he gripped the sides, lowered himself down into the water and said, "Climb onto my shoulders, sir, and you should be able to reach."

The chief engineer obeyed the fourth officer, but when he stretched up, he was still a few inches short of the deck. Harry used every ounce of strength in his body to push Patterson further up until he was able to reach the rim of the hatch and cling on by the tips of his fingers. Water was now pouring into the hold, as the ship listed further and further over. Harry placed a hand under each of Mr. Patterson's buttocks and began to press like a weightlifter until the chief engineer's head appeared above the deck.

"Good to see you, Jim," grunted the captain, as he continued to place every ounce of his weight onto the oar.

"You too, Arnold," replied the chief engineer, as he pulled himself slowly out of the hold.

It was at that moment the last torpedo hit the sinking ship. The oar snapped in half and the iron hatch lid came crashing down on the chief engineer. Like the axe of a medieval executioner, with one slice it cleanly severed his head and slammed shut. Patterson's body fell back into the hold, landing in the water next to Harry.

Harry thanked God he couldn't see Mr. Patterson in the darkness that now surrounded him. At least the water had stopped flooding in, even if it meant there was now no escape.

As the *Devonian* began to keel over, Harry assumed the captain must also have been killed or he surely would have been banging on the hatch trying to find some way of getting him out. As he slumped down into the water, Harry thought how ironic it was that he should go to his grave like his father, entombed in the hollow bottom of a ship. He clung to the side of the hold in one final effort to cheat death. As he waited for the water to rise inch by inch above his shoulders, his neck, his head, myriad faces flashed before him. Strange thoughts take over when you know you only have a few moments left to live.

At least his death would solve problems for so many people he loved. Emma would be released from her pledge to forsake all others for the rest of her days. Sir Walter would no longer have to worry about the implications of his father's will. In time, Giles would inherit the family title and all his father's worldly goods. Even Hugo Barrington might survive now that it would no longer be necessary for him to prove he wasn't Harry's father. Only his dear mother . . .

Suddenly there was an almighty explosion. The *Devonian* split in two and seconds later both halves reared up like a startled horse, before the broken ship unceremoniously sank to the bottom of the ocean.

The captain of the U-boat watched through his periscope until the *Devonian* had disappeared below the waves, leaving in its wake a thousand brightly colored cotton dresses and countless bodies bobbing up and down in the sea, surrounded by potatoes.

54

"CAN YOU TELL me your name?" Harry looked up at the nurse but couldn't move his lips. "Can you hear me?" she asked. Another American accent.

Harry managed a faint nod, and she smiled. He heard a door opening and although he couldn't see who had entered the sick bay, the nurse left him immediately, so it had to be someone in authority. Even if he couldn't see them, he could hear what they were saying. It made him feel like an eavesdropper.

"Good evening, Nurse Craven," said an older man's voice.

"Good evening, Dr. Wallace," she replied.

"How are our two patients?"

"One's showing definite signs of improvement. The other's still unconscious."

So at least two of us survived, thought Harry. He wanted to cheer but, although his lips moved, no words came out.

"And we still have no idea who they are?"

"No, but Captain Parker came in earlier to see how they were, and when I showed him what was left of their uniforms, he wasn't in much doubt they were both officers."

Harry's heart leaped at the thought that Captain Havens might have survived. He heard the doctor walk over to the other bed but he couldn't turn his head to see who was lying there. A few moments later, he heard, "Poor devil, I'll be surprised if he survives the night."

Then you obviously don't know Captain Havens, Harry wanted to tell him, because you won't kill him off that easily.

The doctor returned to Harry's bedside and began to examine him. Harry could just make out a middle-aged man with a serious, thoughtful face. Once Dr. Wallace had finished his examination, he turned away and whispered to the nurse, "I feel a lot more hopeful about this one, although the odds are still no better than fifty-fifty after what he's been through. Keep fighting, young man," he said, turning to face Harry, though he couldn't be sure if the patient could hear him. "We're going to do everything in our power to keep you alive." Harry wanted to thank him, but all he could manage was another slight nod, before the doctor walked away. "If either of them should die during the night," he heard the doctor whisper to the nurse, "are you familiar with the correct procedure?"

"Yes, doctor. The captain is to be informed immediately, and the body is to be taken down to the morgue." Harry wanted to ask how many of his shipmates were already there.

"And I'd also like to be kept informed," added Wallace, "even if I've turned in for the night."

"Of course, doctor. Can I ask what the captain has decided to do with those poor devils who were already dead when we pulled them out of the water?"

"He's given an order that as they were all sailors, they are to be buried at sea, at first light tomorrow morning."

"Why so early?"

"He doesn't want the passengers to realize just how many lives were lost last night," the doctor added as he walked away. Harry heard a door open. "Goodnight, nurse."

"Goodnight, doctor," the nurse replied, and the door closed.

Nurse Craven walked back and sat down by Harry's bedside. "I don't give a damn about the odds," she said. "You're going to live."

Harry looked up at a nurse who was hidden behind her starched white uniform and white cap, but even so, he couldn't miss the burning conviction in her eyes.

—◇—

When Harry next woke, the room was in darkness apart from a glimmer of light in the far corner, probably from another room.

His first thought was of Captain Havens, fighting for his life in the next bed. He prayed that he would survive and they'd be able to return to England together, when the captain would retire and Harry could sign up with any Royal Navy vessel Sir Walter could get him on.

His thoughts turned to Emma once again, and how his death would have solved so many problems for the Barrington family, problems that would now return to haunt them.

Harry heard the door open again and someone with an unfamiliar step walked into the sick bay. Although he couldn't see who it was, the sound of his shoes suggested two things: it was a man, and he knew where he was going. Another door opened on the far side of the room and the light became brighter.

"Hi, Kristin," said a man's voice.

"Hello, Richard," came back the nurse's reply. "You're late," she said, teasing, not angry.

"Sorry, honey. All the officers had to remain on the bridge until the search for survivors was finally abandoned."

The door closed, and the light softened once more. Harry had no way of knowing how much time had passed before the door opened again—half an hour, an hour perhaps—and he heard their voices.

"Your tie's not straight," said the nurse.

"That won't do," the man replied. "Someone might figure out what we've been up to." She laughed as he began walking toward the door. Suddenly he stopped. "Who are these two?"

"Mr. A and Mr. B. The only survivors from last night's rescue operation."

I'm Mr. C, Harry wanted to tell her as they walked toward his bed. Harry closed his eyes; he didn't want them to think he'd been listening to their conversation. She took his pulse.

"I think Mr. B is getting stronger by the hour. You know, I can't bear the thought of not saving at least one of them." She left Harry and walked over to the other bed.

Harry opened his eyes and turned his head slightly to see a tall young man in a smart white dress uniform with gold epaulets. Without warning, Nurse Craven began to sob. The young man placed an arm gently around her shoulder and tried to comfort her. No, no, Harry wanted to shout, Captain Havens can't die. We're going back to England together.

"What's the procedure in these circumstances?" asked the young officer, sounding rather formal.

"I have to inform the captain immediately, and then wake Dr. Wallace. Once all the papers have been signed and clearance has been authorized, the body will be taken down to the morgue and prepared for tomorrow's burial service."

No, no, no, Harry shouted, but neither of them heard him.

"I pray to whatever God," continued the nurse, "that America doesn't become involved in this war."

"That's never going to happen, honey," said the young officer. "Roosevelt's far too canny to get himself involved in another European war."

"That's what the politicians said last time," Kristin reminded him.

"Hey, what's brought this on?" He sounded concerned.

"Mr. A was about the same age as you," she said. "Perhaps he also had a fiancée back home."

Harry realized that it wasn't Captain Havens in the next bed, but Tom Bradshaw. That was when he made the decision.

--◇--

When Harry woke again, he could hear voices coming from the next room. Moments later, Dr. Wallace and Nurse Craven walked into the sick bay.

"It must have been heart-wrenching," said the nurse.

"It wasn't at all pleasant," admitted the doctor. "Somehow it was made worse because they all went to their graves nameless, although I had to agree with the captain, that's the way a sailor would have wanted to be buried."

"Any news from the other ship?" asked the nurse.

"Yes, they've done a little better than us. Eleven dead, but three survivors: a Chinese man and two Englishmen."

Harry wondered if it was possible that one of the Englishmen might be Captain Havens.

The doctor bent down and unbuttoned Harry's pajama top. He placed a cold stethoscope on several parts of his chest and listened carefully. Then the nurse placed a thermometer in Harry's mouth.

"His temperature is well down, doctor," said the nurse after she had checked the vein of mercury.

"Excellent. You might try giving him some thin soup."

"Yes, of course. Will you need my help with any of the passengers?"

"No, thank you, nurse, your most important job is to make sure this one survives. I'll see you in a couple of hours."

Once the door had closed, the nurse returned to Harry's bedside. She sat down and smiled. "Can you see me?" she asked. Harry nodded. "Can you tell me your name?"

"Tom Bradshaw," he replied.

55

"Tom," said Dr. Wallace once he'd completed his examination of Harry, "I wonder if you can tell me the name of your fellow officer who died last night. I'd like to write to his mother, or his wife if he had one."

"His name was Harry Clifton," said Harry, his voice barely audible. "He wasn't married, but I know his mother quite well. I'd planned to write to her myself."

"That's good of you," said Wallace, "but I'd still like to send her a letter. Do you have her address?"

"Yes, I do," said Harry. "But it might be kinder if she heard from me first, and not from a complete stranger," he suggested.

"If you think so," said Wallace, not sounding at all sure.

"Yes, I do," said Harry, a little more firmly this time. "You can always post my letter when the *Kansas Star* returns to Bristol. That's assuming the captain is still planning to sail back to England, now we're at war with Germany."

"*We* are not at war with Germany," said Wallace.

"No, of course we're not," said Harry, quickly correcting himself. "And let's hope it never comes to that."

"Agreed," said Wallace, "but that won't stop the *Kansas Star* making the return journey. There are still hundreds of Americans stranded in England, with no other way of getting home."

"Isn't that a bit of a risk?" asked Harry. "Especially considering what we've just been through."

"No, I don't think so," said Wallace. "The last thing the Germans will want to do is sink an American passenger ship, which would be sure to drag us into the conflict. I suggest you get some sleep, Tom, because I'm hoping that tomorrow the nurse will be able to take you for a turn around the deck. Only one lap to begin with," he emphasized.

Harry closed his eyes but made no attempt to sleep as he began to think about the decision he'd made, and how many lives it would affect. By taking Tom Bradshaw's identity, he had allowed himself a little breathing space to consider his future. Once they learned that Harry Clifton had been killed at sea, Sir Walter and the rest of the Barrington family would be released from any obligations they might have felt bound by, and Emma would be free to begin a new life. A decision he felt Old Jack would have approved of, although the full implications hadn't yet sunk in.

However, the resurrection of Tom Bradshaw would undoubtedly create its own problems, and he would have to remain constantly on his guard. It didn't help that he knew almost nothing about Bradshaw, so that whenever Nurse Craven asked him about his past, he either had to make something up or change the subject.

Bradshaw had proved very adept at deflecting any questions he didn't wish to answer, and had clearly been a loner. He hadn't set foot in his own country for at least three years, possibly more, so his family would have no way of knowing of his imminent return. As soon as the *Kansas Star* arrived in New York, Harry planned to sail back to England on the first available ship.

His greatest dilemma was how to prevent his mother from being put through any unnecessary suffering by thinking she'd lost her only son. Dr. Wallace had gone some way to solving that particular problem when he promised to post a letter to Maisie the moment he arrived back in England. But Harry still had to write that letter.

He had spent hours going over the text in his mind, so that by the time he'd recovered enough to commit his thoughts to paper, he almost knew the script by heart.

New York
September 8th, 1939

My dearest mother,

I have done everything in my power to make sure you receive this letter before anyone can tell you I was killed at sea.

As the date on this letter shows, I did not die when the Devonian was sunk on September 4th. In fact, I was plucked out of the sea by an American ship and am very much alive. However, an opportunity arose for me to assume another man's identity, and I did so, in the hope it would release both you and the Barrington family from the many problems I seem to have unwittingly caused over the years.

It is important that you realize my love for Emma has in no way diminished; far from it. But I do not feel I have the right to expect her to spend the rest of her life clinging to the vain hope that at some time in the future I might be able to prove that Arthur Clifton and not Hugo Barrington was my father. This way, she can at least consider a future with someone else. I envy that man.

I plan to return to England in the near future. Should you receive any communication from a Tom Bradshaw, it will be from me.

I will be in touch with you the moment I set foot in England, but in the meantime, I must beg you to keep my secret as steadfastly as you kept your own for so many years.

Your loving son,

Harry

He read the letter several times before placing it in an envelope marked "Strictly private and confidential." He addressed it to Mrs. Arthur Clifton, 27 Still House Lane, Bristol.

The following morning, he handed the letter over to Dr. Wallace.

—◇—

"Do you think you're ready to try a short walk around the deck?" asked Kristin.

"Sure am," Harry replied, trying out one of the expressions he'd heard her boyfriend use, although he still found it unnatural to add the word "honey."

During those long hours he'd spent in bed, Harry had listened carefully to Dr. Wallace, and whenever he was alone, he tried to imitate his accent, which he'd heard Kristin describe to Richard as East Coast. Harry was thankful for the hours he'd spent with Dr. Paget learning voice skills that he'd assumed would only be of use on stage. He was on stage. However, he still had the problem of how to deal with Kristin's innocent curiosity about his family background and upbringing.

He was assisted by a novel by Horatio Alger and another by Thornton Wilder, the only two books that had been left behind in the sick bay. From these he was able to conjure up a fictional family who hailed from Bridgeport, Connecticut. They consisted of a father who was a small-town bank manager with Connecticut Trust and Savings, a mother who was a dutiful homemaker and had once come second in the town's annual beauty pageant, and an older sister, Sally, who was happily married to Jake, who ran the local hardware store. He smiled to himself when he recalled Dr. Paget's remark that, with his imagination, he was more likely to end up a writer than an actor.

Harry placed his feet tentatively on the floor and, with Kristin's help, pulled himself slowly up. Once he'd put on a dressing gown, he took her by the arm and made his way unsteadily toward the door, up a flight of steps and out onto the deck.

"How long is it since you've been home?" asked Kristin as they began their slow progress around the deck.

Harry always tried to stick to the little he actually knew about Bradshaw, adding a few snippets from the life of his fictitious family. "Just over three years," he said. "My family never complains, because they knew I wanted to go to sea from an early age."

"But how did you come to be serving on a British ship?"

Damn good question, thought Harry. He only wished he knew the answer. He stumbled, to give himself a little more time to come up with a convincing reply. Kristin bent down to assist him.

"I'm fine," he said, once he'd taken Kristin's arm again. Then he began to sneeze repeatedly.

"Perhaps it's time to take you back to the ward," suggested Kristin. "We can't afford to have you catching a cold. We can always try again tomorrow."

"Whatever you say," said Harry, relieved she didn't ask any more questions.

After she'd tucked him up like a mother putting a young child to bed, he quickly fell into a deep sleep.

—◦—

Harry managed eleven laps of the deck the day before the *Kansas Star* sailed into New York Harbor. Although he couldn't admit it to anyone, he was quite excited about the prospect of seeing America for the first time.

"Will you be going straight back to Bridgeport once we've docked?" asked Kristin during his final lap. "Or are you planning to stay in New York?"

"Haven't given it a lot of thought," said Harry, who had in fact given it a great deal of thought. "I suppose it will depend on what time we dock," he added, as he tried to anticipate her next question.

"It's just that, if you'd like to spend the night at Richard's apartment on the East Side, that would be swell."

"Oh, I wouldn't want to put him to any trouble."

Kristin laughed. "You know, Tom, there are times when you sound more like an Englishman than an American."

"I guess after all those years serving on British ships you're bound to eventually get corrupted by the limeys."

"Is that also the reason you felt unable to share your problem with us?" Harry came to a sudden halt: a stumble or a sneeze wasn't going to rescue him this time. "If you'd been just a little more frank in the first place, we'd have been happy to sort out the problem. But, given the circumstances, we had no choice but to inform Captain Parker and leave him to decide what should be done."

Harry collapsed into the nearest deckchair, but as Kristin

made no attempt to come to his rescue, he knew he was beaten. "It's far more complicated than you realize," he began. "But I can explain why I didn't want to involve anyone else."

"No need to," said Kristin. "The captain's already come to our rescue. But he did want to ask how you intended to deal with the bigger problem."

Harry bowed his head. "I'm willing to answer any questions the captain might have," he said, feeling almost a sense of relief that he'd been found out.

"Like the rest of us, he wanted to know how you're going to get off the ship when you don't have any clothes, or a dime to your name?"

Harry smiled. "I figured New Yorkers might consider a *Kansas Star* dressing gown to be pretty nifty."

"Frankly, not too many New Yorkers would notice even if you did walk down Fifth Avenue in a robe," said Kristin. "And the ones that did would probably think it was the latest fashion. But just in case they don't, Richard's come up with a couple of white shirts and a sports jacket. Pity he's so much taller than you, otherwise he'd have been able to supply a pair of pants as well. Dr. Wallace can spare a pair of brown wingtips, a pair of socks and a tie. That still leaves us with the problem of the pants, but the captain has a pair of Bermuda shorts that no longer fit him." Harry burst out laughing. "We hope you won't be offended, Tom, but we also held a little collection among the crew," she added, passing him a thick envelope. "I think you'll find there's more than enough to get you to Connecticut."

"How do I begin to thank you?" said Harry.

"No need to, Tom. We're all so pleased you survived. I only wish we could have saved your friend Harry Clifton as well. Still, you'll be glad to hear that Captain Parker has instructed Dr. Wallace to deliver your letter to his mother personally."

56

Harry was among the first on deck that morning, some two hours before the *Kansas Star* was due to sail into New York Harbor. It was another forty minutes before the sun joined him, by which time he'd worked out exactly how he was going to spend his first day in America.

He had already said farewell to Dr. Wallace, after trying, inadequately, to thank him for all he'd done. Wallace assured him that he would post his letter to Mrs. Clifton just as soon as he arrived in Bristol, and had reluctantly accepted that it might not be wise to visit her, after Harry had hinted that she was of a nervous disposition.

Harry was touched when Captain Parker called into the sick bay to deliver a pair of Bermuda shorts and wish him luck. After he had returned to the bridge, Kristin said firmly, "It's time for you to go to bed, Tom. You'll need all your strength if you're going to travel to Connecticut tomorrow." Tom Bradshaw would have liked to spend a day or two with Richard and Kristin in Manhattan, but Harry Clifton couldn't afford to waste any time now that Britain had declared war on Germany.

"When you wake up in the morning," continued Kristin, "try to get onto the passenger deck before first light, then you can watch the sun rising as we sail into New York. I know you have seen it many times before, Tom, but it never fails to excite me."

"Me too," said Harry.

"And once we've docked," continued Kristin, "why don't you

wait for Richard and me to come off duty and then we can disembark together?"

◄◦►

Dressed in Richard's sports jacket and shirt, a little too large, the captain's Bermuda shorts, a little too long, and the doctor's shoes and socks, a little too tight, Harry couldn't wait to go ashore.

The ship's purser had telegraphed ahead to advise the New York Immigration Department that they had an extra passenger on board, an American citizen called Tom Bradshaw. The NYID had telegraphed back to say that Mr. Bradshaw should make himself known to one of the immigration officials and they would take it from there.

Once Richard had dropped him off at Grand Central, Harry planned to hang around in the station for a little while before heading back to the docks, where he intended to report straight to the union office and find out which ships were due to sail for England. It didn't matter which port they were heading for, as long as it wasn't Bristol.

Once he had identified a suitable vessel, he would sign up for any job on offer. He didn't care if he worked on the bridge or in the boiler room, scrubbed the decks or peeled potatoes, just as long as he got back to England. If there turned out to be no jobs available, he would book the cheapest passage home. He'd already checked the contents of the bulky white envelope Kristin had given him and there was more than enough to pay for a berth that couldn't be smaller than the broom cupboard he'd slept in on the *Devonian*.

It saddened Harry that when he returned to England he wouldn't be able to contact any of his old friends, and he'd have to be cautious even when he got in touch with his mother. But the moment he stepped ashore, his only purpose would be to join one of His Majesty's warships and enlist in the fight against the King's enemies, even though he knew that whenever that ship returned to port he would have to remain on board, like a criminal on the run.

Harry's thoughts were interrupted by a lady. He gazed in admiration when he first saw the Statue of Liberty looming up in front of him through the early-morning mist. He had seen photographs of the iconic landmark but they had not given a true sense of her size as she towered above the *Kansas Star,* welcoming visitors, immigrants and her fellow countrymen to the United States.

As the ship continued on its way toward the harbor, Harry leaned over the railings and looked toward Manhattan, disappointed that the skyscrapers didn't appear to be any taller than some of the buildings he remembered in Bristol. But then, as each minute passed, they grew and grew until they appeared to soar up into the heavens and he had to shade his eyes from the sun as he stared up at them.

A New York Port Authority tugboat came out to join them and guided the *Kansas Star* safely to its berth on number seven dock. When Harry saw the cheering crowds, he began to feel apprehensive for the first time, even though the young man who was sailing into New York that morning was far older than the fourth officer who'd left Bristol only three weeks earlier.

"Smile, Tom."

Harry turned to see Richard looking down into a Kodak Brownie Box camera. He was peering at an upside-down image of Tom, with the Manhattan skyline as a backdrop.

"You'll be one passenger I sure won't forget in a hurry," said Kristin, as she walked across to join him so that Richard could take a second photograph of them together. She had exchanged her nurse's uniform for a smart polka-dot dress, white belt and white shoes.

"Nor me you," said Harry, hoping that neither of them could sense how nervous he was.

"Time for us to go ashore," said Richard, closing the shutter of his camera.

The three of them took the wide staircase down to the lower deck, where several passengers were already streaming off the ship to be reunited with relieved relatives and anxious friends.

As they made their way down the gangway, Harry's spirits were lifted by how many of the ship's passengers and crew wanted to shake him by the hand and wish him luck.

Once they'd stepped onto the dockside, Harry, Richard and Kristin headed toward immigration, where they joined one of four long queues. Harry's eyes darted about in every direction, and he wanted to ask so many questions, but any one of them would have revealed that this was the first time he'd set foot in America.

The first thing that struck him was the patchwork quilt of different colors that made up the American people. He'd only ever seen one black man in Bristol, and remembered stopping to stare at him. Old Jack had told him it was both rude and inconsiderate, adding, "How would you feel if everyone stopped to stare at you just because you were white?" But it was the noise, the bustle and the sheer pace of everything around him that most caught Harry's imagination and made Bristol seem as if it were languishing in a bygone age.

He was already beginning to wish that he'd accepted Richard's offer to stay with him overnight and perhaps spend a few days in a city he was finding so exciting even before he'd left the dockside.

"Why don't I go through first?" said Richard, as they reached the head of the queue. "Then I can pick up my car and meet you both outside the terminal."

"Good idea," said Kristin.

"Next!" shouted an immigration officer.

Richard walked up to the desk and handed over his passport to the official, who glanced briefly at the photo before stamping it. "Welcome home, Lieutenant Tibbet."

"Next!"

Harry stepped forward, uncomfortably aware that he had no passport, no identification and someone else's name.

"My name's Tom Bradshaw," he said with a confidence he didn't feel. "I think the purser of the SS *Kansas Star* telegraphed ahead to warn that I would be coming ashore."

The immigration officer looked closely at Harry, then picked up a sheet of paper and began to study a long list of names. Finally he put a tick by one before turning round and nodding. For the first time, Harry noticed two men standing on the other side of the barrier, wearing identical gray suits and gray hats. One of them gave him a smile.

The immigration officer stamped a piece of paper and handed it to Harry. "Welcome back, Mr. Bradshaw. It's been a long time."

"Sure has," said Harry.

"Next!"

"I'll wait for you," said Harry as Kristin made her way to the desk.

"I'll only be a moment," she promised.

Harry passed through the barrier and entered the United States of America for the first time.

The two men in gray suits stepped forward. One of them said, "Good morning, sir. Are you Mr. Thomas Bradshaw?"

"That's me," said Harry.

The words were hardly out of his mouth before the other man grabbed him and pinned his arms behind his back, while the first man handcuffed him. It all happened so quickly that Harry didn't even have time to protest.

He remained outwardly calm, as he had already considered the possibility that someone might work out that he wasn't Tom Bradshaw, but in fact an Englishman called Harry Clifton. Even so, he had assumed that the worst they could do was serve him with a deportation order and have him shipped back to Britain. And as that was exactly what he'd planned to do anyway, he didn't put up a fight.

Harry spotted two cars waiting by the sidewalk. The first was a black police car, with its back door being held open by another unsmiling man in a gray suit. The second was a red sports car, with Richard sitting on the bonnet, smiling.

The moment Richard saw that Tom had been handcuffed and was being led away, he leaped up and began to run toward him. At the same time, one of the police officers began to read Mr. Bradshaw his rights, while the other continued to grip Harry firmly by the elbow. "You have the right to remain silent.

Anything you say can and will be used against you in a court of law. You have the right to an attorney."

A moment later Richard was striding by their sides. He glared at the officers and said, "What the hell do you think you're doing?"

"If you cannot afford an attorney, one will be appointed to you," continued the first policeman, while the other ignored him.

Richard was clearly amazed by how relaxed Tom appeared, almost as if he wasn't surprised to have been arrested. But he was still determined to do anything he could to assist his friend. He leaped forward and blocked the officers' path and said firmly, "What are you charging Mr. Bradshaw with, officer?"

The senior detective came to a halt, looked Richard in the eye, and said, "First-degree murder."

The story continues in Books Two and Three
of the Clifton Chronicles

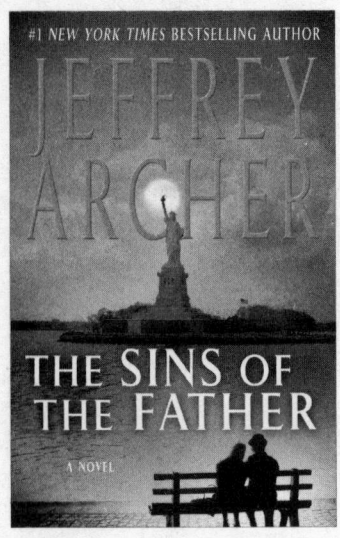

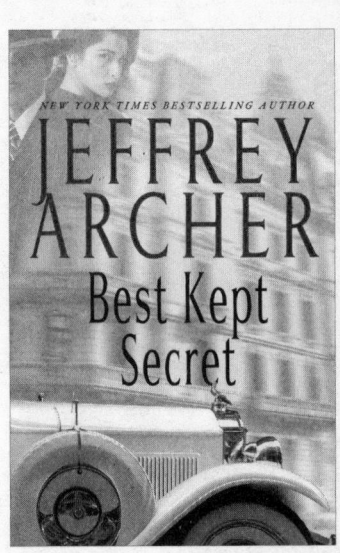

Available Now

Available May 2013